Learn the secrets of great bartending!

From *Aalborg Sours* to *Zooms*, from tropical punch to delicious nonalcoholic drinks, from the classic martini to the consummate margarita, this is the one guide to keep barside for mixing fabulous drinks.

For parties large or small, reach for

*THE COMPLETE BARTENDER*

... the only guide you'll need!

# THE
# COMPLETE
# BARTENDER

·····

# Robyn M. Feller

*Produced by The Philip Lief Group, Inc.*

**BERKLEY BOOKS, NEW YORK**

THE COMPLETE BARTENDER

A Berkley Book / published by arrangement with
The Philip Lief Group

PRINTING HISTORY
Berkley edition / December 1990

Copyright © 1990 by The Berkley Publishing Group.

All rights reserved.
This book, or parts thereof, may not be reproduced
in any form without permission.
For information address: The Berkley Publishing Group,
a division of Penguin Putnam Inc.,
375 Hudson Street, New York, New York 10014.

Visit our website at
www.penguinputnam.com

ISBN: 0-425-12687-0

BERKLEY®
Berkley Books are published by The Berkley Publishing Group,
a division of Penguin Putnam Inc.,
375 Hudson Street, New York, New York 10014.
BERKLEY and the "B" design
are trademarks belonging to Penguin Putnam Inc.

PRINTED IN THE UNITED STATES OF AMERICA

40  39  38  37  36  35  34  33  32  31  30

# Table of Contents

To the Fellers,
who, at times, have driven me to drink

# Acknowledgments

Great thanks to my wonderfully knowledgeable editors, Constance Jones, Julia Banks, Trish Todd, Hillary Cige, and to Philip Lief. And for their assistance during the writing and research of this book: my friend and favorite enologist, Bruce Glassman; The International Bartenders School; The American Bartenders School; The Distilled Spirits Council of the United States; Jimmy Goldmann and Bamboo Bernies; Bobby Caravella and The Shark Bar; Ann Higgins, Caitlin Conlow, Riaz Baksch and Alex Duff, the bartenders at the Mulholland Drive Cafe; all the restaurant owners, managers and bartenders who shared their expertise with me; my friends at T. S. Ma for testing out some of these recipes (sorry, no recipe for Rolling Rock); M. B., fellow barfly and flygirl; and the original SMP band for learning how to bartend with me one hot summer. Thanks also to Frederick and to my family for their support, even when I acted as if I were hung over.

# Introduction

I was first introduced to the art of mixology during a fun, three-week, no-frills course. When asked to explain "exactly how much of this" to use, or to describe "the exact method for doing that," the instructor's philosophy, was—well, Zen. "You just know," he'd respond.

And that's just the point of this book. Except, perhaps, for hard-core bartending jobs at pricey restaurants, mixology is at best an inexact science. There are always going to be differences in the way two people mix a drink. Some go heavy on the alcohol, some light. Some change the ingredients, some change the proportions. Lots of ice vs. one or two cubes. You say old-fashioned, I say lowball. The goal is to make a drink that tastes good to you— and to your guests.

Get to know your liquor supply. Experiment with what you have using the recipes in this book, or try something new. Create your own drinks. The tips you'll find here are based on tried-and-true methods. The recipes, some new, some old, some adapted for today's tastes, are mere guidelines. The step-by-step instructions are intended to make mixing a drink as easy as possible for you.

In the nineties, drinking will be a matter of quality instead of quantity, personal taste instead of fashion statement. The recipes and guidelines in the pages that follow will help you become the bartender *you* want to be, for they'll help you discover how easy and fun it is to mix drinks. The party-planning tips and ideas for creating the perfect bar for your home will enable you to be a master mixologist and the perfect host.

And don't forget: the nineties are a decade of renewed interest in safety and responsibility. We are concerned about our health, our personal welfare and the well-being of our friends. Don't let your friends drink and drive. Many people are drinking more moderately in the interests of fitness. *The Complete Bartender* offers plenty of ideas for lighter and nonalcoholic drinks that fit the mood of the times.

Bartending can be lots of fun if you follow your instincts, do what you like and provide your guests with a safe, good time. Relax and enjoy yourself, and you'll always be the life of the party.

# Stocking Your Bar

━━━━━━━━━━━━━━━━━━━━━━━━━━━━━━━━━━━━━━━━━━━━━━━

The home bar should reflect the owner's personal taste. Not everyone needs to stock every exotic liquor on the market: If all you and your friends ever drink is beer, wine and straight vodka, well then, there's your shopping list. But home bars can grow. Maybe you'll start out with three items and gradually add a few different liquors and a flavorful liqueur or two. Then one day you'll be browsing in a liquor store and you'll pick up a small bottle of whatever it is you've been meaning to try—and so grows your home bar.

Your initial purchases, then, should be based on what you'll use most and what you and your friends like. If you know what you want, you're better off buying in large quantities, since larger bottles are generally less expensive per unit than smaller bottles. But there's no need to go overboard when making your initial purchases; buy reasonable amounts, unless, of course, you are sure that you like something in particular. Then, by all means buy as much as you want, especially if you find it for a good price.

While every bar will be slightly different, here are some basic guidelines. Outlined below is a suggested shopping list for a starter bar. Make any adjustments you like and use the personalized results as your own bar-stocking guidelines. Happy mixing!

## The Basic Home Bar Checklist

━━━━━━━━━━━━━━━━━━━━━━━━━━━━━━━━━━━━━━━━━━━━━━━

*LIQUORS*

| | |
|---|---|
| 1 bottle bourbon | (750 ml) |
| 1 bottle brandy | (750 ml) |

3

| | |
|---|---|
| 1 bottle Canadian whiskey | (750 ml) |
| 1 bottle dry gin | (1¾ liters) |
| 1 bottle rum | (1¾ liters) |
| 1 bottle Scotch whiskey | (750 ml) |
| 1 bottle tequila | (1¾ liters) |
| 1 bottle vodka | (1¾ liters) |

ROCKS

*LIQUEURS*

small bottles of the following:

triple sec

crème de menthe

crème de cacao

Kahlúa

amaretto

Drambuie

Bénédictine

Cointreau

(TALL) COLLINS

MIXING PITCHER

LONG BAR SPOON

*WINE AND BEER*

| | |
|---|---|
| 1 bottle dry vermouth | (small) |
| 1 bottle sweet vermouth | (small) |
| 2 six-packs beer | (1 regular, 1 light) |
| 2 bottles white wine | |
| 2 bottles red wine | |
| 1 bottle rosé wine | (optional) |
| 1 bottle champagne or sparkling wine | |

GOBLET

# The Home Bar of Champions

If the basic stocking suggestions don't appeal to you, perhaps you are looking for liquors that make a bolder statement. Well, take a look on the next page. The spirits mentioned here are more daring—they go beyond the ordinary, allowing you to be a mixologist's mixologist. But you needn't invest in the entire list right off the bat. Go slowly. Find out what you like by tasting, whether at friends' homes or when you go out for a drink.

## LIQUOR

1 bottle brandy
1 bottle V.S.O.P. cognac
1 bottle dry English gin
1 bottle Irish whiskey
1 bottle dark rum (Jamaican)
1 bottle gold rum
1 bottle light rum
1 bottle blended Scotch whiskey
1 bottle Tennessee whiskey
1 bottle gold tequila
1 bottle white tequila
1 or 2 bottles premium vodka (Russian or Scandinavian; store in your freezer)

ROCKS (STEMMED)

COVERED COCKTAIL SHAKER

## LIQUEURS

small bottles of the following:

framboise, kirschwasser, plum brandy (slivovitz) or other flavored brandies of your choice

crème de cassis, sambuca, Galliano, Frangelico, Kahlúa, peppermint schnapps, peach schnapps or any other of your favorite liqueurs, approximately five bottles in all

## WINE

3 aperitif wines, such as Dubonnet, Lillet, Campari
1 bottle cream sherry
1 bottle port
1 bottle madeira
several bottles of your favorite white wines, including at least one table wine and one dessert wine
several bottles of your favorite red wines, ranging from dry to sweet
2 or 3 bottles champagne and/or sparkling wine

# Mixers

Whether you stock a basic bar or one with all the extras, you will need to keep on hand a supply of the following:

Bloody Mary mix
club soda
coffee
cola
cranberry juice cocktail
cream (heavy and light)
cream of coconut
Falernum
ginger ale
grapefruit juice
grenadine
lemon juice
lime juice (Rose's is the most popular—it is not a substitute for fresh lime juice, however, since it contains a sugary syrup)
orange juice
orgeat (almond syrup)
passion fruit juice (or nectar)
piña colada mix
pineapple juice
seltzer
7-Up
sour mix
tomato juice
tonic (quinine) water
water (distilled or spring)

SELTZER BOTTLE

# Odds and Ends

No bar would be complete without the miscellaneous ingredients and garnishes that make mixed drinks truly special. Make sure you include the following in your bar:

bitters (Angostura, orange)
cherries (maraschino)
cinnamon sticks
ice (three types: cubes, cracked and crushed)
lemons
limes
nutmeg
olives
onions (pickled pearl)
oranges
salt
sugar
Tabasco
Worcestershire sauce

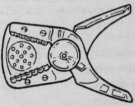

LEMON SQUEEZER

RED WINE

MARTINI PITCHER

# Barware and Glassware

$K$eeping the right tools on hand can make bartending a lot easier. And as anyone who works with their hands can tell you, the right equipment can make the difference between a hassle and a pleasure. The lists below suggest some of the utensils and serving ware that will help make your bartending experience a success.

*EQUIPMENT*

bar spoon (long)
can/bottle opener
champagne bucket
cocktail napkins
corkscrew (winged version or waiter's)
covered cocktail shaker
cutting board
electric blender
ice bucket and tongs
ice scoop (optional)
juice extractor
lemon/lime squeezer
martini pitcher
measures/shot glasses (these vary in size—a jigger is 1½ ounces)
measuring cup
measuring spoons
mixing pitcher
muddler (wooden)

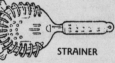

WAITERS CORKSCREW

STRAINER

JUICE EXTRACTOR

WING TYPE CORKSCREW

CAN/BOTTLE OPENER

paring knife/bar knife

picks (for garnishes)

punch bowl and glasses

**BAR KNIFE**

saucers for salt and sugar (if you need to frost the rim of a glass)

seltzer bottle

shaker set: shaker (mixing) glass and metal tumbler

speed pourers (optional)

strainer

straws

swizzle sticks

**WOODEN MUDDLER**

towels

# Glassware

The trend these days is toward multipurpose glassware, so if you choose to have only one or two types, large wineglasses, rocks glasses and highball glasses are good choices. A description of the various types of glassware follows.

**balloon** (large wineglass)  Ranges in size from 9 to 14 ounces.

**beer goblet**  A stemmed balloon-type glass that holds about 12 ounces.

**beer mug**  12 to 16 ounces.

**brandy snifter**  Best to choose those that hold 3, 6 or 12 ounces. They do come larger, though. For straight brandy.

**champagne flute**  For champagne, champagne drinks or wine. Holds 4 to 6 ounces.

**champagne saucer**  Also for champagne, but this type allows bubbles to escape more readily than the fluted or tulip type. Holds about 4 ounces.

**champagne tulip**  For champagne, champagne drinks or wine. Holds 4 to 6 ounces.

**cocktail**  This is your basic glass for drinks "straight up." Ranges in size from 3 ounces to 6 ounces. The large ones can be used for frozen drinks. The 4½-ounce size can be used for martinis, Manhattans and stingers. Sturdy, solid stems are best since you can hold on to the stem without warming the drink.

**Collins** Ranges in size from 10 to 14 ounces. Used for Collins drinks, fizzes, exotic drinks like Mai Tais, Singapore Slings, relatives of Long Island Ice Teas and other mixed drinks that require a bit more room than a highball. Some Collins glasses are frosted for effect.

**double rocks** Holds 14 to 16 ounces. For larger drinks "on the rocks." A gaining trend on the glassware scene.

**goblet** Approximately 12 ounces. Great for tropical drinks, blended drinks, frozen drinks. The 22-ounce **hurricane** glass can also be used for really mammoth drinks.

**highball** Ranges in size from 8 to 12 ounces. Good for most standard mixed drinks. Similar to a Collins glass, but shorter and wider.

**martini** Similar to a cocktail glass, but with a distinctive V shape. Nothing beats a martini in an actual martini glass. About 4 ounces.

**hot drink mug** 10 to 12 ounces. Used for hot drinks, hot coffee drinks, cappuccinos, Irish coffee, etc.

**parfait** A specialty glass, approximately 7½ ounces; can be used for drinks containing ice cream and/or fruit.

**pilsner** 10 to 16 ounces. Used for beer.

**pony (cordial)** Up to 2 ounces. Can be used for liqueurs, brandy and small pousse-cafés.

**pousse-café** A specialty glass for drinks that are "floated," such as Rainbow Pousse-Café or Traffic Light.

**red wine** Holds 6 to 11 ounces. Is more rounded than a white wine glass, in order to direct the bouquet of red wine to the drinker's nose.

**rocks** (stemmed or not stemmed) Ranges in size from 6 to 8 ounces. Also called "lowball" or "old-fashioned." Used for drinks served "on the rocks." If you don't own shot glasses, you can use these to serve straight shots of liquor or liqueur.

**sherry** Holds about 3 ounces. Used for cordials and liqueurs. You can substitute the popular Spanish *copita*.

**shot** Ranges from a fraction of an ounce to 2 ounces (long shot). The standard shot measure these days is 1½ ounces (also called a jigger). Can hold one liquor or can be used for mixed shooters. It also comes in a two-sided metal measuring version, where one side holds 1 ounce and the other side holds 1½ ounces.

**sour** Also called a delmonico glass or a whiskey sour glass. Holds 5 or 6 ounces. Known for its use with sours of all kinds.

**white wine** Can also hold from 6 to 11 ounces, although generally a bit smaller than red wine glasses.

# Measure for Measure

___

Somehow, the ways alcoholic beverages are measured, in both the bottle and the mixing glass, have always managed to confuse most people. Just what *is* a fifth? Which holds more—a pony or a jigger? The charts below should help clear things up.

## Bottle Sizes

___

Remember when you rolled your eyes in math class, wondering why you should bother learning the metric system? Well, your teachers must have known something, because on December 31, 1979, the sizing of liquor bottles in America was converted to metrics.

| | | Spirits | |
|---|---|---|---|
| old name | old size (fl. oz.) | new size (fl. oz.) | new size (metric) |
| miniature | 1.6 | 1.7 | 50 ml |
| half pint | 8.0 | 6.8 | 200 ml |
| pint | 16.0 | 16.9 | 500 ml |
| fifth | 25.6 | 25.4 | 750 ml |
| quart | 32.0 | 33.8 | 1 liter |
| half gallon | 64.0 | 59.2 | 1.75 l |

| **Wines** | | |
|---|---|---|
| old name | new size<br>(fl. oz.) | new size<br>(metric) |
| split | 6.3 | 187 ml |
| tenth | 12.7 | 375 ml |
| fifth | 25.4 | 750 ml |
| quart | 33.8 | 1 liter |
| magnum | 50.7 | 1.5 l |
| double magnum | 101.4 | 3 l |

## Standard Bar Measurements

No, bar measurements don't have anything to do with metrics, but they are confusing enough nonetheless. Keep this chart handy, though, and you'll do all right.

| | |
|---|---|
| 1 teaspoon (barspoon) | ⅛ ounce |
| 1 tablespoon | ⅜ ounce |
| 1 pony | 1 ounce |
| 1 jigger | 1½ ounces |
| 1 wineglass | 4 ounces |
| 1 split | 6 ounces |
| 1 cup | 8 ounces |
| 1 dash | ¹⁄₃₂ ounce |

MEASURING SPOONS

SHOT

MEASURE/SHOT GLASS

# Garnishes

∎ ————————————————————————————— ∎

Garnishes can add flavor or flair to any drink. Here are the garnishes you'll encounter most often, plus a few special ones.

## Types of Garnishes

∎ ————————————————————————————— ∎

**bitters** The leading name in bitters is Angostura, but orange bitters are sometimes called for instead.

**cherries** Maraschino cherries are most often used. They usually are red, but green ones exist, too. Maraschino cherries make great garnishes for tropical drinks and many sours, as well as the standard Manhattan.

**cinnamon sticks** You'll get the most use out of extra-long cinnamon sticks. They can be used to stir and flavor certain hot drinks.

**cucumber** Cucumber slices are popular garnishes for drinks with Pimm's in them.

**lemons** Lemons, one of the most essential garnishes, can be cut into wedges, slices or wheels, and the rinds can be used to make twists. Lemons are especially popular for drinks with club soda in them. Twists are becoming more and more popular as garnishes for martinis.

**limes** Limes, too, can be cut into wedges, slices, wheels or twists. Limes are especially popular for drinks with tonic water in them.

**mint leaves** An absolute must for mint juleps.

**nutmeg** A nice alternative to cinnamon, nutmeg can be sprinkled on hot drinks or certain cream drinks, especially Alexanders.

**olives**  The most popular olives for drinks are small green pitted olives, although other types may be used. This is the quintessential martini garnish. Store in the refrigerator, tightly covered.

**onions**  Pearl onions are used in Gibsons (martinis with pearl onion garnish).

**oranges**  Orange slices are not only decorative but provide a nice flavor to tropical or exotic drinks, sours or even vodka on the rocks.

**pineapple**  Spears, slices or chunks—pineapple can add excitement to many tropical drinks, such as the famous piña colada.

**salt**  Salt is an essential part of a Margarita or a Salty Dog. It also adds zip to Bloody Mary mix. (Salt substitutes may be used for those who are concerned with their salt intake.) A coarse salt works best for frosting glasses.

**sugar**  Superfine granulated sugar is good for making simple sugar syrup, as well as for frosting glasses.

---

# Cutting and Preparing Garnishes

There are several different ways to cut basic fruit garnishes— wedges, slices, wheels and twists. (*Note:* To cut fruit, use a good paring knife and a cutting board.)

To cut lemon or lime wedges, cut off the ends of the fruit and discard. Slice the fruit lengthwise. Take one of the lemon or lime halves and cut that lengthwise as well. Holding the two sections together, cut crosswise so that each cut produces two wedges. Repeat with the other half.

To cut lemon, lime or orange slices, cut off the ends of the fruit and discard. Slice the fruit lengthwise. Take one of the fruit halves and cut across so that each cut produces one slice. Repeat with other half of lemon or lime.

To make fruit ''wheels'' that can be fitted onto the rim of a glass, take a lemon, lime or orange and cut off the ends. Make a cut approximately ¼ inch deep along the length of the fruit. Slice the fruit perpendicular to the original cut. These ''wheels'' can be arranged on the rim of the glass, which will fit inside the small cut in the garnish.

An easy method of making fruit peel twists is to stand the fruit on its end (after cutting off the ends) and cut from top to bottom, staying close to the meat of the fruit. Each cut can be approximately ½ inch wide. When you have finished, you may cut each of those slices into ¼-inch strips.

Olives and pearl onion garnishes may either be placed at the bottom of the drink "solo" or you can spear one to three olives or onions on a toothpick and place in the cocktail glass.

With cherry and orange garnishes, you can spear the cherry with a toothpick and then push the toothpick through the rind of the orange slice. Place on top of the drink.

# Serving Garnishes

For the most part, lemons are used as garnishes when the mixer is club soda. Limes are used when the mixer is tonic water. Limes are also popular with drinks containing cranberry juice (and no other juice) and one liquor, such as a Cape Codder.

A "twist" usually refers to lemon peel only, but recently other fruit twists have become popular. To use a twist, actually twist the peel over the drink to release the essence of the fruit, rub it around the rim of the glass, then drop it into the drink.

# Bartender's Secrets

■————————————————————————————————————————————————■

*TO CHOOSE GLASSWARE:*

■ The trend these days is toward multipurpose glassware. The recipes in this book offer suggestions for the traditional types of glassware to use, but feel free to use whatever you have on hand, provided the drink fits inside. A large wine glass is your best bet if you can afford to buy only one type of glassware. Don't be too concerned if a drink doesn't completely fill the glass, either.

*TO FROST A GLASS, THERE ARE TWO METHODS:*

■ With ice: Dip in water, place in freezer for half an hour. It will get a frosted white look. When removing, hold by the handle or stem so as not to melt the ice with your hand. With salt or sugar (for frosting the rim of a glass only): Moisten the rim of a chilled glass with a lemon or lime wedge. Dip rim into salt or sugar.

*TO CHILL A GLASS:*

■ Refrigerate at least one hour before pouring a drink into it, or
■ Fill glass with ice and cold water and let sit while you are preparing the drink. When you are ready to pour the drink, dump out the ice and water.

*TO MAKE TWISTS AND FLAVOR RIMS:*

■ When a recipe calls for a fruit twist as a garnish, twist the peel above the drink and then drop into the drink.
■ When using a fruit garnish, rub the rim of the glass with the fruit to leave the flavor on the glass.

*TO MAKE DRINKS CALLING FOR ICE:*

■ Although many mixed-drink recipes instruct the bartender to fill a shaker glass with ice, you may use just ¼ cup, or 4 to 5 ice cubes if you prefer.

■ Fresh ice is the key to a great drink. It's a good idea to use a fresh bag of ice when mixing drinks, since freezer odors can ruin the flavor of a drink.

*TO MAKE DRINKS CALLING FOR SODA:*

■ To prevent soda from "exploding," especially if it is on the warm side, turn the cap very slowly—just a tiny bit at a time. Do this over or near a sink in case any soda sprays out.

*TO MAKE DRINKS CALLING FOR WATER:*

■ Always use distilled water or spring water in drinks calling for water. Tap water can make a drink look clouded—and it doesn't taste as good.

*TO MAKE DRINKS CALLING FOR PREMIUM VODKA:*

■ A great vodka will taste even better if it's exceptionally cold. Keep a bottle of the good stuff in your freezer.

*TO MAKE DRINKS CALLING FOR EGG WHITES:*

■ For drink recipes calling for half an egg white, you might be better off doubling the recipe and making two drinks, since an egg white is very difficult to divide.

*TO SHAKE A DRINK:*

■ Drinks containing numerous or difficult-to-mix ingredients are usually shaken. A shaker set is made up of a mixing glass and a metal tumbler. The mixing glass is sometimes referred to as a shaker glass.

■ When using a shaker set, put any ice in the mixing glass, add the other ingredients, fit the metal container snugly over the glass and shake several times. Tip the set so the liquid ends up in the metal tumbler. Use a metal strainer, which fits into the top of the metal tumbler, to strain the liquid into a drink glass.

■ Sometimes a *short shaker* can be used. This is a smaller metal cup that fits directly over the glass from which you will drink. If you don't have a shaker set, a glass with a cover that fits on top or the jug portion of an electric blender will do.

## TO STIR A DRINK:

■ Mixed drinks are usually stirred if they do not contain cream or sour mix, or if only one or two different ingredients are involved.

■ Either half of the shaker set can be used as a mixing cup for drinks that require stirring rather than shaking.

■ Don't overstir drinks made with sparkling beverages such as sodas or champagne. You don't want to spoil the fizz.

## TO POUR A DRINK:

■ If you're making a pitcherful of a mixed drink, set up all the glasses and pour a little into each glass, repeating the process until all are filled the same amount.

■ To pour hot drinks into glasses, put a metal spoon in the glass before pouring. This absorbs the heat so the glass won't break.

## TO POUR A POUSSE-CAFÉ:

■ To float liqueurs or liquors, always put the heaviest one on the bottom of the glass, and float them in order of density and thickness. To do this, hold a bar spoon face-down in the glass and pour the liqueur over the back of the spoon—very slowly.

■ If you have more time, pour the liqueurs into the glass and refrigerate for about an hour. In that time, the liqueurs will find their own place according to their weight, forming the layers you desire.

## TO FLAME LIQUEURS:

■ If it is possible to avoid this process, please do, because it can be dangerous. But if you insist, pre-warm the glass over a low flame, add most of the spirit and warm a teaspoon. Preheat just one teaspoonful of liquor over the flame and then set afire. Pour the flaming liquid into the glass with the remaining liquor—CAREFULLY!

## TO OPEN A BOTTLE OF WINE:

■ Using a sharp knife, remove the seal around the neck of the bottle. Peel the seal off so that the cork is exposed. Insert the tip of the corkscrew into the center of the cork and twist until it is as far down into the cork as possible. Slowly and steadily pull the cork out. It is common etiquette for the server to taste the wine before serving his or her guests.

## TO OPEN A BOTTLE OF CHAMPAGNE OR SPARKLING WINE:

■ Wrap a towel around a well-chilled bottle. With the mouth of the bottle pointed away from people and breakable objects, carefully remove the foil and undo the wire over the cork. Holding the cork in one hand and the rest of the bottle in the other, slowly turn the bottle until you feel the cork loosen. *Slowly* wiggle the cork out. When opening a bottle of sparkling wine or champagne, try for as little sound as possible. While the sound of a cork popping is festive, it allows precious bubbles to escape.

## TO CLEAN GLASSWARE:

■ No matter what type of glassware you use, make sure it's always sparkling clean. When you wash your glassware, air-dry it with the rim down on a towel to avoid spotting.
■ You can also dry with one towel and polish with another.
■ Wash glassware immediately after use.
■ If you can't wash up right away, soak the glasses in warm, sudsy water so that the drink residues don't stick.
■ Don't stack glasses one on top of the other; they might stick together. If they do get stuck together, put the bottom glass in very warm water and fill the top glass with cold water. The bottom glass will expand and the top one contract until the difference frees them up.

# Sour mix

12 oz. lemon juice (juice of approximately 6 lemons)
18 oz. distilled water
¼ cup refined sugar
1 egg white

1. Blend in a blender or shake in a large jar.
2. Refrigerate (it will keep for no more than 7 to 10 days).
3. Always blend or shake before use.

# Sugar syrup (simple syrup)

2 cups sugar
1 cup water

1. Dissolve sugar in water in a saucepan.
2. Simmer for approximately 10 minutes, stirring.
3. Cover and refrigerate until needed.

# On Being a
# Responsible Bartender

We've all heard television news stories about drinking and driving, and we've all read cautionary tales about the dangers of drinking to excess. Drinking and hosting parties are basic social activities, both time-honored and fun, but the very real fact remains that people get drunk from too much alcohol.

When you serve drinks to your guests, you are responsible for the amount of alcohol consumed under your supervision. In some states, in fact, hosts are considered legally liable for whatever may occur as a result of their guests' alcohol consumption. You owe it to your friends to make sure drinking remains a safe and enjoyable experience in your home.

Here are some basic tips to keep in mind so you and your guests can relax and have fun while drinking:

- Always keep a generous supply of nonalcoholic beverages available for guests who either are driving or choose not to drink alcohol. These can include soft drinks, mineral water, fruit and vegetable juices, alcohol-free punches, alcohol-free beers, tea or coffee. "Virgin" drinks are a festive option, especially if you are serving frozen blender drinks. See the chapter on nonalcoholic drinks for recipes you can use to make delicious alcohol-free concoctions.

- Don't make your drinks overly strong. Guests will down strong drinks just as quickly as normal-strength ones, but they will become intoxicated more quickly. Moderation is the key to an enjoyable drinking experience.

21

- Keep tabs on how much your guests have consumed. If someone seems to have had one too many, there is no shame in cutting him or her off. The only shame is in letting someone drink too much at the expense of his or her safety, the safety of others or a congenial atmosphere. If a guest does get drunk, make sure he or she does not drive home.

- If a guest requests a drink that is light on the booze, do oblige. You will not do him or her a favor by loading a drink with alcohol. Never pressure someone into having just one more.

- Always serve food along with alcohol. Alcohol is absorbed into the bloodstream directly from the stomach, and good food provides a balance for drinkers, slowing the rate at which they drink and absorb alcohol. Serving food also adds to the air of hospitality, allowing everyone to have an even better time. Sandwiches, dairy products, meats and fish are good bets.

- Mixers can affect the rate of absorption of alcohol into the system, so take them into account when planning and hosting any get-together. Water dilutes alcohol and slows absorption; carbonated beverages tend to speed it up.

- Don't throw parties whose sole purpose is drinking. If your guests have something else to do, they are less likely to get drunk. Food, conversation, games, videos and business are possible diversions.

- If you have young children and keep a supply of liquor in your home, make sure it is always locked safely away.

- Be aware that as few as one or two drinks can affect the average adult's coordination and ability to think. Alcohol is an anesthetic which could prevent the drinker from realizing he or she is impaired.

# Drinking and Driving

Of course, the safest rule for drinking and driving is: DON'T DO IT. Encourage your guests to use designated drivers, who don't drink at your party and who make sure everyone else gets home safely. For any number of reasons, though, some of your guests may be unable to use the designated driver system from time to time. When you know this is the case, bear in mind the following general guidelines for how long it takes people of different sizes to metabolize the drinks they consume.

| body weight (in pounds) | number of drinks | | | | | |
|---|---|---|---|---|---|---|
| | 1 | 2 | 3 | 4 | 5 | 6 |
| 100–119 | 0 hours | 3 | 6 | 10 | 13 | 16 |
| 120–139 | 0 | 2 | 5 | 8 | 10 | 12 |
| 140–159 | 0 | 2 | 4 | 6 | 8 | 10 |
| 160–179 | 0 | 1 | 3 | 5 | 7 | 9 |
| 180–199 | 0 | 0 | 2 | 4 | 6 | 7 |
| 200–219 | 0 | 0 | 2 | 3 | 5 | 6 |
| Over 220 | 0 | 0 | 1 | 3 | 4 | 6 |

These figures will vary from individual to individual, but they provide valuable insight into just how long it can take for someone to recover from the effects of drinking. When a guest has had a few drinks, encourage him or her to wait before getting behind the wheel. You could save a life.

HIGHBALL

DOUBLE ROCKS

# What's New for the Nineties?

The excesses of the 1980s—fast money, fast talk, extravagant living and overindulgence—have left us exhausted. In the nineties people are returning to quieter lives, classic styles and understated elegance. This trend extends to the bar, heralding both the revival of traditional drinks and the arrival of new drinks suited to an era of good taste and gracious living.

The trend toward simplicity is apparent in what people are drinking—or rather, what they're *not* drinking. Elaborate presentations and super-sugary concoctions are out. Some folks have even given up on alcohol altogether, opting instead for one of the new nonalcoholic beers, plain club soda with lime or, more likely, an imported bottled water with lime.

So what *are* people drinking these days? The basic martini is as popular as always, but it is now served bone-dry. Instead of mixing two parts gin or vodka with one part vermouth, most bartenders serve martinis with but the slimmest hint of vermouth. Drinkers now typically prefer the pure, clean taste of a single, quality liquor to the complexity of multi-ingredient recipes.

High-status brand name liquors are growing with increasing popularity, reflecting the heightened desire for quality rather than quantity. Most people now request a particular brand of liquor. Absolut, Finlandia, Smirnoff and Stolichnaya are vodka musts for the well-stocked bar. Tanqueray, Beefeater and Bombay are the names to remember in gin. Cuervo Especial (Gold) is undoubtedly the leader in the tequila popularity contest, while rum lovers prefer Mount Gay, Bacardi or Myers's. Scotch has made a resurgence as well, with aficionados ordering Dewar's and water or Johnny Walker Black Label on the rocks. Single-malt (unblended) Scotch whiskeys, such as Glenfiddich and The Glenlivet, are also in demand in the United States these days. And Irish whiskeys, such as Old Bushmills and Old Bushmills Black Bush, are capturing a growing audience with their distinctive smoothness. Brandy lovers have found their own new pet drink in armagnac, a cognaclike spirit from France.

A good chilled vodka is probably going to be the most important ingredient in your bar during the 1990s. No need to perform minor miracles with a shaker set—a few ounces of Absolut on the rocks with a splash of cranberry juice could be as complex as you'll have to get. For the diet-conscious or those looking to stay away from lots of alcohol, those proportions could be reversed—a glass of cranberry juice with just a splash of vodka. Flavored vodkas have also remained popular. Some companies are bottling the flavored vodka for you (Absolut Peppar, Absolut Citron), or you might want to flavor the vodka yourself, using herbs, fruits or peppers.

Of course, the "fun" drinks—tropical standbys like the piña colada, the strawberry daiquiri and the always exciting frozen margarita—are here for the duration. The frozen margarita is no longer confined to Mexican restaurants and special occasions and is quickly catching up to gin and vodka tonics as one of the nation's favorite drinks. Escape from life's everyday doldrums is never out of fashion, and what better way to escape than by sipping a drink decorated with a paper umbrella and lots of fresh fruit? Frozen drinks cool you down while conjuring up images of balmy breezes, chaise lounges and the Mexican sun, so they're perfect summer or winter. They owe some of their continuing popularity to the way they taste "virgin"—without any alcohol at all—great!

And even though drinks with silly names are not quite as big as they were in the eighties, for those looking for something truly different, there's plenty of good news. Sour Grapes, a mixture of vodka, Chambord and sour mix, makes a fun shot or a deliciously inviting cocktail; and a Mind Eraser will make you forget all of your troubles. Jell-O shots like the Slimeball, a Midori Jell-O shot, are slippery yet potent. Lube Job and Brain Tumor are two new drinks with Bailey's Irish Cream. The Brain Tumor is intended for the strong of stomach: The idea of the drink is for it to look like a diseased brain (several drops of strawberry liqueur floating on top do the trick).

For those in search of something memorable, albeit rather disgusting, there's the Tiny Bowl, a shot of vodka colored with blue curacao, with one or two raisins added for effect (you figure it out!). Go-Go Juice—a new, blue version of Long Island Ice Tea—and the Summer Share and Bubble Gum shots are fun summer drinks. These newcomers to the bar scene are what the hip barfly just might be ordering.

New fruity blends, including Peachy Keen Freeze, Mandarine Coladas, the Pear Tequila Supreme, Bellini Punch and White Grape, Tangerine and Sparkling Wine Punch, are spiced-up versions of old favorites. There are many, many more fun drinks to choose from: Just take a look at the Index of New Drinks for the Nineties on p. 541.

What's the word on beer? Well for some, the taste of a familiar domestic brand will never be replaced, but for many, the new breed of "microbreweries" has given domestic beer new life. Small outfits from Seattle to Boston and from San Francisco to Brooklyn produce an astounding array of high-quality beer increasingly available to consumers throughout the country. And of course, imported is in—the more exotic, the better. Beers from Mexico, Japan, Brazil, Thailand and just about any other country you can name have found their way to the United States, pleasing the palates of sophisticated drinkers.

Especially popular are the newer "dry" beers. These beers don't have a strong aftertaste of alcohol, so they are especially refreshing. Light beers, too, remain very popular, mainly because of their lower calorie content. Imported lights that combine good taste with health benefits have become extremely popular. And the market for nonalcoholic beers is expanding rapidly, with new products coming out all the time.

The line on wine is also straightforward. Wine snobbery has gone out of style, replaced by an "I know what I like" approach. The hard-and-fast "white wine with white meat, red wine with red meat" rule has gone the way of the dinosaurs. The only rule now is to serve wine that will complement your food and suit your taste. Lighter, crisper wines like Chardonnay, Beaujolais and white Zinfandel are all the rage. Domestic wines have mushroomed in popularity, and the proliferation of new domestic vintners has made a tremendous variety of good domestic wines available. People are no longer impressed by hefty price tags and unpronounceable foreign names—these days, if it's reasonably priced and it tastes good, your guests will congratulate you.

What's new for the nineties, then, is whatever *you* like. And as for serving your drinks, keep your glassware simple too. Sparkling clean, easy-to-hold, basic shapes work fine. Don't worry too much about whether you're using the "right" type of glass. If the drink fits . . .

# Party Planning

■ ─────────────────────────────────────────────────────────────── ■

When planning your next bash, be it an intimate cocktail party, dinner for six or a full-fledged extravaganza, your first rule of thumb should be that the drinks you serve should reflect the tastes of your guests. If you'll be entertaining a room full of beer drinkers, then your planning will be no more complex than making sure you have enough to go around. If, on the other hand, your crowd has a penchant for exotic mixed drinks, you should make sure you have all the necessary ingredients on hand in large enough quantities.

Your guests will not expect you to have a bar as complete as the most upscale establishment in town, but they will expect you to keep up with demand. Too much instead of too little will help ensure the success of your party. Count on each of your guests consuming about three or four drinks over the course of a four-hour party. Have plenty of glassware on hand—at least two glasses per guest, although if it's possible to keep more handy you'll be even better off.

While all the recipes in this book call for a particular type of glass, there's really no need for you to run out and buy every type of glass there is. A basic highball glass and a rocks glass should serve nearly all your needs. Also, large wineglasses can be used for virtually any type of drink. If you're looking for versatility, that's the one to keep around.

There is no way to overemphasize the great importance of fresh ice for your party. Approximately 1½ to 2 pounds per guest should be adequate. Buy your ice in bags to ensure freshness. Who knows what is lurking in the depths of your home freezer? Freezer odors can spoil the taste of your drink masterpieces.

Make sure to serve foods that will not spoil during the course

28

of your party. Otherwise you'll have lots of leftovers and drunk guests. Remember, too, that the amount of liquor and the type of drinks you'll be serving will vary, depending on the time of day as well as the type of party. Daytime parties usually warrant a smaller liquor supply.

What to serve? Punch is inappropriate at cocktail parties, but it is perfect for a holiday party or other special occasion, such as an anniversary or bridal shower. Dinner parties are good times for trying out wines. Brunches are perfect for champagne drinks, such as Mimosas, Kir Royales or the newer Poinsettia. Also nice to serve are highball drinks with juice mixers. Cocktail parties are your chance to get a bit more creative. If your guests don't fall into a particular pattern of drinking (such as all vodka drinkers or all gin drinkers), then experiment with your new-found knowledge of mixing drinks.

Here's a list of basic supplies to help you plan a successful party. The good news is that even if you have leftovers, these liquors will store well in your bar and you'll be even better prepared the next time around. This list assumes that an average bottle (750 ml) of liquor will provide twenty drinks of 1½ ounces each (1½ ounces is the size of the average shot). When selecting your liquors, get the best you can afford. Premium brands make a party an even more special occasion, and your guests will enjoy them.

# Cocktail Party Shopping List

■                                                           ■

*LIQUOR, BEER AND WINE*

2 bottles vodka (note: this is extremely conservative considering vodka's popularity. Absolut is the favorite brand, but any of the other premium vodkas will serve your purposes just as well)

1 bottle dry gin

1 bottle Scotch

1 bottle American whiskey

1 bottle rum

1 bottle tequila

1 small bottle dry vermouth

1 small bottle sweet vermouth

2 bottles white wine

2 bottles red wine

1 or 2 cases of beer (it's nice to have a mix of regular beer and light beer)

3 or 4 bottles of your favorite liqueurs (Kahlúa, amaretto and crème de cacao are ingredients in many popular drinks)

*MIXERS*

5 or 6 bottles club soda

5 or 6 bottles tonic water

4 or 5 bottles cola

2 or 3 bottles diet soda

2 to 3 bottles 7-Up

3 bottles orange juice

2 bottles tomato juice

2 bottles grapefruit juice

ICE BUCKET & TONGS

2 bottles pineapple juice

3 to 4 bottles cranberry juice cocktail

4 quarts sour mix (see recipe, p. 20)

1 bottle Rose's (or other brand) lime juice

4 bottles fresh spring water

*GARNISHES*

1 jar olives

1 jar maraschino cherries

limes

lemons

oranges

*SUPPLIES*

cocktail napkins

straws

stirrers/swizzle sticks

COCKTAIL SHAKER SET

*EQUIPMENT*

blender

shaker set

# Theme Parties

Looking to host a party with some real kick? Spiking the punch is one approach, but it's a lot more fun when you also add a dash of imagination. Just come up with a clever theme for your bash, and it's sure to be a hit.

Sporting events, news events, television shows and popular movies; historical themes, nostalgia and international motifs—each can be incorporated into a great party. With a little planning, the proper ambience and the appropriate beverage, you can celebrate almost any occasion in style. Here are a few suggestions to get you started:

## A Kentucky Derby Party

Turn on the TV for the pre-race show, then cheer on your favorite horse while you and your guests enjoy pitchers of Mint Juleps (recipe p. 304). For authenticity, serve the drinks in silver tumblers, and offer your guests some Derby Pie.

Red roses, wall decorations modeled after the competitors' racing silks and broadbrimmed hats like those worn by Kentucky belles add festive touches. If you like, each guest can pick a horse and lay an informal bet to win a small prize—perhaps a bottle of fine Kentucky bourbon.

# A Mexican Fiesta

Put some mariachi music on the stereo, hang a sombrero on the wall, and serve up some margaritas (on the rocks, p. 292 or frozen, p. 199), Mexican beer (such as Tecate or Corona) with lime squeezed in for extra zip, tequila shots (Cuervo Gold is recommended) or tequila poppers (recipe p. 424).

When downing a shot of tequila, put some salt on the skin at the base of your thumb and forefinger, lick the salt off, do the shot, and finish off by sucking the juice of a wedge of lime. *Qué bueno!*

Some food suggestions include nachos, salsa and do-it-yourself tacos. Have your guests bring the various ingredients for tacos and set up a buffet.

# English Croquet Party

Savor the spirit of *Brideshead Revisited* by hosting your own Edwardian lawn party. Set up the croquet wickets, hand out the mallets and let your guests have at it. When they've worked up a thirst, offer them a gin and tonic (recipe p. 206), a gin rickey (recipe p. 208) or a gimlet (recipe p. 204).

Ask your guests to wear white linen or flannel, boaters, bucks and other summer attire. Have on hand finger sandwiches of watercress, cucumber or egg, as well as biscuits, scones and other pastry delights. A little chamber music piped outdoors will provide the perfect ambience for a civilized afternoon.

# A Spanish *Tapas* Party

Get some pitchers of sangria (red or white, p. 385) flowing, and your guests will be doing the flamenco all evening. Flamenco music is, in fact, a great backdrop for a party. Keep a dance instruction book or video on hand so everyone can try their skill at this sexy dance.

Alongside the sangria, serve a variety of the Spanish finger foods known as *tapas*. These can range from simple olives to marinated seafood. You might also want to offer your guests a paella (made with rice, chicken and seafood), a Spanish omelette (egg, onion and potatoes) or any other typically Spanish food you enjoy.

# Dorm Party Revisited

Do you miss your college days? Do you long for the easy fun and rowdiness of no-hassle dorm parties? Well, why not host your own grown-up dorm party? All you need is a keg of beer in the bathtub and a punch made with fruit juice, club soda, vodka, gin and rum (see the chapter on punch for ideas), served up by the bucket, of course. Decorations? Don't bother.

Snacks should include cheese curls, nuts, pretzels, potato chips and onion dip made from soup mix. And as for music, break out all your old records and make a party tape of all your favorites— whatever you were listening to and dancing to at your alma mater. This kind of bash calls for a crowd and a dance floor, so get ready to party till the sun comes up!

# A Super Bowl Party

Whether your team's made it to post-season play or not—whether you even follow football or not—you can have a blast watching the most spectacular sporting event of the year. Get out your team banners and invite your favorite couch potatoes over for a lazy afternoon of camaraderie.

Cases of beer are a must at any Super Bowl gathering, but old standards like rum and coke (Cuba Libre, recipe p. 158) and screwdrivers (recipe p. 392) add much-appreciated variety. To go with the drinks, hearty food like chili, cheese dogs and pizza hit the spot.

# A Night in the Tropics

You can throw a tropical theme party any time of year, but during the dead of winter it's especially nice to host a little getaway.

Tropical favorites such as Mai Tais (recipe p. 288), Zombies (recipe p. 480) and Piña Coladas (recipe p. 344) are always big hits. You can also try something a little different. Prepare Fogcutters (recipe p. 190), Blue Hawaiians (recipe p. 115) or Wombat shooters (recipe p. 471) for your guests and leave them with an evening they'll never forget.

Bowls and platters of fresh tropical fruits should be available for your guests' pleasure, as well as food on a Polynesian or Caribbean theme, anything from jerk chicken to roast pork. Reggae, hula or calypso music—or just your favorite party music—will add to the fun. If your friends are a little crazy, ask them to come dressed in beach wear, whether it's bikinis or Hawaiian shirts. Find some exotic flowers at your florist and decorate in an island motif to make your party a smash.

These are only a few of the countless theme possibilities you can use to create fantastic parties. From Halloween to Mardi Gras, from *Gone with the Wind* to *Star Wars,* themes can suit all your moods and entertain all your guests.

COCKTAIL

PARFAIT

WHITE WINE

# Holiday Celebrations

Wₑ all know that eggnog is
served at Christmas parties and champagne flows freely on New
Year's Eve, but there are plenty of other drinks that can add a
festive touch to any holiday. If you look beyond the traditional
winter holiday season, there are many overlooked holidays during
the year that deserve something special, too.

Almost any holiday offers a good excuse to get creative in the
bar. Here are some suggestions for drinks that can make your
holiday parties occasions to be remembered. Check the recipe
section for instructions on how to make each of them.

New Year's Day: Poinsettia; Bellini Punch; Mimosa

Washington's Birthday: Cherry Daiquiri (frozen); Washington

Mardi Gras: New Orleans; Daiquiris of any sort; Hurricane

Valentine's Day: Love; Big Blue Sky; Cupid's Kiss; Sweetie Baby

Leap Year (February 29): Leap Year Special

Ground Hog Day: Mudslide

Saint Patrick's Day: Leprechaun's Libation; St. Patrick's Day Mocha Java

Tax Day (April 15): Income Tax cocktail

Easter: Easter Egg Hatch (nonalcoholic)

Memorial Day: Big Blue Sky; Summer Share

Flag Day: Betsy Ross

Midsummer's Eve: shots of aquavit (akvavit); shots of Swedish Punsch
(see Glossary); Fjord; May Blossom Fizz; Midnight Sun; Strawberry
Shortcake

Canada Day: Canada Cocktail

**Independence Day:** Stars and Stripes; Rainbow Sherbet Punch (made with red, white and blue sherbet)

**Halloween:** Cat's Eye; Zombie (made in a punch bowl); Black Witch

**Thanksgiving:** Turkey Shooter; Cranberry Vodka Punch

**Christmas:** Eggnog; Sherry Eggnog; Cold Weather Punch; Fish House Punch; Cranberry Pineapple Vodka Punch; Thanksgiving Cocktail

**New Year's Eve:** White Grape, Tangerine and Sparkling Wine Punch; Champagne Cocktail; Kir Imperial; Champagne-Maraschino Punch

---

CHAMPAGNE TULIP    CHAMPAGNE SAUCER    CHAMPAGNE FLUTE

# Making Toasts

The practice of toasting the health and wealth of others spans the globe and the centuries. It is customary in most social situations, both formal and informal, to offer a word or two before taking that first sip.

In the most casual of circumstances, a mere clink of glasses before drinking is sufficient. Usually, however, the spirit of toasting, of drinking to someone or with someone, means uttering an expression of friendship, of good wishes or of respect.

If you are asked to give a formal toast at an event, there's no need to sweat it. Come up with some appropriate expression of how you really feel about the toastee (make it nice—there's a reason Don Rickles's roasts can't be broadcast) and rehearse it, in front of the mirror if that will make you more at ease. Or if you're not comfortable with your own words, take the words out of the mouths of those who knew how to do it (i.e., check your favorite book of quotations).

What follows is a collection of some toasts; modern, not so modern, serious and silly.

## Toasts over the Years

"Down the hatch!"

"Over the lips, past the gums, look out liver, here it comes."

"Here's to my enemies' enemies."

"Here's looking up your kilt."

"Here's looking up your old address."

"Here's looking at you, kid."
> Humphrey Bogart to Ingrid Bergman in *Casablanca*,
> 1942, Warner Bros.

"Here's mud in your eye!"

"May all your troubles be little ones."
> Anonymous—to be offered to a bride and groom

"The good die young—Here's hoping you live to a ripe
old age."
> Anonymous

"Here's to the whole world, lest some stupid persons take
offense."
> Anonymous

"There's many a toast I'd like to say,
If only I could drink it;
So fill your glass to anything,
And thank the Lord, I'll drink it!"
> Wallace Irwin

"Here's to your health,
and your family's good health,
and may you all live long and prosper."
> Joseph Jefferson

"Let us wet our whistles."
> Petronius

"Here's to good friends,
tonight is kind of special."
> Loewenbrau beer commercial

"May you live all the days of your life."
> Jonathan Swift, *Polite Conversation*

"Let the toast pass,
Drink to the lass,
I'll warrant she'll prove
an excuse for the glass."
> Richard Brinsley Sheridan

"Let us toast the fools; But for them
the rest of us could not succeed."
    Mark Twain


"Here's to you, as good as you are,
And here's to me, as bad as I am;
And as bad as I am, and as good as you are,
I'm as good as you are, as bad as I am."
    Old Scottish toast


# ■ Toasting Around the World ■

| | | |
|---|---|---|
| AUSTRALIA | Cheers! | |
| CHINA | Kan pei! | Bottoms up! |
| DENMARK | Skal! | A salute to you! |
| FINLAND | Kippis! | Cheers! |
| FRANCE | A votre sante | To your health! |
| | A la votre | And to yours (response) |
| GERMANY | Prosit! | Cheers! |
| GREAT BRITAIN | Cheers! | |
| GREECE | Stin ygia sou! | To your health! |
| HAWAII | Kamau! | Here's How! |
| HUNGARY | Egeszsegedre! | To your health! |
| ICELAND | Skal! | A salute to you! |
| IRELAND | Slainthe is saol agat! | Health and life to you! |
| ISRAEL | L'chaim! | To life! |
| ITALY | Alla tua salute | To your health |
| | Cin-cin! | All good things for you! |
| JAPAN | Kan pai! | Bottoms up! |
| MEXICO | Salud! | Health! |
| MOROCCO | Sahrtek! | To your health! |
| NORWAY | Skal! | A salute to you! |
| PHILIPPINES | Mabuhay! | Long life! |

| | | |
|---|---|---|
| POLAND | Na zdrowie! | To your health! |
| PORTUGAL | A sua saude! | To your health! |
| ROMANIA | Noroc! | Good luck! |
| SAUDI ARABIA | Hanian! | Congratulations! |
| SCOTLAND | Slainte mhoiz! | Good health! |
| SINGAPORE | Yam seng! | To your continuing success! |
| SPAIN | Salud! | To your health! |
| SWEDEN | Skal! | A salute to you! |
| TURKEY | Serefinize! | To your honor! |
| U.S.S.R. | Za vashe z-dorovye! | To your health! |
| U.S.A. | Cheers!<br>Bottoms up!<br>Here's to you! | |
| YUGOSLAVIA | Ziveli! | To your health! |

CHAMPAGNE BUCKET

BALLOON OR LARGE WINE GLASS

40

# Frozen Blender Drinks

The blender, that standard gift at bridal showers and most ordinary of household appliances, has at last emerged from the realm of the boring. In fact, as an addition to the home bar, the electric blender makes the art of mixology all the more exciting.

The blender offers a simple, hassle-free way to make drinks. It requires no special training, no advanced degree in mixing drinks, and the results—well, they speak for themselves. This amazing gadget produces frosty delights to please any palate in just a few seconds, right before your eyes. Suitable for whipping up rich, creamy concoctions, refreshing, high-energy tropical drinks or low-calorie, nonalcoholic fruity treats, the electric blender can be your most prized piece of bar equipment.

The blended drink makes a glorious sight at any party. Guests are sure to be impressed with a fabulous frozen margarita (which is quickly becoming the nation's most popular drink). Or you can dazzle them with the incredible sensation of a frozen mango daiquiri, the likes of which they'd never dreamed possible. For a glimpse of the full range of blender drinks you can make, see Index by Type at the back of this book.

If you don't already have one, buy a good sturdy blender for your bar. All you really need is two speeds—high and low—so don't worry about finding a blender with twenty-four settings or any fancy functions. Clean it carefully before using it, then go wild. Once you've gotten used to your blender, experiment with your favorite drink recipes. You never know what you'll discover. For instance, many of the recipes in this book call for a shaker to mix drinks. Try using a blender instead—you might be surprised with the results. Add some fruit here, some cream there. The possibilities are truly infinite.

As a general rule, drinks containing ingredients that don't readily mix—such as cream, sour mix, eggs, ice cream or syrupy ingredients like grenadine or heavy liqueurs—need to be shaken vigorously at least, but blending yields superior smoothness. Remember: The blender is on your side. The results can be almost miraculous if you know how to use it, and the techniques are easy to learn. If you think of your blender as your co-host, it will never let you down.

Here are some basic tips for a great blending experience:

## For blending cream drinks

Fill blending cup one-quarter full of ice
Measure liqueurs first
Add cream
Blend at medium speed for 5–10 seconds or until smooth

## For blending sours

Fill blending cup one-quarter full of ice
Measure liqueurs first
Measure other alcohols next
Add sour mix
Add any other ingredients
Blend at medium speed for 5–10 seconds or until smooth

## For blending tropical drinks

Fill blending cup one-quarter full of ice
Add fresh fruit (if any)
Measure liqueurs
Measure other alcohols next

Add sour mix (if any)
Add any other ingredients
Blend at medium speed for 10–15 seconds or until smooth

---

Average blending times are mentioned above, but use your discretion. You will be able to tell if a drink is ready. When the drink is completely blended, you should not hear the rattle of ice cubes.

And now a few words about your blender:

- Before you use a new blender for the first time, fill it with warm water, and with the lid on, turn the machine on for about 25 seconds. This will remove any dirt or residues in the blender.

- Be certain the machine is turned off before you plug it in.

- Always remove foreign objects such as bar spoons or bar strainers from the blender before you use the machine. Do not insert utensils into the blender cup while the machine is operating.

- Always make sure the blade assembly is attached securely to the bottom of the blender cup. You don't want any leaks!

- Do not pour boiling water into the blender container. It might cause the cup to crack.

- Don't fill the container beyond its capacity, since the efficiency of the machine will be reduced.

- Make sure the lid is on tight before you turn the machine on.

- Don't remove the lid of the blender while the machine is running.

- Never reach into the blender while it is in use. Make sure hair or loose clothing do not get caught.

- Make sure the blades have ceased to spin before removing the container from the base of the machine.

- Always be sure the switch is turned to the OFF position when you are finished.

- To clean your blender after use, fill the mixing container with warm water, put the lid on, and turn the machine on for about 25 seconds. This will loosen any particles stuck to the inside of the container. Then remove and rinse the blender cup in warm water.

■ Always wash the container immediately after use. Don't let residues sit for too long, or they will be more difficult to remove.

■ When washing the inside of the blender, take care not to cut yourself on the metal blades.

If you keep these common-sense safety tips in mind, you'll find out how much fun it is to create a great blender drink. Enjoy!

**ELECTRIC BLENDER**

# The Perfect Punch

Punch, a sometimes bizarre mixture of ingredients that complement and set each other off, is a great way to entertain the masses. It's cheaper and easier to make one large concoction than it is to handle your guests one drink at a time. The punch tradition, which dates back to the eighteenth and nineteenth centuries, when rum was all the rage, has made a resurgence. Today, however, the main ingredient can be any liquor, depending on what you and your guests like, or on the occasion and the season. But, of course, rum is still a favorite component of punch, since it lends itself to mixing well with other ingredients. (Some punch aficionados won't even consider something a punch unless it has rum as its main ingredient!)

For traditional punches, the rum-based varieties are probably your best bet. As for choosing which rum (or other liquor, for that matter) to purchase, a cheaper variety will usually work well, since some of the nuances will be camouflaged. The assortment of juices, sugars, fruits and sodas, or the milk, cream or eggs that the liquor mingles with in the punch bowl can disguise a less expensive rum. But there is no substitute for fine quality, and some discerning palates may notice the difference. So if it is within your means to go for the more expensive brands, you should do it.

In cold weather substantial punches, milk-based punches and hot punches are particular favorites. The traditional Cold Weather Punch, Fish House Punch (first made at the Fish House Club near Philadelphia to cheer our nation's founders), Hot Rum and Cider Punch or, of course, Eggnog (for Christmas parties) are absolute favorites.

A champagne-based punch, such as the Bellini Punch, a peach and champagne blend, are great for New Year's celebrations, weddings or engagement parties.

While punches are not appropriate fare for a typical cocktail party (which, of course, calls for cocktails), they are certainly right for special-occasion parties, especially holiday get-togethers or birthday and anniversary parties.

The greatest advantage to serving a punch is that once the punch is made, you can just relax and enjoy the party while your guests help themselves. And since the majority of punches contain just a fraction of alcohol, you'll save money on liquor. Do make sure, however, that you have enough of the mixture reserved so that you can refill the punch bowl when it runs low, but remember, don't mix fresh punch with whatever remains in the bowl. Empty the bowl and prepare the punch with new ice. Otherwise, the taste will be weakened.

Nonalcoholic punches are great for parties where there will be nondrinkers or children. For the kids, a Rainbow Sherbet punch is always lots of fun.

Sangrias and other wine-based punches, and punches with loads of fruit and exotic juices are particularly popular these days. Especially when the weather starts getting warmer, guests call for something refreshing and lighter. A Strawberry Bowle (or any Bowle, using seasonal fruit) or a Polynesian Punch Bowl are extra-special refreshers. Juleps or coolers can be made in large quantities simply by multiplying your ingredients. And milk punches are a rich and smooth treat.

Ice cubes are not recommended for preserving your punch's chill. The preferred method of keeping your punch cool is a block of ice placed in the punch bowl. Ingredients in cold punches are usually best if chilled ahead of time (see individual recipes). Generally, for cold punches, a two-quart block of ice is recommended for every gallon of punch. Another tip: sodas and carbonated beverages do their best if added to the punch just before you're ready to serve it.

Try some of the single-serving punch recipes in this book. They're great for experimenting with new tastes before you venture to serve a crowd.

# Low-Calorie Drinks

In this age of health and fitness, almost everyone watches what and how much they eat and drink. Alcoholic beverages have gotten a bad rap as a source of empty calories, but there are plenty of options open to the weight-conscious bartender. The first step toward having fun without putting on the pounds is to know the facts about the caloric content of the drinks you serve. The following charts should give you an idea of how many calories are in your favorite drinks. (Numbers are approximate.)

## Spirits

| | |
|---|---|
| 80-proof liquors (1½ fluid ounces) | 97 calories |
| 86-proof liquors (1½ fl. oz.) | 105 calories |
| 90-proof liquors (1½ fl. oz.) | 110 calories |
| 94-proof liquors (1½ fl. oz.) | 116 calories |
| 100-proof liquors (1½ fl. oz.) | 124 calories |
| Aromatic bitters (1 tsp.) | 13 calories |
| Beer (lager type, 12 fl. oz.) | 151 calories |
| Beer (light, 12 fl. oz.) | 98 calories |
| Champagne (25 proof, 3½ fl. oz.) | 91 calories |
| Liqueurs (1 fl. oz.) | 66–106 calories |
| (e.g. 1 fl. oz. crème de menthe = 100 calories; 1 fl. oz. sloe gin = 68 calories; 1 fl. oz. amaretto = 82 calories) | |
| Vermouth, dry (1 fl. oz.) | 33 calories |

| Vermouth, sweet (1 fl. oz.) | 44 calories |
| Wine, dry (3½ fl. oz.) | 87 calories |
| Wine, sweet, dessert or aperitif (2 fl. oz.) | 80 calories |
| Wine, sherry (2 fl. oz) | 80 calories |

# Mixers

| Club soda | 0 calories |
| Cola (12 fl. oz. can) | 144 calories |
| Cranberry juice cocktail (2 fl. oz.) | 37 calories |
| Diet cola (12 fl. oz. can) | 0 calories |
| Fresh lemon juice (1 tbs.) | 4 calories |
| Fresh lime juice (1 tbs.) | 4 calories |
| Fresh orange juice (2 fl. oz.) | 28 calories |
| Ginger ale (12 fl. oz. can) | 113 calories |
| Heavy cream (1 tablespoon) | 53 calories |
| Pineapple juice, unsweetened (2 fl. oz.) | 34 calories |
| Tomato juice (2 fl. oz.) | 12 calories |
| Tonic water (12 fl. oz. can) | 113 calories |

Many of the drinks in this book are relatively low in calories, and you can lower the calorie counts of many simply by using less alcohol. For instance, if a recipe calls for 1½ ounces of vodka, limit it to one ounce and you've already cut out 32 calories if you're using 80-proof vodka. See the index of low-calorie drinks for a representative sampling of drinks that contain approximately 110 calories or less. Refer to the recipe section for instructions on how to make them.

# Beer

**B**eer appreciation is fast becoming an American passion, not to mention an international affair. The drinking of this foamy brew is no longer restricted to fraternity house parties and weekend football games. As imported beer has skyrocketed in popularity, along with light beer and the newer "dry" beer varieties, beer has taken on a new image of quality. The many different styles and flavors of beer offer great variety to the aficionado. Different beers are available to suit any occasion, taste and mood. And there is some especially good news about beer: Despite what you may believe, it has fewer calories than many other spirits. An average bottle contains just 150 calories, and light beers have even less.

Beer is made by cooking and fermenting grain, including malt, barley, rice, corn and others. It is then flavored with hops, which give it its bitter flavor. The brewing process varies from beer to beer depending on what ingredients are used, and on fermenting techniques and temperatures. An astounding array of brews results, as the following list of beer types shows.

## Types of Beer

*Ale*—a brew made with top-fermenting yeast; has a distinctive fruitiness; sharper and stronger than lager.

*Beer*—includes all beer, lager, porter and stout.

*Bitter*—a well-hopped ale, usually on draft; typically acidic, with a color that varies from bronze to deep copper.

*Bock*—the German term for a strong beer.

*Cold-filtered*—beer that is not pasteurized like other bottled and canned beers, giving it the fresh taste of draft beer.

*"Dark beer"*—usually refers to a dark brew of the Munich type; heavier, deeper flavor.

*Dry beer*—cold filtered and dry brewed for a beer that leaves no aftertaste.

*Lager*—any beer made by bottom fermentation; in Britain, typically golden; in continental Europe, can be dark; in Germany and the Netherlands, indicates everyday beer.

*Light beer*—lager-type beers that have a lower alcohol and calorie content.

*Nonalcoholic brew, or Near beer*—a new breed of beers that have no alcohol in them.

*Pilsner*—a golden-colored, dry, bottom-fermenting beer; flowery aroma, dry finish.

*Sake*—although often considered a wine, sake is actually a beer, since it is a refermented rice brew; has a high alcohol content.

*Porter*—an ale with a rich, heavy foam; sweeter than ale.

*Steam beer*—a term coined by the San Francisco company that produces Anchor Steam; has elements of both ale and lager.

*Stout*—extra-dark, top-fermenting brew; can sometimes be sweetish and has a very strong taste.

---

With all these beers available, you have plenty of possibilities to choose from. Do you prefer light-bodied, light-tasting, low-calorie beer, or a fuller-tasting brew? Does the familiar taste of Budweiser or Miller do it for you, or does a more exotic Mexican style—such as Corona or Sol—or a heavy, rich Irish style like Guinness Stout whet your whistle? Wherever your tastes take you, exploring the options can be lots of fun.

The quality of American beers is going up, and some of the best domestic beers available today come from regional breweries and microbreweries throughout the country. These smaller operations have experienced a resurgence in recent years, delivering beers of exceptional quality to local or regional markets. The development offers a real advantage for beer drinkers, and not only because they now have more to choose from. Because many of these independent breweries supply relatively small amounts of product to limited geographic areas, their beer does not have to travel far and therefore offers greater freshness and better flavor to the consumer. Among the beers currently available:

Anchor Steam, brewed by Anchor Brewing Company in San Francisco, has a strong malt flavor, creamy head and somewhat sweet taste. Their Anchor Liberty Ale is golden but somewhat cloudy, and has a sweet aroma of hops and an exotic, perfumy flavor.

Coors, the beer of the West, is produced in Golden, Colorado. It is light and easy to drink, and is now available nationwide.

Dixie Beer from New Orleans offers lots of flavor in a crisp, clean brew.

Lone Star Beer, from Texas, of course, is dry with a pleasant malt taste.

New Amsterdam Amber Beer comes from New York City's Old New York Beer Company. It's full bodied, aromatic and a real crowd pleaser in the metropolitan area.

Rolling Rock Premium Beer, widely available on the East Coast, has become the preferred drink of hip young urbanites.

Redhook Extra Special Bitter Ale, from the Redhook Ale Brewery in Seattle, is spicy, bitter and dark amber.

Sierra Nevada Pale Ale is amber colored with a light, lemony flavor. It is produced by Sierra Nevada Brewing Company in Chico, California.

Samuel Adams Boston Stock Ale, from the Boston Beer Company, is clear, light amber and fruity. Their Samuel Adams Boston Lager is also good; it is clear and light amber, has a fruity scent and delivers clean, sweet taste.

---

Light beers are extremely popular in this nation of fitness buffs. Some of the offerings out there include:

Amstel Light (95 calories) from Holland; the leader of the lights
Budweiser Light Beer (108 calories)
Coors Light (110 calories)
Kirin Light (105 calories) from Japan
Michelob Light (134 calories)
Miller's Lite (96 calories)
Stroh Light (115 calories)

---

The latest trend is to "dry" beers, which eliminate a lot of the aftertaste traditionally associated with beer. Among the more popular beers in this category are:

Bud Dry
Michelob Dry
Kirin Dry
Sapporo Dry

For draft beer lovers whose home bar does not include the equipment to tap a keg, cold-filtered beer is an excellent alternative. Choose from the following:

Busch Light Draft
Miller's Genuine Draft
Sapporo, one of Japan's finest exports

More and more imports, from almost any country you can think of, are appearing on the market today. No bar is complete without at least one imported selection, but you should have no trouble finding something you like among the hundreds of foreign beers offered for sale in America. Here are just a few of the many excellent imports:

Australia—Foster's Lager
Austria—Gosser Export Beer
Belgium—Westmalle "Triple" Abbey Trappist Beer; St. Sixtus Belgium Abbey Ale
Canada—Carling Black Horse Ale; Labatt's 50 Ale; Labatt's Crystal Lager Beer; Labatt's Pilsner Blue; Molson's Ale; Moosehead Canadian Beer
China—Tsing Tao
Czechoslovakia—Pilsner Urquell
Denmark—Carlsberg Royal Lager Beer
France—Kronenbourg 1664 Imported Beer; "33" Export Brew
Germany—Beck's Beer and Beck's Dark; Lowenbrau; St. Pauli Girl Beer

Great Britain—Bass Pale Ale I.P.A.; Newcastle Brown Ale; Watney's Red Barrel

Holland—Heineken Lager Beer; Grolsch Natural Holland Beer

Ireland—Guinness Extra Stout; Guinness Gold Lager; Harp Lager

Jamaica—Red Stripe

Japan—Kirin Beer; Sapporo Lager Beer

Mexico—Dos Equis XX Beer; Corona; Tecate Cerveza; Sol; Chihuahua

Norway—Aas Bok Beer; Rignes Special Beer

Switzerland—Cardinal Lager Beer

---

An increasing number of surprisingly good nonalcoholic brews are making their way into stores nationwide. The better choices include:

Haacke Best

Kaliber, produced by the Guinness Brewing Company

Moussy

Wartech Nonalcoholic Brew

---

Once you've decided which beers to include in your home bar, storing and serving them correctly is a snap. Store beer upright in your refrigerator and away from the light. Keep in mind that it's not a good idea to re-chill beer once it has been removed from refrigeration.

Beers should be served cold, but not *too* cold, or they lose some of their flavor. As a general guideline, most American light-bodied beers are good at about 42 degrees F, typical imported beers are best at 47–50 degrees, and full-bodied ales offer peak flavor at 55 degrees.

Beer can be served in mugs, goblets or pilsner glasses, depending on the occasion. If you like, frost the glasses by placing them in your freezer at least an hour before serving. To serve beer—whether from a bottle, can or tap—pour it slowly into a glass tilted at a forty-five-degree angle so the stream of beer flows down its side. This prevents excessive head from forming. When the glass is about two-thirds full, straighten the glass and pour the beer into the center until full, leaving a head of about three-fourths of an inch. If you prefer your beer without a head, keep the glass tilted until full.

Beer is a perfect accompaniment to a casual gathering of friends. Pour a few, raise your glass and savor the unique joys of this cool and frothy refreshment.

BEER MUG     PILSNER GLASS     BEER GOBLET

# Wine

The trend in wine for the nineties is to forget the hard-and-fast rules that have long dictated the drinking of wine. Now we all can enjoy the wine that we like with the foods we like—anytime we like. Those unfamiliar with the many subtleties of wine, and those who are simply not experts, have been scared away in the past. The good news is that there's no longer a stigma attached to simply finding a wine you enjoy and then sticking with it. But, of course, experimentation is bound to lead to some wonderful new discoveries.

Those on the cutting edge, then, are drinking whatever tastes right to them. The basic guideline, however, is that lighter wines best complement lighter foods, and fuller-bodied wines go with heavier foods.

As for serving wine, it is a common misconception that white wine should be served ice cold and red wine rather warm. Actually, both should be served at approximately the same temperature (red wine, usually 60 degrees F; white wine at about 55 degrees). An exception to the red wine rule is Beaujolais wines, which are usually better if chilled slightly, since these wines lack a high acid balance and chilling helps to compensate for the low acidity. Also, the better the quality of your wine, the less you should chill it, since chilling masks the flavor.

What about the old rule that you should let a bottle of red wine "breathe" before serving? When wine is exposed to the air, it "ages" and mellows. Breathing can thus enhance the flavor of any wine that is too astringent or tannic. Simply removing the cork from the bottle and letting it stand for a while will accomplish nothing, since only a very small portion of the wine makes contact with the air. Pour the wine into a glass or a decanter, allowing it to mix with the air, and let it stand for a while. The exposure to air will soften the flavor.

The most popular wines are produced in France, the United States (especially California, but also in Oregon, Washington and New York), Italy, Germany, Australia, Spain, Portugal, Argentina and Chile. The following list names the most popular categories of wine, the grapes they are made from, the general characteristics of those wines, and some suggestions for what sort of foods taste good with them. The descriptions are meant to give only a basic impression of each wine; any number of good books on wine can give you much more detailed information. What reminds one person of cedar, for instance, might evoke a pine forest for someone else. It's a good idea when tasting a new wine to keep a notebook and jot down anything memorable about the wine, so that you'll be able to recall later on what it tasted and smelled like to you.

# French Wines

These are named for the region they are grown in. For example, if you pick up two bottles of white Burgundy, one might say Meursault and one might be a Macon-Villages. They are both made from the Chardonnay grape, but they come from different areas in Burgundy. Here are the general categories of wine produced in France:

# Red Wines

1. Red Bordeaux: Made from a mix of three grapes, usually Cabernet Sauvignon, Merlot and Cabernet Franc. Their general flavor characteristics are cassis and cherry, sometimes eucalyptus, woody or cedarlike; some have a tobacco flavor. Commonly served with simply roasted meats or fowl. Good with mushrooms, cheese dishes and other medium to full-flavored dishes.

2. Red Burgundy: Made from the Pinot Noir grape. Characteristically less tannic, softer and fruitier than Bordeaux, emphasizing fruit flavors such as strawberries and boysenberries;

jammy, plummy and woody are other possible descriptions. Good with roasted meats and lighter dishes such as fish. Also good with cheeses and other earthy foods.

3. Rhone Wines: Made from a mix of many different grapes, depending on the region. The most common is the Syrah grape. Some Rhone wines contain up to twenty different kinds of grapes. They are typically bigger, heavier, full-bodied wines; tannic with a higher alcohol content. Other characteristics are pepperiness, cherry flavor, spiciness, jamminess and fruitiness. Go well with heavily spiced, full-flavored foods, such as barbecue, spicy pasta dishes, sausages and stews.

4. Beaujolais: Made from the Gamay grape. There are two types of Beaujolais. One, Beaujolais Nouveau, receives a lot of attention each November when it's released. It is shipped almost immediately after bottling and is very light, fresh and fruity and contains very little acidity. It's an easy wine for beginning wine drinkers to like. The other, referred to simply as Beaujolais, or "Cru Beaujolais," has a bit more body, acid and concentration of flavor, although it is also considered a light, fruity wine. Both have a grapeyness and are berry flavored and jammy. They are often best if served a bit chilled and are good paired with light, simple summer fare. A great picnic wine.

# White Wines

1. White Burgundy: Made from Chardonnay grapes. These are oaky and buttery, with hints of lemon, spice and flowers. There's a great range in style among white burgundies, from fuller, heavier bodied to lighter wines. They go well with fish dishes, especially salmon, and cream sauces, as well as light pastas and various kinds of lightly prepared meats, such as veal.

2. White Bordeaux: Made primarily from the Sauvignon Blanc grape. It is lighter, crisper, more acidic. Often described as herbacious, grassy, appley and lemony. Goes best with lighter, simpler foods.

   A subcategory of White Bordeaux is Sauterne, which is a dessert wine made primarily from the Semillon grape. It is sweet, honeyed and syrupy, and is excellent with desserts, especially fresh fruit or custards, or as an aperitif.

3. Loire: Made from the Chenin Blanc or Sauvignon Blanc grape. They are light, crisp, acidic wines, known for their flintiness or smokiness, as well as grassy or herbaceous characters. These benefit from being served a little colder and are drunk fairly young, usually three to four years from the date on the bottle. They tend to go well with seafood, especially oysters, clams, crabs and scallops and other light fish or salad dishes. Also great with vegetable soup.

4. Alsatian: This is a huge category of wine, but the two most famous types are made from the Riesling grape and the Gewurztraminer grape. These wines are much like the German-style whites—steely, highly acidic and crisp, with a spiciness and fruitiness. These wines go well with Chinese food and Indian food, as well as pork, quiche or German cuisine.

(*Note:* Many mistake "fruitiness" to mean sweetness, particularly in Alsatian and German wines. Typically, in fact, these wines are very dry on the tongue, with very little sugar.)

# Champagne

This is the sparkling wine made in the Champagne region of France, from a mix of grapes—predominantly Chardonnay and Pinot Noir. There are two types, vintage and nonvintage. Vintage means that the wine was made predominantly from grapes of a particularly excellent year. While vintage champagnes are more expensive, the difference in quality between vintage and nonvintage (a blend of grapes and wines from different years to conform to a house style) is small, so average drinkers gain little from the extra cost of vintage champagne. Champagne varies from light, crisp and acidy to heavy, toasty and yeasty. Try different brands of champagne to learn which is to your liking.

Champagne goes with just about everything, except perhaps Mexican and other very spicy foods. It also makes a wonderful aperitif. Like other wines, champagne is also best served not too cold. And even though the loud pop associated with opening a champagne bottle is a festive tradition, the quieter the event, the better. The louder the sound, the more gases and bubbles escape, ruining champagne's wonderful effervescent quality. Slip the cork out as gently and as slowly as possible.

# American Wines

In the United States, the primary identifier of wines is the type of grape. The most popular are from California, which in some cases now equals and even surpasses France in the quality of wine produced. Many other states, particularly in the Northwest, also produce surprisingly good wines.

# Red Wines

1. Cabernet Sauvignon: This is made from the same grape as the primary grape in French Red Bordeaux, and it has the same basic characteristics—cassis, cherry, sometimes eucalyptus, woody, cedarlike. It goes with the same foods.

2. Pinot Noir: This is the American version of a red burgundy. Recently, Oregon has gained acclaim for the quality of its pinot noirs.

3. Zinfandel: This wine is indigenous to America but similar to the Rhone wines of France—big, full-bodied, peppery and heavy. It goes well with heavy foods, such as barbecue, chile and garlicky foods.

# White Wine

1. Chardonnay-based wines: Made from the same grape used to produce French white Burgundy. One of the most popular wines in America, it has a unique complexity and clarity. This wine emphasizes the more oaky and fruity aspects, while these qualities of the French version are more balanced by acidity. It complements the same foods.

2. Sauvignon blanc–based wines: Made from the same grapes used in French white Bordeaux. There's more acid and fruitiness and less wood in these wines than in the French white Bordeaux, but they complement the same foods.

## Sparkling Wines

Made in the champagne style, American sparkling wines cannot legally call themselves champagne. Nonetheless, these wines can be quite excellent—much a match for their French counterparts. The same serving guidelines apply.

## Other U.S. Wines

1. White Zinfandel: This wine has recently become very popular. It is light, crisp and easy to drink, and goes well with any light fare.
2. Rosé: A light pink wine made from red grapes. The skins are removed before fermentation begins, so only some of their color remains in the wine. Rosé is light, crisp and not necessarily sweet.
3. Blush: A mixture of white and red wine, with white the predominant ingredient. The wine has all the characteristics of the white used as its base.

## Italian Wines

There are no hard-and-fast rules for wine labeling in Italy, but wines are usually named for the town near where the grapes come from. The name may also refer to the grape variety used. Italian wines go very well with most Italian foods, but they can be served as an accompaniment to any type of meal, depending on the individual characteristics of the wine.

# Red Wines

1. Barolo: Made from the nebbiolo grape. It is full, warm, robust; has a slightly greater alcohol content than its very close relative, Barbaresco. This wine must be aged for a minimum of three years before it is bottled. It goes with full-bodied, spicy foods, such as tomato sauces, lasagna, roasted meats and pizza.

2. Barbaresco: Also made from the nebbiolo grape. It has many of the same qualities as Barolo but is a bit lighter, not as tannic and more fruity. Aged for a minimum of two years, it goes with same foods as Barolo.

3. Chianti: The best known of Italian red wines, it is a simple red wine, not very tannic and lighter bodied. The predominant grape variety is Sangiovese. It is best with basic Italian foods such as pizza.

4. Valpolicella: A relatively light and fruity wine, it nevertheless has some substance. Age improves this wine only up to a point; it should be drunk five to eight years after the date on the bottle. The more basic Corvina and Molinara grapes are its ingredients. It goes well with simple Italian foods.

# White Wines

In general, Italian whites are crisp, light, fruity and not very woody. They tend to be clean and acidy, almost lemony. Their flavors stand up well to vinaigrettes and seafood dishes.

1. Pinot Grigio: A fine, full-bodied wine that ranges in color from pale straw to copper. This is a very simple wine made from the pinot gris grape. It complements deep-fried seafood dishes and other simple foods.

2. Orvieto: Made from the Trebbiano grape, this is a medium-bodied dry wine. It goes well with seafood.

3. Frascati: Also made from the Trebbiano grape, with the malvasia. A medium-bodied, dry wine, it goes with lighter Italian foods, particularly seafood.

4. Soave: A crisp, fruity wine made from the garganega and Trebbiano grapes. Light and simple, it goes well with the same light fare.

# German Wines

Riesling is the most popular German wine, made from the riesling grape. It ranges from very dry to very sweet and is similar to the Alsatian wines of France. A rating system of six categories delineates the sweetness of each riesling, with the first (*Kabinett*) being the driest and the sixth (*Eiswein*) being the sweetest. This information is given on the bottle, so you can choose accordingly. The wine should be served a bit colder than others. Depending on its sweetness, it can be served with anything from desserts (sweeter) to Indian and Chinese food (drier).

# Australian Wines

There is no formal labeling system for Australian wines, because wine making is a fairly recent development there and the country is so large. Most Australian wines are classified by grape variety. In red wine, look for Cabernet Sauvignon, Shiraz (the equivalent of the syrah in the Rhone wines of France) or one that combines Cabernet Sauvignon with Shiraz. Australian Shiraz is rich, complex and smoky or spicy—truly one of the most enjoyable reds available today.

In white wine, some of the best are Chardonnay or wines that combine Sauvignon Blanc with Semillon. The results are not as sweet in Australia as in France, but the wine is heavily wooded, oaky and fuller flavored.

# Spanish Wines

Spain is known mostly for its red wines. The most popular table wine from Spain is Rioja, a full-bodied and often very woody wine. The predominant grape is the Tempranillo, but some varieties of Rioja also contain Graciano, Mazuelo and Garnacho.

# Fortified Wine

Fortified wine contains brandy or other spirits, added in order to increase alcohol content or to stop the fermentation process. These wines are typically sweet, although some are dry. The drier ones are sometimes used as aperitifs as well as dessert wines or after-dinner drinks. More and more, fortified wines can be found not only on their own but mixed in cocktails, such as the Madeira Cocktail, the Prince of Wales, the Tuxedo, the Affinity Cocktail, the Adonis, the Soviet Cocktail and the Sherry Twist. Madeira, marsala, port and sherry fall into the fortified wine category.

## Madeira

Named for the island on which it is produced, these wines are fortified with brandy made from madeira wine. They can range in taste from light and dry to heavy and sweet. The types are:

Sercial ("rainwater")—light, dry

Verdelho—light, dry; rare

Bual—golden, sweet

Malmsey—deep gold, very sweet

## Marsala

Developed in the 1800s, these wines come from Marsala on Sicily, Italy. The wines are warm golden yellow in hue and have a caramel aroma. For the most part they are used for cooking. The important types are:

Fine—must have at least 17 percent alcohol and be aged for a minimum of four months

Superiore—sweet and dry; must have at least 18 percent alcohol and be aged for a minimum of two years

Vergine—extremely dry; must have at least 18 percent alcohol and be aged for a minimum of five years

Speciale—made with eggs and other flavorings; must have at least 18 percent alcohol and be aged for at least six months

# Port

Originally from Portugal and now associated with England, most ports are red; all are sweet. The types are:

Vintage—bottled two years in wood after the vintage and aged for decades; this is a fortified wine of the most excellent quality

Ruby—young and fruity; bright in color

Tawny—paler, less sweet and softer than ruby port

White—made from white grapes; similar in taste to ruby

PONY GLASS

# Sherry

Authentic sherry is made in Spain; sherry-like wines are made, however, in a variety of places, including Australia, Cyprus and California. The types range from pale and dry to deeply rich and sweet. They are:

Manzanilla—very pale and dry; serve chilled

Fino—pale and dry; serve chilled

Amontillado—pale gold and not as dry as fino; fuller in body; serve at room temperature straight or on the rocks

Oloroso—golden, full-bodied, can be dry but is usually sweet; cream sherry is the most common variety; sweeter olorosos should be served at room temperature, drier ones on the rocks

# Vermouth

Although vermouth is technically a wine, it is usually considered an aperitif. See the section on aperitifs for discussion.

# Aperitifs

∎ ▬▬▬▬▬▬▬▬▬▬▬▬▬▬▬▬▬▬▬▬▬▬▬▬▬ ∎

The term "aperitif" may sound fancy, but it actually refers to nothing more than any drink taken before a meal—a drink intended to "open up the appetite." Light spirits such as wine, champagne or fortified wine make superb openings to a meal. But there are many other exciting aperitifs on the market, including vermouths and bitters. Aperitifs can be enjoyed on their own, chilled, on the rocks or as ingredients in a large variety of mixed drinks.

Chilled vermouth offers an enjoyable way to ease yourself into a meal. A processed wine-based beverage, vermouth also contains sugar additives, herbal and plant flavorings and extra alcohol. At one time, dry vermouth was produced by the French and sweet vermouth by the Italians. Today the lines are less clear-cut, and both countries produce both varieties. Vermouth can be enjoyed on its own and is especially good on the rocks or with soda. Dry vermouth is a main ingredient in martinis; sweet vermouth is a main ingredient in Manhattans. Two of the more popular vermouths are Martini & Rossi and Cinzano, both from Italy. They come in dry and sweet varieties.

Other favorite aperitifs include Lillet Aperitif from France, which comes in white and red types. This wine-based drink with an orange flavoring has a rather delicate flavor. Dubonnet Aperitif Wine is manufactured both in France and in the United States. Its red (rouge) version is sweet, its white (blanc) dry.

Bitters might also appeal to you. Most bitters have, as one would assume, a bitter note to them, and many, although not all, have some alcohol content. They are generally derived from formulas that include some combination of aromatic plants, such as barks, seeds, roots, flowers, herbs, fruits and, many times, quinine. Many bitters have medicinal uses. In fact, a glass of club soda with some Angostura bitters is a great way to relieve an upset stomach. Bright red Campari, which comes from Italy, is one of the leading bitters aperitifs. It is very appealing to the eye, but watch out—it has a 96 proof alcohol base. It tastes bitter but is aromatic and has a very slight hint of underlying sweetness.

Another to try is Amer Picon, a French product based on orange, quinine and gentian roots. England offers orange bitters and peach bitters; Italy produces Punt e Mes Bitters, which are wine-based with quinine and have a sweet and bitter taste. Angostura bitters from Trinidad are a popular component of many mixed drink recipes, but some adventurous drinkers take them straight. In the same vein are Peychauds's Bitters from Louisiana, which are slightly more pungent than Angostura.

Anise-flavored Pernod (90 proof, so watch out) from France is the best known of its type. It is best taken five parts water to one part liquor, and turns cloudy when mixed. Ouzo is another favorite among fans of anise, and is sometimes served with three coffee beans floating on top.

Those looking for a truly great aperitif might try mixing up a Campari and Soda, an Americano, a Negroni or a Vermouth Cassis. Some others to try are the Knockout, the Addington, the Puntegroni, the Cat's Eye, the Bitter Bikini, the Via Veneto, the Dubonnet Cocktail, the Dubonnet Negroni, the Depth Charge, Pernod and Water and the Kiss Me Quick. Kir or Kir Royale are two more ways to whet your palate. Check the Index by Ingredients for various spirits to find additional recipes.

Remember, too, that as the rules of drinking become less formal, aperitifs can be consumed before, during or after a meal—or just by themselves. Drink what you want when you want.

SOUR GLASS

MARTINI GLASS

SHERRY

# After-Dinner Drinks

Coffee drinks, pousse-cafés, pony glasses filled with your favorite liqueur or snifters of brandy or cognac make the perfect conclusion to a meal. As this partial list of options shows, after-dinner drinks are typically liqueur based. Their soothing quality induces a sense of relaxation and well-being after the evening meal, promoting good digestion. While it is acceptable today to drink these drinks anytime, after dinner is still the preferred time for most. A fine after-dinner drink can inspire friendly conversation or simply wipe away the cares of the day.

Coffee, which makes a superb ending to a great meal, offers the perfect complement to many liqueurs. Try a Spanish Coffee, Mexican Coffee, Viennese Coffee or any other coffee drink (see coffee drink index, p. 507) to top off your dining experience. Mixed liqueur drinks, such as a B & B or Jelly Bean, Dirty Mother or Sicilian Kiss are adventurous alternatives for those seeking something a little different. And if you like pousse-cafés, why not try a Rainbow Pousse-Café or a Traffic Light? The recipe section of this book contains many possibilities to choose from. For those who prefer the simplicity of just one liqueur, however, cordials running the gamut from amaretto to Drambuie to Frangelico, and from Grand Marnier to Chambord to Tia Maria make for some sweet evening thoughts.

If a mellower, more complex flavor is more to your liking, brandy, the leading category of after-dinner drinks, offers a wide range of tastes. The term brandy comes from the Dutch word *brandewijn,* meaning ''burned wine,'' which refers to the heating of wine for distillation into spirits. The results of this process are liqueurs with an aroma as rewarding as their flavor, so brandies should always be served in a snifter.

While brandies come from a variety of regions, such as Spain, Italy and California, it is France that most people think of as the finest source, thanks largely to that nation's production of two very special forms of brandy. Subtle, sophisticated cognac and pungent, smooth armagnac are distilled under the strictest regulations, aged in oak barrels and carefully blended to perfection. Both have an alcohol content of 40 to 43 percent, but they differ in that cognac is distilled twice and armagnac just once. Armagnac thus has a larger, and often sweeter, flavor. It is also distinguished from cognac by vintaging—it can be vintaged, while cognac cannot.

Among the better-known brands of cognac are Courvoisier, Hennessey, Rémy-Martin and Martell. But despite cognac's enduring appeal, armagnac has recently overtaken it in popularity, with such brands as Sempé attracting a great deal of attention.

Reading the labels on bottles of these fine spirits is somewhat overwhelming to the untrained eye, but this simple key should unravel the mystery:

*V.S.* = Very Special or Very Superior, equivalent to the three stars designation; the least expensive blend, aged at least 2½ years (most brandies are aged from 3 to 5 years)

*V.O.* = Very Old, aged at least 4½ years

*V.S.O.P.* = Very Superior Old Pale, aged at least 4½ years but generally for 7 to 10 years

*Vieille Réserve* = a finer grade of brandy, aged as long as V.S.O.P.

*Extra* or *Napoleon* = designates the very finest brandies, 6½ years or older

---

Aside from cognac and armagnac, other brandies include those made from apples, such as Calvados, from Normandy, and applejack, a less refined version from the United States. A strong, woody-tasting brandy known as *marc* in France is called *grappa* in Italy, while Spain produces a brandy that is a sweeter and heavier alternative to cognac and armagnac.

Another type of brandy is true fruit brandy, known as *eau-de-vie* or *alcools blanc*. These are not the same as the colored, sweet brandies more familiar to Americans. Instead, true fruit brandies are unsweetened and usually clear. Aged in the bottle, they deliver a purer and more sophisticated flavor to the palate than their syrupy cousins. Cherry, plum, pear, raspberry and strawberry types are some of the best known and widely used true fruit brandies. Unlike cognac and armagnac, these fruit brandies should be served slightly chilled.

Cordials and liqueurs are another group of after-dinner drinks most everyone can enjoy. These alcoholic beverages are particularly sweet, and are flavored with any of a number of herbs, seeds, fruits, nuts and other special flavorings. Cream liqueurs, such as Bailey's Original Irish Cream, add cream to the spirits as a stabilizer. Another distinct category is crèmes such as crème de noyaux, crème de cassis and crème de cacao. These liqueurs have an exceptionally high sugar content, which results in a consistency quite similar to cream.

Some other popular liqueurs are aquavit (akvavit), distilled from rye and caraway; Benedictine, made from a secret formula of herbs; Galliano, a piquant herb-based liqueur; peppermint schnapps, a refreshing eye-opener; crème de fraises, derived from strawberries; crème de banana, formulated from bananas; a Danish cherry drink called Cherry Heering; Cointreau, distilled from orange peels; coffee-flavored Kahlúa; and Southern Comfort, a whiskey-based drink with peaches added.

Liqueurs are traditionally served in pony glasses after a meal, but today, more and more liqueurs can be found in exciting mixed drinks. From the famed Grasshopper, made with crème de menthe, to Kahlúa and Cream; from the Good and Plenty, a combination of ouzo and anisette, to the Jelly Bean, mixed from anisette and blackberry brandy: Liqueurs add a delicious dimension to mixed drinks.

Whatever your pleasure in after-dinner drinks, a sip of spirits following the evening meal is indeed a pleasure.

HOT DRINK MUG

BRANDY SNIFTER

POUSSE CAFE

# Drink Recipes

# A

## Aalborg Sour

**2 oz. Aalborg akvavit (or substitute any Scandinavian akvavit/aquavit)**
**1 oz. sour mix**

1. Fill mixing glass with ice
2. Add akvavit and sour mix
3. Shake
4. Strain into a cocktail glass
5. Add ice (optional)

## Abbey Cocktail (1)

**1½ oz. gin**
**¾ oz. orange juice**
**1 or 2 dashes orange bitters**

1. Fill mixing glass with ice
2. Add gin, orange juice and orange bitters
3. Shake
4. Strain into a chilled cocktail glass
5. Garnish with a cherry or an orange peel

# Abbey Cocktail (2)

1½ oz. gin
¾ oz. orange juice
¼ oz. sweet vermouth
1 or 2 dashes Angostura bitters

1. Fill mixing glass with ice
2. Add gin, orange juice, sweet vermouth and bitters
3. Shake
4. Strain into a chilled cocktail glass
5. Add ice
6. Garnish with a cherry

# Absolut Santo

3 oz. Absolut vodka
dash Chambord

1. Fill mixing glass with ice
2. Add Absolut vodka and Chambord
3. Shake
4. Strain into a chilled martini glass

(Courtesy of Sign of the Dove, New York City)

# Acapulco

1¾ oz. rum
¼ oz. triple sec
1 egg white
½ oz. lime juice
¼ tsp. sugar
mint leaves

1. Fill mixing glass with ice
2. Add rum, triple sec, egg white, lime juice and sugar
3. Shake

4. Strain into a rocks glass
5. Add ice
6. Garnish with 2 or 3 torn mint leaves

# Acapulco

1¾ oz. rum
¼ oz. triple sec
1 egg white
½ oz. lime juice
¼ tsp. sugar
mint leaves

1. Fill mixing glass with ice
2. Add rum, triple sec, egg white, lime juice and sugar
3. Shake
4. Strain into a rocks glass
5. Add ice
6. Garnish with 2 or 3 torn mint leaves

# Addington

1½ oz. sweet vermouth
1½ oz. dry vermouth
4 oz. club soda

1. Fill highball glass with ice
2. Add sweet vermouth and dry vermouth
3. Fill with club soda
4. Stir
5. Garnish with a lemon twist

# Admiral Cocktail

1 oz. bourbon
1½ oz. dry vermouth
½ oz. lemon juice

1. Fill mixing glass with ice
2. Add bourbon, dry vermouth and lemon juice
3. Shake
4. Strain into a chilled cocktail glass
5. Garnish with a lemon twist

# Adonis

**1½ oz. dry sherry**
**¾ oz. sweet vermouth**
**dash orange bitters**

1. Fill mixing glass with ice
2. Add sherry, sweet vermouth and orange bitters
3. Stir
4. Strain into a chilled cocktail glass
5. Garnish with an orange peel

# Adrienne's Dream

**2 oz. brandy**
**½ oz. peppermint schnapps**
**½ oz. white crème de cacao**
**½ oz. lemon juice**
**½ tsp. sugar**
**1 oz. club soda**

1. Fill mixing glass with ice
2. Add brandy, peppermint schnapps, white crème de cacao, lemon juice and sugar
3. Shake
4. Strain into a Collins glass
5. Add ice
6. Top with club soda
7. Garnish with a mint sprig

# Adult Hot Chocolate

1½ oz. peppermint schnapps
1 cup hot chocolate
whipped cream

1. Pour peppermint schnapps into a mug
2. Add hot chocolate
3. Top with a dollop of whipped cream, if desired

# Affair

2 oz. strawberry schnapps
2 oz. cranberry juice cocktail
2 oz. orange juice
1 oz. club soda (optional)

1. Fill highball glass with ice
2. Add strawberry schnapps, cranberry juice cocktail and orange juice
3. Stir
4. Top with club soda, if desired

# Affinity Cocktail

1 oz. scotch whiskey
1 oz. dry sherry
1 oz. port
2 dashes Angostura bitters

1. Fill mixing glass with ice
2. Add scotch, sherry, port and bitters
3. Stir
4. Strain into a chilled cocktail glass
5. Garnish with a lemon twist and a cherry

# After Dinner

1½ oz. apricot brandy
1½ oz. curaçao
2 oz. lime juice

1. Fill a mixing glass with ice
2. Add apricot brandy, curaçao and lime juice
3. Shake
4. Strain into a rocks glass with ice
5. Garnish with lime

# After Eight (shooter)

⅓ oz. Kahlúa
⅓ oz. Bailey's Original Irish Cream
⅓ oz. white crème de menthe

Layer Kahlúa, Bailey's and white crème de menthe in a rocks glass without ice

# After Five (shooter)

⅓ oz. Kahlúa
⅓ oz. peppermint schnapps
⅓ oz. Bailey's Original Irish Cream

Layer Kahlúa, peppermint schnapps and Bailey's in a rocks glass without ice

# A.J.

1½ oz. applejack (apple brandy)
1½ oz. grapefruit juice
3 or 4 dashes grenadine

1. Fill mixing glass with ice
2. Add applejack, grapefruit juice and grenadine
3. Shake
4. Strain into a chilled cocktail glass

# Alabama

1 oz. brandy
1 oz. curaçao
½ oz. lime juice
½ tsp. sugar syrup

1. Fill mixing glass with ice
2. Add brandy, curaçao, lime juice and sugar syrup
3. Shake
4. Strain into chilled cocktail glass
5. Garnish with orange peel

# Alabama Slammer

½ oz. sloe gin
½ oz. Southern Comfort
½ oz. triple sec
½ oz. Galliano
2–3 oz. orange juice

1. Fill mixing glass with ice
2. Add all ingredients
3. Shake
4. Strain into a highball glass
5. Add ice
6. Garnish with a cherry and an orange slice

# Alabama Slammer (shooter)

1½ oz. sloe gin
1½ oz. amaretto
1½ oz. Southern Comfort
1½ oz. orange juice

1. Fill mixing glass with ice
2. Add sloe gin, amaretto, Southern Comfort and orange juice
3. Shake
4. Strain into shot glasses

(Makes about 4 shots)

# Alabazam

2 oz. cognac
1 tbs. curaçao
1 tsp. lemon juice
2 tsp. sugar syrup
2 dashes orange bitters

1. Fill mixing glass with ice
2. Add cognac, curaçao, lemon juice, sugar syrup and orange bitters
3. Shake
4. Strain into a rocks glass filled with ice

# Alaska

1½ oz. gin
1 oz. yellow Chartreuse

1. Fill mixing glass with ice
2. Add gin and yellow Chartreuse
3. Shake
4. Strain into a chilled cocktail glass
5. Garnish with a lemon wedge

# Albermarle

2 oz. gin
½ tbs. powdered sugar
dash raspberry syrup
1½ tbs. lemon juice
club soda

1. Fill mixing glass with ice
2. Add gin, sugar, raspberry syrup and lemon juice
3. Strain into a rocks glass filled with ice
4. Fill with club soda

# Alexander

1 oz. white crème de cacao
1 oz. gin
1 oz. heavy cream

1. Fill mixing glass with crushed ice
2. Add crème de cacao, gin and cream
3. Shake
4. Strain into a chilled cocktail glass
5. Sprinkle with nutmeg (optional)

# Alexander's Sister's Cocktail

1 oz. green crème de menthe
1 oz. gin
1 oz. heavy cream

1. Fill mixing glass with crushed ice
2. Add crème de menthe, gin and cream
3. Shake
4. Strain into a chilled cocktail glass
5. Sprinkle with nutmeg (optional)

# Alfredo

1½ oz. gin
1½ oz. Campari

1. Fill mixing glass with ice
2. Add gin and Campari
3. Shake
4. Strain into a rocks glass filled with ice

# Algonquin

1½ oz. whiskey
1 oz. dry vermouth
1 oz. pineapple juice

1. Fill mixing glass with ice
2. Add whiskey, dry vermouth and pineapple juice
3. Shake
4. Strain into a chilled cocktail glass

# Allegheny

1 oz. bourbon
1 oz. dry vermouth
1½ tsp. blackberry brandy
1½ tsp. lemon juice

1. Fill mixing glass with ice
2. Add bourbon, dry vermouth, blackberry brandy and lemon juice
3. Shake
4. Strain into a chilled cocktail glass
5. Garnish with a twist of lemon

# Alliance

1 oz. gin
1 oz. dry vermouth
2 dashes aquavit (akvavit)

1. In a mixing glass, combine gin, dry vermouth and aquavit with several ice cubes
2. Shake
3. Strain into a rocks glass containing a couple of ice cubes

# Almond Cocktail

2 oz. gin
1 oz. dry vermouth
½ oz. amaretto

1. Fill mixing glass with ice
2. Add gin, dry vermouth and amaretto
3. Stir
4. Strain into a rocks glass filled with ice

# Almond Joy

1 oz. cream of coconut
1 oz. amaretto
1 oz. dark crème de cacao
2 oz. cream

1. Fill mixing glass with ice
2. Add cream of coconut, amaretto, dark crème de cacao and cream
3. Shake
4. Strain into a highball glass filled with ice

# Alto Parlarle

1 oz. orange sherbet
½ oz. Cointreau
chilled dry Italian sparkling wine
dash grenadine

1. In a chilled 8-oz. wineglass, combine orange sherbet and Cointreau
2. Blend together
3. Top with chilled dry Italian sparkling wine
4. Add dash of grenadine to top

# Amaretto and Cream

1½ oz. amaretto
1½ oz. cream

1. Fill mixing glass with cracked ice
2. Add amaretto and cream
3. Shake
4. Strain into chilled cocktail glass

# Amaretto Coffee (Italian Coffee)

1½ oz. amaretto
Hot coffee
Whipped cream

1. Pour amaretto into a mug
2. Fill with hot coffee
3. Add whipped cream to top

# Amaretto Mist

**1½ oz. Amaretto**

1. Add crushed ice to a rocks glass
2. Pour in amaretto
3. Garnish with a lemon twist

# Americana

**1 tsp. bourbon**
**dash orange bitters**
**½ tsp. superfine sugar**
**dry sparkling wine**
**1 slice brandied peach**

1. Combine bourbon, bitters and sugar in a mixing glass
2. Pour into a chilled champagne glass
3. Top with sparkling wine
4. Do NOT stir
5. Garnish with 1 slice brandied peach

# American Beauty

**¾ oz. brandy**
**¾ oz. dry vermouth**
**½ oz. grenadine**
**¾ oz. orange juice**
**½ oz. crème de menthe**

1. Fill mixing glass with ice
2. Add brandy, dry vermouth, grenadine, orange juice and crème de menthe
3. Shake
4. Strain into a chilled cocktail glass

# Americano

1 oz. Campari
1 oz. sweet vermouth
3 oz. club soda

1. Fill a highball glass with ice
2. Add Campari, sweet vermouth and club soda
3. Stir

# Amer Picon Cocktail

1½ oz. Amer Picon
1 tsp. grenadine
½ oz. fresh lime juice

1. Fill mixing glass with ice
2. Add Amer Picon, grenadine and lime juice
3. Shake
4. Strain into a chilled cocktail glass

# Andalusia

1½ oz. dry sherry
½ oz. brandy
½ oz. light rum

1. Fill mixing glass with ice
2. Add sherry, brandy and rum
3. Stir
4. Strain into a chilled cocktail glass

# Angel Face

**1 oz. gin**
**½ oz. apricot brandy**
**½ oz. apple brandy**

1. Fill mixing glass with ice
2. Add gin, apricot brandy and apple brandy
3. Shake
4. Strain into a chilled cocktail glass

# Angel's Kiss

**1 oz. dark crème de cacao**
**1 oz. cream**

1. Pour dark crème de cacao into 2 oz. pony glass
2. Float cream on top by slowly pouring the cream over the back of a long-handled bar spoon (the liquids should not mix)

(*Note:* See further instructions under pousse-cafés.)

# Angel's Tit

**1 oz. dark crème de cacao**
**1 oz. cream**

1. Pour dark crème de cacao into 2 oz. pony glass
2. Float cream on top by slowly pouring the cream over the back of a long-handled bar spoon (the liquids should not mix)
3. Garnish with a cherry on a toothpick centered across the top

(*Note:* See further instructions under poussc-cafés.)

# Anna's Banana

**1½ oz. vodka**
**1 oz. lime juice**
**½ small banana, peeled and sliced**
**1 tsp. honey**

1. Fill blender with 4 oz. ice
2. Add vodka, lime juice, banana slices and honey
3. Blend at medium speed for about 15 seconds, until smooth
4. Pour into a chilled goblet or large wine glass
5. Garnish with a lime slice


# Ante

**1 oz. apple brandy**
**½ oz. triple sec**
**1 oz. Dubonnet**

1. Fill mixing glass with ice
2. Add apple brandy, triple sec and Dubonnet
3. Stir
4. Strain into a chilled cocktail glass


# Anti-Freeze (shooter)

**½ oz. green crème de menthe**
**½ oz. vodka**

1. Fill mixing glass with ice
2. Add green crème de menthe and vodka
3. Shake
4. Strain into a rocks glass

# Aperitivo Cocktail

1½ oz. gin
1 oz. sambuca
3 dashes orange bitters

1. Fill mixing glass with ice
2. Add gin, sambuca and orange bitters
3. Shake
4. Strain into a chilled cocktail glass

# Applecar

1 oz. applejack (apple brandy)
1 oz. triple sec
1 oz. lemon juice

1. Fill mixing glass with ice
2. Add applejack, triple sec and lemon juice
3. Shake
4. Strain into a chilled cocktail glass

# Apple Daiquiri

½ oz. apple juice
½ oz. lime juice
1½ oz. light rum
½ tsp. superfine sugar

1. Fill mixing glass with 4 oz. shaved ice
2. Add apple juice, lime juice, light rum and sugar
3. Shake
4. Strain into a chilled cocktail glass

# Apple Eden

1½ oz. vodka
3 oz. apple juice

1. Pour vodka and apple juice over ice cubes in a rocks glass
2. Stir
3. Garnish with an orange twist

# Apple Ginger Punch

18 oz. apple brandy
2 oz. cherry liqueur
2 oz. kirsch
1 qt. pineapple-grapefruit juice
24 oz. Green ginger wine
1 qt. plus 1 pt. ginger ale
2 red apples
2 yellow apples

1. Chill all ingredients
2. Pour apple brandy, cherry liqueur, kirsch, juice and wine over a block of ice in a large punch bowl
3. Stir
4. Refrigerate for one hour
5. Cut apples into wedges and hold on side
6. When ready to serve, pour in ginger ale
7. Float apple slice on top of punch

# Apple Grog

1½ oz. applejack (apple brandy)
1 tbsp. brown sugar
4 oz. water
2 whole allspice
1 piece cinnamon stick
½ oz. 151-proof rum

1. Pour applejack, sugar and water into a small saucepan
2. Add allspice and cinnamon
3. Bring to boiling point, but do not boil
4. Pour into a heat-resistant mug
5. Float 151-proof rum on top
6. Garnish with a twist of lemon

## Apple Jacques

1½ oz. Lillet
1½ oz. apple brandy

1. Fill mixing glass with ice
2. Add Lillet and apple brandy
3. Shake
4. Strain into a cocktail glass

## Apple Pie

1½ oz. light rum
¾ oz. sweet vermouth
½ oz. apple brandy
1 tsp. lemon juice
dash grenadine
dash apricot brandy

1. Fill mixing glass with ice
2. Add light rum, sweet vermouth, apple brandy, lemon juice,
   grenadine and apricot brandy
3. Shake
4. Strain into a cocktail glass

## Apres Ski

1 oz. peppermint schnapps
1 oz. Kahlúa
1 oz. white crème de cacao

1. Fill mixing glass with ice
2. Add peppermint schnapps, Kahlúa and white crème de cacao
3. Shake
4. Put approximately 1 oz. of crushed ice into a cocktail glass
5. Strain drink into the glass

# Apricot

**1½ oz. apricot brandy**
**¾ oz. orange juice**
**¾ oz. lemon juice**
**dash gin**

1. Fill mixing glass with ice
2. Add apricot brandy, orange juice, lemon juice and gin
3. Shake
4. Strain into a chilled cocktail glass

# Apricot Fizz

**1½ oz. apricot brandy**
**3 oz. sour mix**
**1 oz. club soda**

1. Fill mixing glass with ice
2. Add apricot brandy and sour mix
3. Shake
4. Strain into a Collins glass
5. Add club soda
6. Add ice
7. Garnish with a cherry and an orange slice

# Apricot Sour

**1 oz. lemon juice**
**½ tsp. superfine sugar**
**2 oz. apricot brandy**

1. Pour lemon juice and sugar into mixing glass
2. Stir to dissolve sugar
3. Add apricot brandy and ice cubes
4. Shake
5. Strain into a chilled cocktail glass
6. Garnish with a cherry and an orange slice (or a lemon twist)

# Arawak Punch

1½ oz. gold Jamaican rum
½ oz. pineapple juice
½ oz. cranberry juice
½ oz. lime juice
1 tsp. almond-flavored syrup

1. Fill mixing glass with ice
2. Add all ingredients
3. Shake
4. Pour into a rocks glass
5. Add ice

(*Note:* Recipe may be multiplied by number of servings desired and prepared in a punch bowl.)

# Around the World

1½ oz. gin
1½ oz. green crème de menthe
1½ oz. pineapple juice

1. Fill mixing glass with ice
2. Add gin, crème de menthe and pineapple juice
3. Shake
4. Strain into a rocks glass filled with ice

# Artillery

2 oz. dry gin
1 oz. sweet vermouth

1. Fill mixing glass with ice
2. Add gin and sweet vermouth
3. Shake
4. Strain into a chilled cocktail glass

# Artillery Punch

1 qt. bourbon
1 qt. red wine
1 qt. black tea
1 pt. dark rum
1 pt. orange juice
1 cup brandy
1 cup gin
1 cup lemon juice
Sugar syrup (to taste)

1. Combine all ingredients and allow to chill in refrigerator
2. When ready to serve, pour over ice in a large punch bowl
3. Adjust sweetness and garnish with lemon twists

(Makes approximately 40 servings)

# Assassino

2 oz. whiskey
1 oz. dry vermouth
1 oz. pineapple juice
1 oz. club soda
2–3 dashes Sambuca Romana

1. Fill mixing glass with ice
2. Add whiskey, dry vermouth and pineapple juice
3. Shake
4. Strain into a Collins glass
5. Top with club soda
6. Add ice
7. Add a few dashes Sambuca to top of drink

## Astronaut

1½ oz. Jamaican rum
1½ oz. vodka
1½ tsp. lemon juice
1½ tsp. passion fruit juice

1. Fill mixing glass with ice
2. Add rum, vodka, lemon juice and passion fruit juice
3. Shake
4. Strain into a Collins glass
5. Add ice
6. Garnish with a lemon twist

## Atlantic Breeze

1 oz. light rum
½ oz. apricot brandy
4 oz. pineapple juice
1 oz. lemon juice
dash grenadine
½ oz. Galliano

1. Fill mixing glass with ice
2. Add light rum, apricot brandy, pineapple juice, lemon juice and grenadine
3. Shake
4. Strain into a Collins glass half-filled with ice
5. Top with Galliano
6. Garnish with a cherry and an orange slice

# Aubade

2½ oz. light rum
1 oz. lime juice
½ oz. grenadine
2–3 oz. tonic

1. Fill a highball glass with ice
2. Add rum, lime juice and grenadine
3. Stir
4. Add tonic
5. Stir gently

# Aunt Agatha

2 oz. light rum
4 oz. orange juice
2–3 drops Angostura bitters

1. Fill a rocks glass with ice
2. Add rum and orange juice
3. Stir
4. Float bitters on top
5. Garnish with an orange slice

# Aunt Jemima

½ oz. brandy
½ oz. white crème de cacao
½ oz. Bénédictine

Layer ingredients into a pony glass, beginning with the brandy.

# Aviation

1½ oz. gin
½ tsp. apricot brandy
½ tsp. cherry brandy
½ oz. lemon juice

1. Fill mixing glass with ice
2. Add gin, apricot brandy, cherry brandy and lemon juice
3. Shake
4. Strain into a chilled cocktail glass

# Azteca

1½ oz. light rum (tequila may be substituted)
1 oz. Kahlúa
1 oz. white crème de cacao
1–2 dashes curaçao

1. Fill mixing glass with ice
2. Add rum (or tequila), Kahlúa, white crème de cacao and curaçao
3. Shake
4. Strain into a chilled cocktail glass

# B

## B & B

½ oz. Bénédictine
½ oz. brandy

1. Pour the Bénédictine into a cordial glass
2. Float the brandy on top

## Baby Ruth (shooter)

½ oz. Frangelico
½ oz. vodka
2 or 3 peanuts

1. Layer Frangelico and vodka in a shot glass
2. Add peanuts

## Bacardi

1½ oz. Bacardi light or gold rum
½ oz. lime juice
3 dashes grenadine

1. Fill mixing glass with ice
2. Add Bacardi, lime juice and grenadine
3. Shake
4. Strain into a chilled cocktail glass

# Bahama Mama

1½ oz. light rum
1½ oz. gold rum
1½ oz. dark rum
2 oz. sour mix
2 oz. pineapple juice
2½ oz. orange juice
dash grenadine

1. Put a dash of grenadine in the bottom of a Collins glass or a hurricane glass
2. Fill a mixing glass with ice
3. Pour in light rum, gold rum, dark rum, sour mix, pineapple juice and orange juice
4. Shake
5. Pour into the Collins or hurricane glass
6. Garnish with a cherry and an orange slice

# Bailey's and Coffee

1½ oz. Bailey's Original Irish Cream
hot coffee
whipped cream

1. Pour Bailey's into a mug
2. Fill with hot coffee
3. Add whipped cream to top

# Bamboo Cocktail

1½ oz. dry sherry
¾ oz. dry vermouth
dash orange bitters

1. Fill mixing glass with ice
2. Add dry sherry, dry vermouth and orange bitters
3. Stir
4. Strain into a chilled cocktail glass

# Banana Banshee

1 oz. white crème de cacao
1 oz. banana liqueur
1 oz. cream

1. Fill mixing glass with ice
2. Add crème de cacao, banana liqueur and cream
3. Shake
4. Strain into a chilled cocktail glass

# Banana Boat

1½ oz. tequila
½ oz. banana liqueur
1 oz. lime juice

1. In a blender, combine tequila, banana liqueur, lime juice and 2 oz. crushed ice
2. Blend at medium speed for approximately 15 seconds, or until smooth
3. Pour into a sour glass

# Banana Daiquiri (frozen)

1½ oz. light rum
½ oz. lime juice
1 oz. banana liqueur
¼ banana, sliced
1 tsp. sugar or honey (optional)
½ oz. cream

1. In a blender, put ½ cup crushed ice
2. Add rum, lime juice, banana liqueur, banana, sugar and cream
3. Whip at low speed until smooth
4. Pour into an oversized wineglass, sour glass or chilled champagne glass
5. Garnish with a lime slice

# Banana Mama

1½ oz. light rum
½ oz. dark rum
1 oz. banana liqueur
1 oz. cream of coconut
1 oz. fresh or frozen strawberries
2 oz. pineapple juice

1. In blender, combine light rum, dark rum, banana liqueur, cream of coconut, strawberries and pineapple juice with 3 oz. crushed ice
2. Blend until smooth
3. Pour into a goblet

# Banana Moo

1½ oz. banana liqueur
1½ oz. cream

1. Fill mixing glass with ice
2. Add banana liqueur and cream
3. Shake
4. Strain into a rocks glass filled with ice

# Banana Split

1½ oz. banana liqueur
¾ oz. white crème de cacao
¾ oz. crème de noyaux
dash milk
several dashes cherry brandy

1. In blender, combine banana liqueur, white crème de cacao, creme de noyaux and milk with 3 oz. ice
2. Blend until smooth
3. Pour into a pilsner glass
4. Top with cherry brandy
5. Garnish with a cherry

# Banana Tree

1 oz. banana liqueur
½ oz. white crème de cacao
½ oz. Galliano
½ banana, peeled and sliced
5 oz. vanilla ice cream
4 drops vanilla extract

1. Fill blender with banana liqueur, white crème de cacao, Galliano, banana slices, vanilla ice cream and vanilla extract (Add ¼ cup crushed ice to make it thicker, if desired)
2. Blend until smooth
3. Pour into a large goblet or wineglass
4. Garnish with a slice of banana, with skin

# Barbados Bowl

8 ripe bananas
8 oz. lime juice
1 cup sugar
12 oz. light rum
12 oz. dark rum
1 qt. plus 12 oz. pineapple juice
12 oz. mango nectar
2 limes, sliced

1. Chill all ingredients, except bananas
2. Thinly slice 6 bananas
3. Place banana slices, lime juice and sugar in a blender
4. Blend for a few seconds, until mixture is smooth
5. Pour over a block of ice in a large punch bowl
6. Pour in light rum, dark rum, pineapple juice and mango nectar
7. Stir
8. Refrigerate one hour before serving
9. Cut the remaining bananas into thin slices
10. Cut limes into thin slices
11. Float fruit on top of punch

# Barbarella

**2 oz. Cointreau**
**1 oz. sambuca**

1. Fill mixing glass with ice
2. Add Cointreau and sambuca
3. Shake
4. Strain into a rocks glass filled with ice

# Barbary Coast

**¾ oz. light rum**
**¾ oz. scotch**
**¾ oz. gin**
**¾ oz. crème de cacao**
**¾ oz. light cream**

1. Fill mixing glass with ice
2. Add all ingredients
3. Shake
4. Strain into a large cocktail glass filled with ice

# Barnum

**1 oz. gin**
**½ oz. apricot brandy**
**2 dashes bitters**
**dash lemon juice**

1. Fill mixing glass with ice
2. Add gin, apricot brandy, bitters and lemon juice
3. Shake
4. Strain into a rocks glass filled with ice

# Bay Breeze

1½ oz. vodka
4 oz. pineapple juice
1 oz. cranberry juice

1. Fill a highball glass with ice
2. Add vodka, pineapple juice and cranberry juice
3. Stir

# Beauty Spot Cocktail

1 oz. gin
½ oz. dry vermouth
½ oz. sweet vermouth
1 tsp. orange juice
dash grenadine

1. Put a dash of grenadine in a chilled cocktail glass
2. Fill mixing glass with ice
3. Add gin, dry vermouth, sweet vermouth and orange juice
4. Shake
5. Strain into glass

# Beer Buster

1 oz. chilled vodka
2 dashes Tabasco
draft beer

1. Combine chilled vodka, Tabasco and cold beer (usually draft beer) in a chilled beer mug
2. Stir

102

# Bee's Knees

1½ oz. light rum
1 tsp. honey
1 tsp. fresh lemon juice

1. Fill mixing glass with ice
2. Add light rum, honey and fresh lemon juice
3. Shake
4. Strain into a chilled cocktail glass

# Bee-Stung Lips

2 oz. light rum
1 tsp. honey
1 tsp. heavy cream

1. Fill mixing glass with ice
2. Add rum, honey and cream
3. Shake
4. Strain into a chilled cocktail glass

# Bellini

1 fresh peach
brut champagne

1. Puree a peach in a blender
2. Pour into a champagne glass
3. Add ice cold champagne

# Bellini Punch

fresh peaches
iced brut champagne
1 tbs. lemon juice
sugar

1. In a blender, puree enough peaches to fill the bottom of punch bowl
2. Pour mixture into bowl
3. Add approximately 3 times as much champagne
4. Add lemon juice and sugar (to taste)
5. Stir thoroughly

# Belmont

1½ oz. gin
¾ oz. raspberry syrup
½ oz. cream

1. Fill mixing glass with ice
2. Add gin, raspberry syrup and cream
3. Stir well
4. Strain into a chilled cocktail glass

# Bennett

1½ oz. gin
½ oz. fresh lime juice
1-2 dashes Angostura bitters
1 tsp. powdered sugar

1. Fill mixing glass with ice
2. Add gin, lime juice, bitters and powdered sugar
3. Shake
4. Strain into a chilled cocktail glass

# Bentley

1½ oz. apple brandy
1½ oz. Dubonnet

1. Fill mixing glass with ice
2. Add apple brandy and Dubonnet
3. Stir
4. Strain into a chilled cocktail glass

# Bent Nail

1½ oz. Canadian whiskey
½ oz. Drambuie
1 tsp. kirsch

1. Fill mixing glass with ice
2. Add whiskey, Drambuie and kirsch
3. Shake
4. Strain into a cocktail glass

# Bermuda Highball

1 oz. gin
1 oz. brandy
½ oz. dry vermouth
ginger ale or club soda

1. Fill a highball glass with ice
2. Add gin, brandy and dry vermouth
3. Fill with ginger ale or club soda
4. Stir

# Betsy Ross

**1½ oz. brandy**
**1½ oz. port**
**2 dashes Angostura bitters**
**2 drops blue curaçao**

1. Fill mixing glass with ice
2. Add brandy, port, bitters and blue curaçao
3. Stir
4. Strain into a brandy snifter

# Between the Sheets

**¾ oz. brandy**
**¾ oz. triple sec**
**¾ oz. light rum**
**¾ oz. sour mix**

1. Fill mixing glass with ice
2. Add brandy, triple sec, rum and sour mix
3. Shake
4. Strain into a rocks glass filled with ice

# B-52 ✳

**1 oz. Bailey's Original Irish Cream**
**1 oz. Kahlúa**
**1 oz. Grand Marnier**

1. Fill mixing glass with ice
2. Add Bailey's, Kahlúa and Grand Marnier
3. Shake
4. Strain into a rocks glass filled with ice

# Bible Belt

2 oz. Jack Daniel's
2 oz. Rose's lime juice
2 oz. sour mix
1 oz. triple sec

1. Fill mixing glass with ice
2. Add Jack Daniel's, Rose's lime juice, sour mix and triple sec
3. Shake
4. Frost the rim of a highball glass with sugar
5. Strain mixture into the glass
6. Add ice if necessary

(Courtesy of The Cowgirl Hall of Fame, New York City)

# Big Blue Sky

½ oz. light rum
½ oz. blue curaçao
½ oz. cream of coconut
2 oz. pineapple juice

1. Fill blender with light rum, blue curaçao, cream of coconut, pineapple juice and 3 oz. crushed ice
2. Blend until smooth
3. Pour into a goblet

# Bitter Bikini

1½ oz. Campari
1 oz. dry vermouth
½ oz. triple sec

1. Fill mixing glass with ice
2. Add Campari, dry vermouth and triple sec
3. Shake
4. Strain into a rocks glass filled with ice (preferably crushed ice)

# Blackberry Demitasse

1 oz. blackberry brandy
½ oz. brandy
1 tbsp. blackberry jelly
½ oz. water
½ tsp. lemon juice

1. Heat blackberry brandy, brandy, blackberry jelly, water and lemon juice in a small saucepan (do NOT bring to a boil)
2. Stir well (jelly should be dissolved)
3. Pour into a demitasse cup
4. Garnish with a slice of lemon

# Black-Cherry Rum Punch

24 oz. light rum
4 oz. dark rum
2 oz. 151-proof rum
2 cans (17 oz. each) pitted black cherries in heavy syrup
4 oz. Peter Heering
4 oz. crème de cassis
4 oz. orange juice
8 oz. sour mix
2 limes
1 qt. chilled club soda

1. In a large punch bowl add light rum, dark rum, 151-proof rum, cherries, Peter Heering, crème de cassis, orange juice and sour mix
2. Slice limes into thin slices and add to mixture
3. Add a block of ice
4. Stir well
5. Refrigerate for about one hour
6. When ready to serve, pour in club soda
7. Stir gently

# Black-Eyed Susan

2 oz. Grand Marnier
½ oz. white crème de menthe
½ oz. brandy

1. Fill mixing glass with ice
2. Add Grand Marnier, white crème de menthe and brandy
3. Shake
4. Strain into a chilled cocktail glass


# Black Hawk

1½ oz. blended whiskey
1½ oz. sloe gin

1. Fill mixing glass with ice
2. Add blended whiskey and sloe gin
3. Stir
4. Strain into a chilled cocktail glass
5. Garnish with a cherry


# Black Lady

2 oz. Grand Marnier
½ oz. Kahlúa
1 tbs. brandy

1. Fill mixing glass with ice
2. Add Grand Marnier, Kahlúa and brandy
3. Shake
4. Strain into a chilled cocktail glass

# Black Licorice

½ oz. sambuca
½ oz. Kahlúa

Pour sambuca and Kahlúa into a brandy snifter or a pony glass

# Black Magic

1½ oz. vodka
¾ oz. Kahlúa
1–2 dashes lemon juice

1. Fill a rocks glass with ice
2. Add vodka, Kahlúa and lemon juice
3. Garnish with a lemon twist

# Black Manhattan

1½ oz. Old Bushmills Black Bush Irish whiskey
¼ oz. sweet vermouth

1. Fill mixing glass with ice
2. Add Old Bushmills Black Bush Irish whiskey and sweet vermouth
3. Stir
4. Strain into a chilled martini glass or rocks glass filled with ice
5. Garnish with a cherry

# Black Marble

4 oz. Stolichnaya vodka (or other Russian or Polish vodka)

1. Fill a rocks glass with ice
2. Pour in Stolichnaya
3. Garnish with a black olive and an orange slice

# Black Russian

**2 oz. vodka**
**1 oz. Kahlúa**

1. Fill rocks glass with ice
2. Add vodka and Kahlúa
3. Stir

# Blackthorn

**1½ oz. sloe gin**
**1½ oz. sweet vermouth**

1. Fill mixing glass with ice
2. Add sloe gin and sweet vermouth
3. Stir
4. Strain into a chilled cocktail glass

# Black Velvet

**Guinness Stout**
**champagne**

1. Combine equal amounts of Guinness (preferably on draft) and champagne in a chilled Collins glass
2. Stir

# Black Witch

**1½ oz. gold rum**
**¼ oz. dark rum**
**¼ oz. apricot brandy**
**½ oz. pineapple juice**

1. Fill mixing glass with ice
2. Add gold rum, dark rum, apricot brandy and pineapple juice
3. Shake
4. Strain into a chilled cocktail glass

# Blanche

1 oz. Cointreau
1 oz. curaçao
1 oz. anisette

1. Fill mixing glass with ice
2. Add Cointreau, curaçao and anisette
3. Stir
4. Strain into a chilled cocktail glass

# Blinker

1½ oz. blended whiskey
3 oz. grapefruit juice
½ oz. grenadine

1. Fill mixing glass with ice
2. Add whiskey, grapefruit juice and grenadine
3. Strain into a rocks glass filled with ice

# Blizzard

3 oz. bourbon
1 oz. cranberry juice
1 tbs. lemon juice
2 tbs. sugar syrup
3 oz. crushed ice

1. Pour all ingredients into a blender
2. Blend at low speed for about 15 seconds (until smooth)
3. Pour into a large wineglass or a highball glass

# Blood and Sand

1 oz. scotch
¾ oz. cherry brandy
¾ oz. sweet vermouth
¾ oz. orange juice

1. Fill mixing glass with ice
2. Add scotch, cherry brandy, sweet vermouth and orange juice
3. Stir
4. Strain into a chilled cocktail glass

# Bloody Maria

1½ oz. tequila
3 oz. tomato juice
½ oz. lemon juice
3 drops Tabasco sauce
3 drops Worcestershire sauce
pinch celery salt
pinch pepper
dab horseradish (squeeze out liquid)

1. Combine tequila, tomato juice, lemon juice and seasonings (to taste) in a well-chilled mixing glass
2. Shake
3. Pour into an oversized wineglass or a chilled Collins glass
4. Garnish with a lime slice or a celery stalk

(*Note:* A Bloody Maria may also be served on the rocks and stirred in the glass, or it may be shaken with ice and strained into the glass.)

# Bloody Mary

1½ oz. vodka
3 oz. tomato juice
½ oz. lemon juice

**3 drops Tabasco sauce**
**3 drops Worcestershire sauce**
**pinch celery salt**
**pinch pepper**
**dab horseradish (squeeze out liquid)**

1. Combine vodka, tomato juice, lemon juice and seasonings (to taste) in a well-chilled mixing glass
2. Shake
3. Pour into an oversized wineglass or a chilled Collins glass
4. Garnish with a lime slice or a celery stalk

(*Note:* A Bloody Mary may also be served on the rocks and stirred in the glass, or it may be shaken with ice and strained into the glass.)

# Blue Carnation

**½ oz. white crème de cacao**
**½ oz. blue curaçao**
**2 oz. cream**

1. Fill mixing glass with ice
2. Add white crème de cacao, blue curaçao and cream
3. Shake
4. Strain into a chilled cocktail glass

# Blue Denim

**½ oz. dry vermouth**
**½ oz. bourbon**
**2 dashes Angostura bitters**
**dash blue curaçao**

1. Fill mixing glass with ice
2. Add dry vermouth, bourbon, Angostura bitters and blue curaçao
3. Shake
4. Strain into a rocks glass filled with ice
5. Garnish with a twist of lemon

# Blue Hawaiian

1 oz. light rum
2 oz. pineapple juice
1 oz. blue curaçao
1 oz. cream of coconut

1. Fill blender with 3 oz. crushed ice
2. Pour in rum, pineapple juice, blue curaçao and cream of coconut
3. Blend at low speed for about 15 seconds (until smooth)
4. Pour into a goblet
5. Garnish with a cherry and an orange slice

# Blue Margarita

2 oz. tequila
¾ oz. blue curaçao
2 oz. sour mix
½ oz. lime juice
salt for glass (optional)
Lemon or lime wedge (if you use salt)

1. Rub the rim of a margarita or large cocktail glass with the lemon or lime wedge (if you are going to salt the rim)
2. Turn the rim of the glass in a bed of salt (if desired)
3. Fill a mixing glass with ice
4. Add tequila, blue curaçao, sour mix and lime juice
5. Shake
6. Strain into the glass
7. Add ice cubes (if desired)
8. Garnish with a cherry or a lime wedge

# Blue Moon

1½ oz. gin
½ oz. dry vermouth
1 tsp. blue curaçao
dash Angostura bitters

1. Fill mixing glass with ice
2. Add gin, dry vermouth, blue curaçao and bitters
3. Shake
4. Strain into a chilled cocktail glass

# Blue Shark

1 oz. white tequila
1 oz. vodka
¾ oz. blue curaçao

1. Fill mixing glass with ice
2. Add tequila, vodka and blue curaçao
3. Shake
4. Strain into a chilled cocktail glass

# Boardwalk Breezer

1½ oz. dark rum
½ oz. banana liqueur
½ oz. lime juice
4 oz. pineapple juice
dash grenadine

1. Fill mixing glass with ice
2. Add dark rum, banana liqueur, lime juice and pineapple juice
3. Shake
4. Strain into a Collins glass
5. Add ice
6. Top with a dash of grenadine
7. Garnish with a cherry and an orange slice

# Bobby Burns

1 oz. scotch
1 oz. dry vermouth
1 oz. sweet vermouth
dash Bénédictine

1. Fill mixing glass with ice
2. Add scotch, dry vermouth, sweet vermouth and Bénédictine
3. Stir
4. Strain into a chilled cocktail glass

# Bocci Ball

1½ oz. amaretto
6 oz. orange juice
club soda (if desired)

1. Fill a highball glass with ice
2. Add amaretto and orange juice
3. Stir
4. Splash club soda on top (optional)

# Boilermaker

2 oz. whiskey
1 glass of beer

1. Drink a straight shot of whiskey
2. Chase it down with a glass of your favorite beer

(*Note:* If you prefer, mix the whiskey and beer in a highball glass and drink them together.)

# Bolero

**1½ oz. light rum**
**¾ oz. apple brandy**
**¼ tsp. sweet vermouth**

1. Fill mixing glass with ice
2. Add light rum, apple brandy and sweet vermouth
3. Stir
4. Strain into a chilled cocktail glass

# Bombay

**1 oz. brandy**
**1 oz. dry vermouth**
**½ oz. sweet vermouth**
**½ tsp. curaçao**
**dash of Pernod**

1. Fill mixing glass with ice
2. Add brandy, dry vermouth, sweet vermouth, curaçao and Pernod
3. Shake
4. Strain into a chilled rocks glass filled with ice

# Booster

**2 oz. brandy**
**½ oz. curaçao**
**1 egg white**

1. Fill mixing glass with ice
2. Add brandy, curaçao and egg white
3. Shake
4. Strain into a chilled cocktail glass

# The Bottom Line

1½ oz. vodka
½ oz. lime juice
4 oz. tonic

1. Fill a highball glass with ice
2. Add vodka and lime juice
3. Fill with tonic
4. Garnish with a lime slice

# Bourbon Daisy

1½ oz. bourbon
½ oz. Southern Comfort
½ oz. lemon juice
½ oz. grenadine
1 oz. club soda

1. Fill mixing glass with ice
2. Add bourbon, Southern Comfort, lemon juice and grenadine
3. Shake
4. Strain into a Collins glass
5. Add ice
6. Top with club soda
7. Garnish with a pineapple spear or a cherry and an orange slice

# Bourbon Old-Fashioned

1 tsp. sugar
2 dashes bitters
1 tsp. water
3 oz. bourbon

1. Put sugar, bitters and water in rocks glass
2. Muddle to dissolve sugar
3. Add 1 or 2 ice cubes to glass

4. Pour in the bourbon
5. Add more ice (if desired)
6. Twist a lemon peel over the drink and add as garnish
7. If desired, may also garnish with a cherry and an orange slice

# Bourbon Sour

1½ oz. bourbon
3 oz. sour mix

1. Fill mixing glass with ice
2. Add bourbon and sour mix
3. Shake
4. Strain into a sour glass
5. Add ice
6. Garnish with a cherry and an orange slice

# Brain

1 oz. Kahlúa
1 oz. peach schnapps
1 oz. Bailey's Original Irish Cream

Layer Kahlúa, peach schnapps and Bailey's in a rocks glass filled with ice

# Brain Eraser

1 oz. vodka
½ oz. Kahlúa
½ oz. amaretto
club soda

1. Fill rocks glass with ice
2. Add vodka, Kahlúa and amaretto
3. Top with club soda
4. Drink it in one shot through a straw

# Brain Tumor

**2 oz. Bailey's Original Irish Cream**
**6 drops strawberry liqueur**

1. Fill a rocks glass with ice
2. Pour in Bailey's
3. Drop in strawberry liqueur
4. Do NOT stir
(Drink is supposed to resemble an unhealthy brain.)

# Brandy Alexander

**½ oz. white crème de cacao**
**½ oz. brandy**
**½ oz. heavy cream**
**nutmeg or cinnamon**

1. Fill mixing glass with ice
2. Add crème de cacao, brandy and cream
3. Shake
4. Strain into a chilled cocktail glass
5. Sprinkle nutmeg or cinnamon on top

# Brandy Cobbler

**2½ oz. brandy**
**1 tsp. peach liqueur (curaçao may be substituted)**
**2 tsp. lemon juice**
**1 tsp. sugar syrup (to taste)**

1. Fill a chilled highball glass or goblet about with cracked ice
2. Add brandy, peach liqueur, lemon juice and sugar syrup
3. Stir (the glass should frost)
4. Garnish with a cherry and an orange slice

# Brandy Eggnog

2½ oz. brandy
1 cup milk
2 tbs. powdered sugar
1 egg

1. Combine all ingredients with ice
2. Shake well
3. Strain into a mug
4. Garnish with a sprinkle of nutmeg

# Brandy Gump

½ oz. brandy
½ oz. fresh lemon juice
2–3 drops grenadine

1. Fill mixing glass with ice
2. Add brandy and lemon juice
3. Shake
4. Strain into a chilled cocktail glass
5. Add a couple of drops of grenadine

# Brandy Ice

1½ oz. brandy
½ oz. white crème de cacao
2 scoops French vanilla ice cream
2 oz. shaved ice

1. Combine all ingredients in a blender
2. Blend until smooth
3. Pour into a large brandy snifter
4. Garnish with shaved sweet chocolate

# Brandy Manhattan

**2 oz. brandy**
**½ oz. sweet vermouth**
**dash Angostura bitters**

1. Fill mixing glass with some ice
2. Add brandy, sweet vermouth and bitters
3. Stir gently
4. Strain into chilled martini glass
5. Garnish with a cherry

# Brandy Milk Punch

**2 oz. brandy**
**5 oz. cold milk**
**pinch sugar**

1. Add a few ice cubes to a highball glass
2. Add brandy, milk and generous pinch of sugar
3. Stir
4. Sprinkle with nutmeg or cinnamon

# Brandy Old-Fashioned

**2½ oz. brandy**
**1 cube sugar**
**1–2 dashes Angostura bitters**

1. In a rocks glass, combine bitters and sugar cube
2. Pour in the brandy
3. Stir until sugar cube is dissolved
4. Add ice

# Brass Monkey

½ oz. vodka
½ oz. light rum
orange juice

1. Fill a highball glass with ice
2. Add vodka, rum and orange juice
3. Stir

# Brassy Blonde

1½ oz. whiskey
1½ oz. grapefruit juice
1 tsp. strawberry liqueur
1 oz. club soda

1. Fill a Collins glass with ice
2. Add whiskey, grapefruit juice and strawberry liqueur
3. Stir
4. Top with club soda
5. Stir again

# Brave Bull ✳

1½ oz. tequila
1 oz. Kahlúa

1. Fill a rocks glass with ice
2. Add tequila and Kahlúa
3. Stir

# Breakfast Eggnog

**1 egg**
**1 oz. brandy**
**½ oz. curaçao**
**4 oz. cold milk**

1. Fill mixing glass with ice
2. Add egg, brandy, curaçao and cold milk
3. Shake well
4. Strain into a chilled highball glass

# Bronx Cheer

**2 oz. apricot brandy**
**6 oz. raspberry soda**

1. Fill a Collins glass with ice
2. Add apricot brandy and raspberry soda
3. Stir
4. Garnish with an orange slice

# Brown

**1¼ oz. bourbon**
**1¼ oz. dry vermouth**
**2 dashes orange bitters**

1. Fill mixing glass with ice
2. Add bourbon, dry vermouth and bitters
3. Shake
4. Strain into rocks glass filled with ice

# Brown Bomber

½ oz. peanut liqueur
½ oz. white crème de cacao
2 oz. cream

1. Fill mixing glass with ice
2. Add peanut liqueur, white crème de cacao and cream
3. Shake
4. Strain into a chilled cocktail glass

# Bubble Gum (shooter)

1½ oz. vodka
1½ oz. banana liqueur
1½ oz. peach schnapps
1½ oz. orange juice

1. Fill mixing glass with ice
2. Add vodka, banana liqueur, peach schnapps and orange juice
3. Shake
4. Strain into shot glasses

(Makes about 4 shots)

# Bucks Fizz

1½ oz. gin
½ tsp. sugar
2 oz. orange juice
1 oz. sour mix
1 oz. club soda

1. Fill mixing glass with ice
2. Add gin, sugar, orange juice and sour mix
3. Shake
4. Strain into a Collins glass
5. Add club soda
6. Fill with ice
7. Garnish with a cherry and an orange slice

# Buffalo Sweat (shooter)

**1½ oz. bourbon**
**dash of Tabasco sauce**

1. Pour bourbon into a shot glass
2. Add a dash Tabasco

# Bull Frog

**1½ oz. vodka**
**limeade**

1. Fill a highball glass with ice
2. Add vodka and limeade
3. Stir
4. Garnish with a slice of lime

# Bull Shot

**1½ oz. vodka**
**1 tsp. lemon juice**
**3–4 drops Worcestershire sauce**
**dash Tabasco sauce**
**Beef bouillon, chilled**

1. Fill a rocks glass with ice
2. Add vodka, lemon juice, Worcestershire and Tabasco
3. Fill with bouillon
4  Stir

# Butterscotch Collins

1 tsp. sugar
water
1½ oz. scotch
½ oz. Drambuie
2 oz. lemon juice
1 oz. soda

1. Dissolve sugar in water
2. Pour over ice in a Collins glass
3. Add scotch, Drambuie and lemon juice
4. Stir
5. Top with soda
6. Garnish with a cherry and an orange slice

# B.V.D.

1½ oz. gin
¾ oz. light rum
¾ oz. dry vermouth

1. Fill mixing glass with ice
2. Add gin, light rum and dry vermouth
3. Stir
4. Strain into a chilled cocktail glass

# C

## Cablegram

**2 oz. blended whiskey**
**1 tsp. sugar syrup**
**½ oz. lemon juice**
**ginger ale**

1. Fill mixing glass with cracked ice
2. Add whiskey, sugar syrup and lemon juice
3. Shake
4. Pour into a highball glass
5. Fill with ginger ale

## Cadiz

**¾ oz. blackberry brandy**
**¾ oz. dry sherry**
**½ oz. triple sec**
**¼ oz. cream**

1. Fill mixing glass with ice
2. Add blackberry brandy, dry sherry, triple sec and cream
3. Shake
4. Strain into a rocks glass filled with ice

## Café Bonaparte

**1½ oz. brandy**
**cappuccino (espresso and steamed milk)**

1. Pour brandy into a hot drink glass
2. Fill with cappuccino

# Café Foster

**1 oz. Bacardi Black Label rum**
**½ oz. crème de banana**
**hot coffee**
**vanilla-flavored whipped cream**

1. Pour Bacardi and crème de banana into a coffee mug or glass
2. Fill with hot coffee
3. Top with whipped cream

(Courtesy of Cafe L'Erope, Sarasota, Florida)

# Café Marnier

**1½ oz. Grand Marnier**
**strong coffee or espresso**

1. Pour Grand Marnier into a coffee mug
2. Add hot coffee so that mug is three-fourths full
3. Stir
4. Add whipped cream, if desired

# Café Theatre

**½ oz. Bailey's Original Irish Cream**
**½ oz. white crème de cacao**
**dash Frangelico liqueur (amaretto may be substituted)**
**dash dark crème de cacao**
**hot coffee**

1. Pour Bailey's and white crème de cacao into a coffee mug
2. Add enough coffee so that the cup is almost filled
3. Add a dash each of Frangelico and dark crème de cacao
4. Top with whipped cream
5. Garnish with a cinnamon stick

# Café Zurich

1½ oz. anisette
1½ oz. cognac
½ oz. amaretto
hot coffee
1 tsp. honey
whipped cream

1. Pour anisette, cognac and amaretto into a coffee mug
2. Add hot coffee so that mug is three-fourths filled
3. Allow honey to float on top of drink
4. Stir
5. Add whipped cream, if desired

# Caipirinha

2 or 3 lime wedges
dash sugar
½ oz. sour mix
3 oz. Brazilian rum

1. Mash the lime wedges with sugar in a mixing glass
2. Add ice, rum and sour mix
3. Shake
4. Pour into a highball glass
5. Garnish with lime slice

# Cajun Bloody Mary

1 oz. Absolut Peppar vodka (or other pepper-flavored
     vodka)
Bloody Mary mix (see recipe for Bloody Mary or Virgin
     Mary)

1. Fill a highball glass with ice
2. Add Absolut Peppar vodka
3. Fill with Bloody Mary mix
4. Stir
5. Garnish with a celery stalk or lime or a hot pepper (if you dare)

(*Note:* For an extra spicy experience, rub hot spices along the rim of the glass.)

## California Driver

**1 oz. vodka**
**3 oz. orange juice**
**3 oz. grapefruit juice**

1. Fill a highball glass with ice
2. Add vodka, orange juice and grapefruit juice
3. Stir

## California Ice Tea

**½ oz. vodka**
**½ oz. gin**
**½ oz. light rum**
**½ oz. triple sec**
**½ oz. white tequila**
**½ oz. sour mix**
**1 oz. orange juice**
**1 oz. pineapple juice**

1. Fill mixing glass with ice
2. Add all ingredients
3. Shake
4. Strain into a Collins glass
5. Add ice
6. Garnish with a lemon slice

# California Lemonade

½ oz. vodka
½ oz. gin
½ oz. brandy
2 oz. sour mix
2 oz. orange juice
¼ oz. grenadine

1. Fill mixing glass with ice
2. Add all ingredients
3. Shake
4. Strain into a Collins glass
5. Add ice

# California Root Beer

1 oz. Galliano
1 oz. Kahlúa
2 oz. club soda
1 oz. cola
splash beer (optional)

1. Fill a rocks glass with ice
2. Pour in Galliano and Kahlúa
3. Add club soda and cola
4. Stir
5. Splash beer on top (if desired)

# Calypso (also called Jamaican Coffee)

¾ oz. Tia Maria
¾ oz. Jamaican rum
hot coffee

1. Pour Tia Maria and rum into a coffee mug
2. Add hot coffee
3. Top with whipped cream (if desired)

# Campari and Soda

**2 oz. Campari**
**2 oz. club soda**

1. Fill a highball glass with ice
2. Add Campari and club soda
3. Stir
4. Garnish with an orange peel (twist)

# Campobello

**1½ oz. gin**
**1 oz. sweet vermouth**
**1 oz. Campari**

1. Fill mixing glass with ice
2. Add gin, sweet vermouth and Campari
3. Shake
4. Strain into a cocktail glass

# Canada Cocktail

**1½ oz. Canadian whiskey**
**½ oz. triple sec**
**2 dashes Angostura bitters**
**1 tsp. sugar**

1. Fill mixing glass with ice
2. Add Canadian whiskey, triple sec, bitters and sugar
3. Shake
4. Strain into a chilled cocktail glass

# Cape Codder

**1½ oz. vodka**
**6 oz. cranberry juice**

1. Fill a highball glass with ice
2. Add vodka and cranberry juice
3. Stir
4. Garnish with a wedge of lime

# Cape Grape

**1½ oz. vodka**
**4 oz. grapefruit juice**
**1 oz. cranberry liqueur**

1. Fill a highball glass half full of ice
2. Add vodka, grapefruit juice and cranberry liqueur
3. Stir slowly
4. Garnish with a twist of grapefruit peel

# Cappuccino Mocha

**hot espresso**
**steamed milk**
**¾ oz. Kahlúa**
**¾ oz. crème de cacao**

1. Fill coffee mug with hot espresso (about half full)
2. Add Kahlúa and crème de cacao
3. Top with steamed milk
4. Dust with cinnamon or chocolate

# Capri

**¾ oz. white crème de cacao**
**¾ oz. banana liqueur**
**¾ oz. cream**

1. Fill mixing glass with ice
2. Add white crème de cacao, banana liqueur and cream
3. Shake
4. Strain into a rocks glass filled with ice

# Caramel Nut

1 oz. white crème de cacao
1 oz. caramel liqueur
5 oz. vanilla ice cream, soft

1. In blender, combine white crème de càcao, caramel liqueur and ice cream
2. Blend at medium speed until smooth
3. Pour into a large goblet or wineglass
4. Garnish with whipped cream
5. Top with chopped nuts, if desired

# Carroll Cocktail

1½ oz. brandy
¾ oz. sweet vermouth

1. Fill mixing glass with ice
2. Add brandy and sweet vermouth
3. Stir
4. Strain into a chilled cocktail glass
5. Garnish with a cherry

# Caruso

½ oz. gin
½ oz. dry vermouth
½ oz. crème de menthe

1. Fill mixing glass with ice
2. Add gin, dry vermouth and crème de menthe
3. Stir
4. Strain into a chilled cocktail glass

# Casablanca

2 oz. light rum
1½ tsp. triple sec
1½ tsp. lime juice
1½ tsp. cherry liqueur

1. Fill mixing glass with ice
2. Add rum, triple sec, lime juice and cherry liqueur
3. Shake
4. Strain into a chilled cocktail glass

# Cat's Eye

2 oz. dry vermouth
½ oz. yellow Chartreuse
2 dashes orange bitters

1. Fill mixing glass with ice
2. Add dry vermouth, yellow Chartreuse and orange bitters
3. Shake
4. Strain into a chilled cocktail glass

# Cerebral Hemorrhage

1 oz. Kahlúa
1 oz. peach schnapps
1 oz. Bailey's Original Irish Cream
⅛ oz. grenadine

1. Layer Kahlúa, peach schnapps and Bailey's in a rocks glass filled with ice
2. Add several drops of grenadine

# Chablis Cooler

1 oz. vodka
1 tsp. grenadine
½ oz. lemon juice
dash vanilla extract
3 oz. California chablis
club soda

1. Put 4 ice cubes in a wineglass
2. Add vodka, grenadine, lemon juice and vanilla extract
3. Pour in chablis
4. Stir gently
5. Top with club soda

# Chambord Daiquiri

¾ oz. Chambord
¾ oz. light rum
juice of ½ lime
1 tsp. powdered sugar
3 or 4 black raspberries (optional)

1. In a blender, combine 1 cup crushed ice with Chambord, light rum, lime juice and powdered sugar
2. Throw in raspberries (optional)
3. Blend for approximately 30 seconds or until smooth
4. Pour into a champagne glass

# Chambord Royale Spritzer

1½ oz. Chambord
chilled champagne
club soda

1. Pour Chambord into wineglass
2. Add a splash of champagne
3. Top with club soda

# Champagne Cocktail

1 cube sugar
dash bitters
twist of lemon
chilled champagne

1. Put sugar cube, bitters and lemon twist in the bottom of a champagne glass
2. Fill glass with chilled champagne

# Champagne-Maraschino Punch

6 oz. maraschino liqueur
6 oz. brandy
1 tsp. orange bitters
2 oranges
1 lemon
4 fifths iced brut champagne

1. Slice oranges and lemon into thin slices
2. Place sliced fruit, maraschino liqueur, brandy and orange bitters in punch bowl
3. Refrigerate for one hour
4. When ready to serve, add a large chunk of ice to the punch bowl and pour mixture over it
5. Pour in the champagne
6. Stir gently

# Champagne Punch

16 oz. triple sec
1 bottle (500 ml) rum
8 oz. maraschino liqueur
3 cups chilled pineapple juice, unsweetened
8 oz. club soda
8 oz. ginger ale
4 bottles (750 ml. each) champagne (or sparkling wine)

1. In a punch bowl, combine triple sec, rum, maraschino liqueur and pineapple juice
2. Stir
3. Refrigerate fcr one hour
4. Add a block of ice
5. Add club soda, ginger ale and champagne or sparkling wine
6. Stir again

## Champagne Sherbet Punch

**2 bottles dry champagne or sparkling wine (750 ml each)**
**1 bottle chilled white wine**
**1 qt. orange or raspberry sherbet**

1. In a punch bowl, combine champagne or sparkling wine and white wine
2. Add a block of ice
3. Add scoops of sherbet

## Charro

**1 oz. tequila**
**1⅓ oz. evaporated milk**
**⅔ oz. strong coffee**

1. Fill mixing glass with 4 oz. crushed ice
2. Add tequila, evaporated milk and coffee
3. Shake
4. Strain into a rocks glass half filled with ice

## Cheap Man's Piña Colada

**1½ oz. Malibu**
**3 oz. pineapple juice**
**dash milk**

1. In blender, combine Malibu, pineapple juice and milk with 3 oz. crushed ice
2. Blend until smooth
3. Pour into a goblet
4. Garnish with a pineapple spear or an orange slice

## Cherry Bomb (also called Fireworks)

½ oz. vodka
½ oz. light rum
½ oz. tequila
3 oz. pineapple juice
1 oz. cream of coconut
2 tsp. milk
1 drop grenadine

1. Fill mixing glass with ice
2. Add vodka, light rum, tequila, pineapple juice, cream of coconut, milk and grenadine
3. Shake well
4. Strain into a Collins glass half filled with ice
5. Garnish with a cherry

## Cherry Cola

2 oz. dark rum
½ oz. cherry brandy
2 oz. cola

1. Fill a rocks glass with ice
2. Add rum, cherry brandy and cola
3. Stir
4. Garnish with a lemon twist

# Cherry Daiquiri (frozen)

1½ oz. light rum
½ oz. cherry brandy
½ oz. lime juice
2–3 dashes kirsch

1. Put 4 oz. ice in blender
2. Add light rum, cherry brandy, lime juice and kirsch
3. Blend at medium speed for about 15 seconds, until smooth
4. Pour into a goblet or large wineglass
5. Garnish with a lime slice

# Chicago

1½ oz. brandy
1 dash curaçao
1 dash Angostura bitters
cold brut champagne
lemon wedge
superfine granulated sugar

1. Rub rim of a goblet or large wineglass with lemon wedge
2. Roll rim of glass in a dish of the sugar so that the rim is evenly frosted
3. Fill mixing glass with cracked ice
4. Add brandy, curaçao and bitters
5. Shake
6. Strain into prepared glass
7. Fill with champagne

# Chi-Chi

1½ oz. light rum
½ oz. blackberry brandy
5 oz. pineapple juice

1. Fill mixing glass with ice
2. Add rum, blackberry brandy and pineapple juice
3. Shake
4. Strain into a highball glass filled with ice
5. Garnish with a spear of pineapple

# Chinese Cocktail

1½ oz. Jamaican rum
1 tbsp. grenadine
1 tbsp. maraschino liqueur
1 tbsp. triple sec
1 dash Angostura bitters

1. Fill mixing glass with ice
2. Add all ingredients
3. Shake
4. Strain into a cocktail glass

# Chiquita Cocktail

½ oz. banana liqueur
½ oz. Cointreau
½ oz. light cream

1. Fill mixing glass with ice
2. Add banana liqueur, Cointreau and light cream
3. Shake
4. Fill a sour glass halfway with crushed ice
5. Strain drink into the sour glass

# Chocolate Banana Banshee

¾ oz. banana liqueur
¾ oz. white crème de cacao
¾ oz. Kahlúa
1 oz. cream (milk may be substituted)

1. Fill mixing glass with ice
2. Add banana liqueur, crème de cacao, Kahlúa and cream
3. Shake
4. Strain into a highball glass
5. Add ice

# Chocolate Black Russian

1½ oz. Kahlúa
¾ oz. vodka
5 oz. chocolate ice cream

1. In blender, combine Kahlúa, vodka and ice cream
2. Blend at medium speed until smooth
3. Pour into a large goblet or wineglass

# Chocolate-Covered Cherry (shooter)

½ oz. Kahlúa
½ oz. amaretto
½ oz. white crème de cacao
drop grenadine

1. Fill mixing glass with ice
2. Add Kahlúa, amaretto and white crème de cacao
3. Shake
4. Strain into a shot glass
5. Put a drop of grenadine through the center

# Chocolate Rum

1 oz. white rum
2 tsp. white crème de cacao
2 tsp. white crème de menthe
2 tsp. heavy cream
1 tsp. rum (151 proof)

1. Fill mixing glass with ice
2. Add white rum, crème de cacao, crème de menthe and heavy cream
3. Shake
4. Strain into a rocks glass filled with ice
5. Top with 151-proof rum

# Cinzano

3 oz. Cinzano dry vermouth
3 dashes orange bitters
3 dashes Angostura bitters

1. Fill mixing glass with ice
2. Add Cinzano dry vermouth, orange bitters and Angostura bitters
3. Stir
4. Strain into a chilled cocktail glass
5. Garnish with a twist of orange peel

# City Slicker

2 oz. brandy
1 oz. curaçao
dash Pernod

1. Fill mixing glass with ice
2. Add brandy, curaçao and Pernod
3. Shake
4. Strain into a chilled cocktail glass

# Clamdigger

1½ oz. vodka
3 oz. clam juice
3 oz. tomato juice
dash Tabasco sauce
dash Worcestershire sauce
salt and pepper (to taste)

1. Fill a highball glass with ice
2. Pour in all ingredients
3. Stir
4. Garnish with a lime slice

# Claret Cup

2 tbsp. sugar
¼ cup water
2 bottles red wine, chilled (25.4 oz. each)
4 oz. Cointreau
4 oz. crème de cassis
2½ oz. port
2½ oz. lemon juice
1 bottle club soda, chilled (33.8 oz.)

1. In a small saucepan, combine the sugar and water
2. Bring to a boil
3. Simmer for 5 minutes
4. Allow mixture to cool completely
5. In a large punch bowl, combine red wine, Cointreau, crème de cassis, port, lemon juice and the sugar mixture
6. Cover and refrigerate until cold
7. When ready to serve, pour in club soda
8. Garnish with slices of lemon and orange

# Claridge

1 oz. gin
1 oz. dry vermouth
½ oz. apricot brandy
½ oz. Cointreau

1. Fill mixing glass with ice
2. Add gin, dry vermouth, apricot brandy and Cointreau
3. Shake
4. Strain into a chilled cocktail glass

# Classic

1½ oz. brandy
¼ oz. Cointreau
¼ oz. maraschino liqueur
1 tsp. lemon juice

1. Fill mixing glass with ice
2. Add brandy, Cointreau, maraschino liqueur and lemon juice
3. Shake
4. Strain into a chilled cocktail glass

# Climax

½ oz. white crème de cacao
½ oz. amaretto
½ oz. triple sec
½ oz. vodka
½ oz. banana liqueur
1 oz. cream

1. Fill mixing glass with ice
2. Add white crème de cacao, amaretto, triple sec, vodka, banana liqueur and cream
3. Shake
4. Strain into a chilled cocktail glass

# Club Med

1½ oz. vodka
¾ oz. Chambord
½ oz. lemon juice
3 oz. pineapple juice

1. Fill mixing glass with ice
2. Add vodka, Chambord, lemon juice and pineapple juice
3. Shake
4. Strain into a Collins glass
5. Add ice

# Cocoa-Colada

1½ oz. Myers's Rum
1 oz. Kahlúa
2 oz. pineapple juice
1 oz. coconut cream

1. In blender, combine rum, Kahlúa, pineapple juice and coconut cream with 1 scoop ice
2. Blend until smooth
3. Pour into a 16-oz. soda glass
4. Garnish with a slice of orange

(Courtesy of Sugar Reef, New York City)

# Coco-Loco

1 whole coconut, in shell
1 oz. tequila
1 oz. rum
1 oz. gin
½ oz. grenadine

1. Cut a 3-inch hole in top of coconut
2. With juice of coconut still inside, pour in tequila, rum, gin and grenadine
3. Add several ice cubes and stir
4. Garnish with a slice of lemon or lime (squeeze in juice and then throw in)
5. Drink with a long straw

(If you prefer to serve this drink in a glass, drill two holes in coconut and drain liquid into a mixing glass over several ice cubes, add liquors and grenadine and stir well. Then, pour into a goblet or highball glass, add lemon or lime.)

# Coconut Cola

**1½ oz. Malibu rum liqueur**
**cola**

1. Fill a highball glass with ice
2. Add Malibu
3. Fill with cola
4. Garnish with a wedge of lime

# Coco-Toastie

**1 oz. light rum**
**½ oz. Malibu**
**3 oz. vanilla ice cream**
**2 tbsp. whipping cream**

1. In blender, combine light rum, Malibu, vanilla ice cream and whipping cream
2. Blend until smooth
3. Pour into a chilled cocktail glass
4. Garnish with toasted shredded coconut

# Coffee Alexander

**1 oz. Kahlúa**
**1 oz. dark crème de cacao**
**1 oz. cream**

1. Fill mixing glass with ice
2. Add Kahlúa, dark crème de cacao and cream
3. Shake
4. Strain into a chilled cocktail glass

# Coffee Cooler

**1½ oz. vodka**
**1 oz. Kahlúa**
**1 oz. heavy cream**
**4 oz. iced coffee**
**½ tsp. sugar syrup (optional)**
**1 scoop coffee ice cream**

1. Fill mixing glass with ice
2. Add vodka, Kahlúa, heavy cream, iced coffee and sugar syrup
3. Shake
4. Strain into a rocks glass
5. Add some ice and the coffee ice cream

# Coffee Keokee

**¾ oz. brandy**
**¾ oz. Kahlúa**
**hot coffee**

1. Pour brandy and Kahlúa into a coffee mug
2. Add hot coffee
3. Top with whipped cream (if desired)

# Cold Deck

1½ oz. brandy
¾ oz. sweet vermouth
¾ oz. peppermint schnapps

1. Fill mixing glass with ice
2. Add brandy, sweet vermouth and peppermint schnapps
3. Shake
4. Strain into a chilled cocktail glass

# Cold Weather Punch

two medium-sized lemons
½ cup sugar
1 tsp. ground ginger
1 bottle (750 ml) dark rum
1 bottle (750 ml) brandy
8 oz. sherry
3 pints boiling water

1. In a small earthenware bowl, combine the rinds of the lemons (save the rest of the lemon) with the sugar
2. Soften the lemon rinds using a muddler or the back of a spoon
3. Add the juice of the two lemons and the ginger
4. Mix well
5. Switch mixture to a larger earthenware bowl
6. Add, in order, rum, brandy, sherry and boiling water
7. Mix and let sit for approximately 20 minutes
8. Garnish with grated nutmeg
9. Serve immediately

# Colorado Bulldog

1½ oz. vodka
¾ oz. Kahlúa
3 oz. cola

1. Fill a highball glass with ice
2. Add vodka, Kahlúa and cola
3. Stir

# Columbia Cocktail

1½ oz. light rum
¾ oz. raspberry syrup
½ oz. lemon juice

1. Fill mixing glass with ice
2. Add light rum, raspberry syrup and lemon juice
3. Shake
4. Strain into a chilled cocktail glass

# Conchita

1 oz. tequila
1 oz. grapefruit juice
2–3 drops lemon juice

1. Fill a rocks glass with ice
2. Add tequila, grapefruit juice and lemon juice
3. Stir

# Concorde

2 oz. cognac
2 oz. chilled pineapple juice
champagne

1. Combine cognac and chilled pineapple juice in a mixing glass
2. Stir
3. Strain into a champagne glass filled with cracked ice
4. Fill rest of glass with champagne

# Continental

4 oz. rye
½ oz. Jamaican rum
1½ oz. sweet cream
1½ oz. lemon juice

1. Fill mixing glass with ice
2. Add rye, rum, sweet cream and lemon juice
3. Shake
4. Strain into a Collins glass
5. Add ice

# Cool Breeze

1½ oz. vodka
3 oz. unsweetened pineapple juice
3 oz. cranberry juice cocktail
1 oz. ginger ale

1. Fill a highball glass with ice
2. Add vodka, pineapple juice and cranberry juice
3. Stir
4. Top with ginger ale

# Cooler by the Lake

3 oz. white wine
2 oz. cranberry juice cocktail
¼ oz. peach schnapps
¼ oz. sugar syrup
¼ oz. sour mix
club soda

1. Fill a 10-oz. glass with ice
2. Add white wine, cranberry juice cocktail, peach schnapps, sugar syrup and sour mix
3. Stir well
4. Fill with club soda

5. Stir again, gently
6. Garnish with a slice of fresh peach

(Courtesy of the Ritz-Carlton Hotel, Chicago, Il.)

# Coronado

■ ————————————————————— ■

1½ oz. gin
½ oz. curaçao
2 oz. unsweetened pineapple juice
3 dashes kirsch

1. Fill mixing glass with ice
2. Add gin, curaçao, pineapple juice and kirsch
3. Shake
4. Strain into a rocks glass filled with ice

# Costa del Sol

■ ————————————————————— ■

2 oz. gin
1 oz. apricot brandy
1 oz. Grand Marnier

1. Fill mixing glass with ice
2. Add gin, apricot brandy and Grand Marnier
3. Shake
4. Strain into a rocks glass

# Country Club Cooler

■ ————————————————————— ■

4 oz. Lillet blanc (dry vermouth may be substituted)
1 tsp. grenadine
club soda

1. Pour Lillet and grenadine into a Collins glass
2. Add several ice cubes
3. Stir
4. Top with club soda
5. Garnish with a lemon twist

# Cranberry Pineapple Vodka Punch

2 qts. chilled cranberry juice cocktail
1 qt. 14 oz. chilled pineapple juice (unsweetened)
8 oz. vodka
16 oz. chilled ginger ale
16 oz. chilled club soda
several fresh pineapple spears

1. In a punch bowl, combine cranberry juice cocktail, pineapple juice, vodka, ginger ale and club soda
2. Add a block of ice
3. Garnish with pineapple spears

(Makes approximately 20 servings)

# Cranberry Splash

4 oz. vodka
cranberry juice cocktail

1. Pour vodka into a rocks glass filled with ice
2. Add a splash of cranberry juice
3. Garnish with a slice of lime (optional)

# Cranberry Vodka

premium vodka
fresh cranberries

1. Fill a large, clean jar with fresh cranberries
2. Add a premium vodka
3. Cover and let stand for 3 days, turning the jar several times daily
4. Remove most of the fruit and refrigerate
5. Serve the vodka over ice in a wineglass or rocks glass

# Cranberry-Vodka Punch

2 qts. chilled cranberry juice cocktail
1 bottle (750 ml) vodka
2 cups chilled ginger ale
2 cups chilled club soda

1. In a large punch bowl, combine cranberry juice cocktail and vodka
2. Stir
3. Add a block of ice
4. Pour in ginger ale and club soda
5. Garnish with slices of fresh fruit

# Cream Supreme

1 oz. triple sec
1 oz. white crème de cacao
1 oz. cream (milk may be substituted)

1. Fill mixing glass with ice
2. Add triple sec, crème de cacao and cream
3. Shake
4. Strain into a highball glass
5. Add ice
6. Garnish with an orange slice

# Cream Soda

1½ oz. amaretto
club soda

1. Fill a highball glass with ice
2. Add amaretto
3. Fill with club soda
4. Stir

# Creamy Mimi

1 oz. vodka
1 oz. sweet vermouth
2 tsp. triple sec
2 tsp. white crème de cacao

1. Fill mixing glass with 3 oz. crushed ice
2. Add all ingredients
3. Shake
4. Strain into a rocks glass
5. Add ice (if desired)

# Cricket

1 oz. white crème de cacao
1 oz. green crème de menthe
1 oz. cream
dash brandy

1. Fill mixing glass with ice
2. Add white crème de cacao, green crème de menthe, cream and brandy
3. Shake
4. Strain into a chilled champagne glass

# Cruise Control

1 oz. light rum
½ oz. apricot brandy
½ oz. Cointreau
½ oz. lemon juice
1 oz. club soda

1. Fill mixing glass with ice
2. Add rum, apricot brandy, Cointreau and lemon juice
3. Shake
4. Strain into a highball glass half filled with ice
5. Top with club soda

# Cuba Libre
# (commonly called Rum and Coke)

**1½ oz. light rum**
**6 oz. cola**

1. Fill a highball glass with ice
2. Add rum and cola
3. Stir
4. Garnish with a lime wedge or slice

# Cuban Cooler

**2 oz. light rum**
**ginger ale**

1. Fill a highball glass with ice
2. Add rum
3. Fill glass with ginger ale
4. Garnish with a lemon twist

# Cupid's Kiss

**½ oz. crème de noyaux**
**¼ oz. white crème de cacao**
**1 oz. cream**
**1 strawberry**

1. Fill mixing glass with ice
2. Add crème de noyaux, white crème de cacao and cream
3. Shake
4. Pour into a tulip glass
5. Garnish with a strawberry

(Courtesy of Timbers Charhouse, Highland Park, Illinois)

# Czar

1 oz. vodka
1 oz. Grand Marnier
½ oz. lime juice
dash orange bitters
3 oz. dry sparkling white wine

1. Fill mixing glass with ice
2. Add vodka, Grand Marnier, lime juice and orange bitters
3. Shake
4. Strain into a large wineglass
5. Top with sparkling wine

# Czarina

½ oz. vodka
¼ oz. dry vermouth
¼ oz. apricot brandy
dash Angostura bitters

1. Fill mixing glass with ice
2. Add vodka, dry vermouth, apricot brandy and bitters
3. Shake
4. Strain into a chilled cocktail glass

# D

## Daiquiri

**2 oz. light rum**
**1 oz. lime juice**
**1 tsp. sugar**

1. Fill mixing glass with ice
2. Add rum, lime juice and sugar
3. Shake
4. Strain into a cocktail glass
5. Garnish with a lime slice

## Daisy

**2 oz. tequila**
**1 oz. lemon juice**
**2 tsp. grenadine**
**splash club soda**

1. Fill mixing glass with ice
2. Add tequila, lemon juice and grenadine
3. Shake
4. Strain into a rocks glass
5. Add ice
6. Top off with a splash of club soda

# Damn-the-Weather

**1 oz. gin**
**¼ oz. triple sec**
**½ oz. sweet vermouth**
**½ oz. orange juice**

1. Fill mixing glass with ice
2. Add gin, triple sec, sweet vermouth and orange juice
3. Shake
4. Strain into a cocktail glass
5. Add ice
6. Garnish with a cherry

# Dandy

**1½ oz. Canadian or rye whiskey**
**1½ oz. Dubonnet**
**3 dashes Cointreau**
**dash Angostura bitters**

1. Fill mixing glass with ice
2. Add whiskey, Dubonnet, Cointreau and bitters
3. Stir
4. Strain into a chilled cocktail glass

# Danish Mary

**1 oz. aquavit (akvavit)**
**Bloody Mary mix**

1. Fill highball glass with ice
2. Add aquavit and Bloody Mary mix (see Bloody Mary recipe, p. 113)
3. Stir
4. Garnish with a celery stalk or a lime slice

# Darb

1 oz. gin
1 oz. dry vermouth
1 oz. apricot brandy
½ oz. lemon juice
1 tsp. sugar

1. Fill mixing glass with ice
2. Add gin, dry vermouth, apricot brandy, lemon juice and sugar
3. Shake
4. Strain into a cocktail glass

# Dark Eyes

1½ oz. vodka
¼ oz. blackberry brandy
2 tsp. lime juice

1. Fill mixing glass with ice
2. Add vodka, blackberry brandy and lime juice
3. Shake
4. Strain into a brandy snifter

# Davis

1½ oz. light rum
1½ oz. dry vermouth
1 oz. lime juice
2 dashes raspberry syrup

1. Fill mixing glass with ice
2. Add rum, dry vermouth, lime juice and raspberry syrup
3. Shake
4. Strain into a rocks glass
5. Add ice

# Death in the Afternoon

1½ oz. Pernod
chilled champagne

1. Pour Pernod into a chilled champagne glass
2. Fill the glass with champagne

# Deep Throat (shooter)

½ oz. Kahlúa
½ oz. vodka
whipped cream

1. Pour Kahlúa and vodka into a shot glass
2. Top with whipped cream

# Delmonico

¾ oz. gin
½ oz. dry vermouth
½ oz. sweet vermouth
½ oz. brandy

1. Fill mixing glass with ice
2. Add gin, dry vermouth, sweet vermouth and brandy
3. Stir
4. Strain into a cocktail glass
5. Garnish with a lemon twist

# Dempsey

1½ oz. gin
1 oz. apple brandy
2 dashes grenadine
2 dashes Angostura bitters

1. Fill mixing glass with ice
2. Add gin, apple brandy, grenadine and bitters
3. Shake
4. Strain into a rocks glass filled with ice

# Depth Bomb

**1½ oz. apple brandy**
**1½ oz. brandy**
**¼ tsp. grenadine**
**¼ tsp. lemon juice**

1. Fill mixing glass with ice
2. Add apple brandy, brandy, grenadine and lemon juice
3. Shake
4. Strain into a chilled cocktail glass

# Depth Charge

**1½ oz. gin**
**1½ oz. Lillet**
**2 dashes Pernod**

1. Fill mixing glass with ice
2. Add gin, Lillet and Pernod
3. Shake
4. Strain into a chilled cocktail glass

# Derby Special

**1½ oz. light rum**
**½ oz. Cointreau**
**1 oz. orange juice**
**½ oz. lime juice**

1. Add approximately 4 oz. cracked ice to a blender
2. Pour in light rum, Cointreau, orange juice and lime juice
3. Blend at medium speed until smooth
4. Pour into a highball glass

# De Rigueur

**1½ oz. whiskey**
**¾ oz. grapefruit juice**
**1 tsp. honey**

1. Fill mixing glass with ice
2. Add whiskey, grapefruit juice and honey
3. Shake
4. Strain into a chilled cocktail glass

# Diamond Fizz

**1½ oz. gin**
**juice of ½ lemon**
**1 tsp. powdered sugar**
**chilled champagne**

1. Fill mixing glass with ice
2. Add gin, lemon juice and sugar
3. Shake
4. Strain into a large wineglass
5. Add a few ice cubes
6. Fill with champagne

# Diamond Head

**1½ oz. gin**
**½ oz. curaçao**
**2 oz. pineapple juice (unsweetened)**
**1 tsp. sweet vermouth**

1. Fill mixing glass with cracked ice
2. Add gin, curaçao, pineapple juice and sweet vermouth
3. Shake
4. Strain into a chilled cocktail glass

# Diana

**3 oz. white crème de menthe**
**1 oz. brandy**

1. Fill a rocks glass with ice
2. Add white crème de menthe and brandy
3. Stir

# Dinah Cocktail

**1½ oz. blended whiskey**
**1 oz. sour mix**
**½ tsp. powdered sugar**

1. Fill mixing glass with ice
2. Add whiskey, sour mix and sugar
3. Shake
4. Strain into a cocktail glass
5. Garnish with a mint leaf

# Diplomat

**2 oz. dry vermouth**
**1 oz. sweet vermouth**
**2 dashes maraschino liqueur**

1. Fill mixing glass with ice
2. Add dry vermouth, sweet vermouth and maraschino liqueur
3. Stir
4. Strain into a chilled cocktail glass
5. Garnish with a twist of orange peel

# Dirty Mother (also called a Separator)

**1½ oz. brandy**
**¾ oz. Kahlúa**

1. Fill a rocks glass with ice
2. Add brandy and Kahlúa
3. Stir

# Dirty White Mother

1½ oz. brandy
½ oz. Kahlúa
1 oz. cream

1. Fill a rocks glass with ice
2. Add brandy and Kahlúa
3. Float cream on top

# Doctor

1½ oz. Swedish Punsch
2 oz. lime juice

1. Fill mixing glass with ice
2. Add Swedish Punsch and lime juice
3. Shake
4. Strain into a rocks glass
5. Add ice

# Dr. Pepper

½ oz. amaretto
½ oz. 151-proof rum
cold beer

1. Pour amaretto and 151-proof rum into a beer glass or mug
2. Fill with beer

# Dodge Special

1½ oz. dry gin
1½ oz. Cointreau
dash grape juice

1. Fill mixing glass with ice
2. Add gin, Cointreau and grape juice
3. Stir
4. Strain into a cocktail glass

# Dominican Coco Loco

1½ oz. light rum
½ oz. amaretto
1 tsp. grenadine
½ oz. pineapple juice (unsweetened)
1 oz. coconut cream
several dashes milk

1. In blender, combine all ingredients with 3 oz. crushed ice
2. Blend until smooth
3. Pour into a goblet or large wineglass
4. Garnish with a pineapple slice

(*Note:* This drink can also be served in a pineapple.)

# Dorado

2 oz. tequila
1½ oz. lemon juice
1 tbs. honey

1. Fill mixing glass with ice
2. Add tequila, lemon juice and honey
3. Shake
4. Strain into a highball glass filled with ice

# Douglas

**2 oz. English gin**
**1 oz. dry vermouth**

1. Fill a rocks glass with ice
2. Add English gin and dry vermouth
3. Stir
4. Garnish with a lemon twist

# Down the Hatch

**2 oz. whiskey**
**3 dashes blackberry brandy**
**2 dashes orange bitters**

1. Fill mixing glass with ice
2. Add whiskey, blackberry brandy and orange bitters
3. Shake
4. Strain into a cocktail glass

# Drawbridge

**5 oz. dry white wine**
**club soda**
**splash of blue curaçao**

1. Fill a wineglass with ice
2. Pour in white wine
3. Top with club soda
4. Add a splash of blue curaçao
5. Garnish with a lemon twist

# Dream

**2 oz. brandy**
**¾ oz. curaçao**
**¼ oz. Pernod**

1. Fill mixing glass with ice
2. Add brandy, curaçao and Pernod
3. Shake
4. Strain into a cocktail glass


# Dream Cocktail

**1½ oz. brandy**
**½ oz. Cointreau**
**½ tsp. anisette**

1. Fill mixing glass with ice
2. Add brandy, Cointreau and anisette
3. Stir
4. Strain into a chilled cocktail glass over 2 or 3 ice cubes


# Dubonnet Cocktail

**1 oz. gin (or vodka)**
**1 oz. Dubonnet (red)**

1. Fill mixing glass with ice
2. Add gin or vodka and Dubonnet
3. Stir
4. Strain into a chilled cocktail glass or a rocks glass filled with ice

# Dubonnet Fizz

1½ oz. gin
1½ oz. Dubonnet
½ oz. cherry brandy
½ oz. lemon juice
club soda

1. Fill a highball glass with ice
2. Add gin, Dubonnet, cherry brandy and lemon juice
3. Stir
4. Top with club soda
5. Stir again
6. Garnish with a cherry

# Dubonnet Manhattan

1 oz. Dubonnet
1 oz. whiskey

1. Fill mixing glass with ice
2. Add Dubonnet and whiskey
3. Shake
4. Strain into a cocktail glass
5. Garnish with a cherry

# Dubonnet Negroni

1½ oz. Dubonnet
1½ oz. gin
1½ oz. Campari

1. Fill mixing glass with ice
2. Add Dubonnet, gin and Campari
3. Stir
4. Strain into a wineglass
5. Garnish with a lemon twist

# Duchess

¾ oz. Pernod
¾ oz. dry vermouth
¾ oz. sweet vermouth

1. Fill mixing glass with ice
2. Add Pernod, dry vermouth and sweet vermouth
3. Shake
4. Strain into a rocks glass
5. Add ice
6. Garnish with a cherry

# Dundee

1½ oz. gin
2 tbs. scotch
2 tsp. Drambuie
1 tsp. lemon juice

1. Fill mixing glass with ice
2. Add gin, scotch, Drambuie and lemon juice
3. Shake
4. Strain into a rocks glass and add ice
5. Garnish with a cherry and a lemon twist

# Dunlop

3 oz. light rum
1½ oz. sherry
2 dashes Angostura bitters

1. Fill mixing glass with ice
2. Add rum, sherry and bitters
3. Shake
4. Strain into a rocks glass filled with ice

# Dutch Coffee

1½ oz. Vandermint Liqueur
hot coffee

1. Pour Vandermint Liqueur into a coffee mug
2. Add hot coffee
3. Top with whipped cream

# Dutch Velvet

½ oz. chocolate mint liqueur
½ oz. banana liqueur
2 oz. cream

1. Fill mixing glass with ice
2. Add chocolate mint liqueur, banana liqueur and cream
3. Shake
4. Strain into a chilled cocktail glass
5. Garnish with 1 tsp. shaved chocolate, if desired

# E

## Earthquake

1½ oz. rye whiskey
1½ oz. gin
1½ oz. Pernod

1. Fill mixing glass with ice
2. Add rye, gin and Pernod
3. Shake
4. Strain into a chilled cocktail glass

## East India Cocktail

1½ oz. brandy
1 tsp. light rum
½ tsp. triple sec
½ tsp. pineapple juice (unsweetened)
dash bitters

1. Fill mixing glass with ice
2. Add brandy, rum, triple sec, pineapple juice and bitters
3. Shake
4. Strain into a chilled cocktail glass
5. Garnish with a lemon twist

## Eclipse (1)

1½ oz. sloe gin
1 oz. gin

**3–4 dashes grenadine**
**1 maraschino cherry**

1. Put a cherry in a rocks glass
2. Cover cherry with grenadine
3. In a separate glass, shake sloe gin and gin with ice
4. Strain the gins into the rocks glass (they should float on the grenadine, not mix with it)

# Eclipse (2)

**1½ oz. Old Bushmills Black Bush Irish whiskey**
**seltzer**

1. Fill a highball glass with ice
2. Add Old Bushmills Black Bush Irish whiskey
3. Stir
4. Garnish with a slice of orange

# Egghead

**1½ oz. vodka**
**4 oz. orange juice**
**1 egg**

1. In blender, add vodka, orange juice, egg and 3 or 4 ice cubes
2. Blend at medium speed for about 15 seconds
3. Pour over 4 or 5 ice cubes in a rocks glass

# Eggnog (standard recipe)

**1 dozen eggs**
**2 cups superfine granulated sugar**
**1 pt. Jamaican rum**
**1 pt. cognac**
**3 pts. milk**
**1 pt. cream**
**nutmeg or cinnamon**

1. Separate eggs
2. Beat yolks and sugar until thick
3. Add rum, cognac, milk and cream
4. Stir mixture
5. Set aside and chill in refrigerator
6. When ready to serve, put this mixture into a punch bowl
7. Do NOT add ice cubes
8. Beat egg whites (until they are stiff) and fold into egg mixture
9. Do NOT beat or stir
10. Sprinkle top with nutmeg

(Makes approximately 28–30 servings)

# El Cid

**1½ oz. tequila**
**1 oz. lime juice**
**½ oz. almond-flavored syrup**
**tonic water**
**dash of grenadine**

1. Pour tequila, lime juice and almond syrup into a Collins glass
2. Stir well
3. Fill with tonic water
4. Add a dash of grenadine to top
5. Garnish with a lime slice

# El Diablo

**1½ oz. tequila**
**½ oz. crème de cassis**
**1½ tsp. lime juice**
**1 oz. ginger ale**

1. Fill a Collins glass with ice
2. Add tequila, crème de cassis and lime juice
3. Fill with ginger ale
4. Stir

# El Presidente Edwardo

1½ oz. gold rum
½ oz. curaçao
1 oz. dry vermouth
dash grenadine

1. Fill mixing glass with ice
2. Add rum, curaçao, dry vermouth and grenadine
3. Shake
4. Strain into a chilled cocktail glass

# El Salvador

1½ oz. light rum
¾ oz. Frangelico
½ oz. lime juice
1 tsp. grenadine

1. Fill mixing glass with ice
2. Add light rum, Frangelico, lime juice and grenadine
3. Shake
4. Strain into a chilled cocktail glass

# Emerald Isle Cooler

3 scoops vanilla ice cream
1 oz. green crème de menthe
1 oz. Irish whiskey
1 oz. club soda

1. In blender, combine vanilla ice cream, green crème de menthe
   and Irish whiskey
2. Blend until smooth
3. Pour into a chilled highball glass
4. Add club soda
5. Stir gently

# Empire

**1½ oz. gin**
**½ oz. apple brandy**
**¾ oz. apricot brandy**

1. Fill mixing glass with ice
2. Add gin, apple brandy and apricot brandy
3. Stir
4. Strain into a chilled cocktail glass

# Eve

**½ tsp. Pernod**
**1 tbsp. cognac**
**2 tsp. sugar**
**2 tsp. curaçao**
**chilled pink sparkling wine**

1. Pour Pernod into a large wineglass
2. Turn glass so that Pernod coats the sides
3. Add cognac
4. In a small bowl, combine sugar and curaçao, allowing sugar to dissolve
5. Add to wineglass
6. Stir
7. Add 3 or 4 ice cubes
8. Fill with chilled pink sparkling wine

# Everglades Special

**1 oz. light rum**
**1 oz. white crème de cacao**
**1 oz. light cream**
**2 tsp. Kahlúa (or other coffee liqueur)**

1. Fill mixing glass with ice
2. Add rum, white crème de cacao, light cream and Kahlúa
3. Shake
4. Strain into a chilled cocktail glass
5. Add ice

# Everything But

1 oz. whiskey
1 oz. gin
1 oz. lemon juice
1 oz. orange juice
1 egg
1 tsp. apricot brandy
½ tsp. powdered sugar

1. Fill mixing glass with ice
2. Add all ingredients
3. Shake
4. Strain into a sour glass
5. Add ice (if desired)

# Express

1½ oz. Grand Marnier
½ oz. Absolut vodka

1. Fill mixing glass with ice
2. Add Grand Marnier and Absolut vodka
3. Shake
4. Strain into a chilled martini glass

(Courtesy of Sign of the Dove, New York City)

# Eye-Opener

1½ oz. light rum
1 tsp. triple sec
1 tsp. white crème de cacao
3 dashes anise-flavored liqueur
1 tsp. Falernum syrup (or sugar syrup)
1 egg yolk

1. Fill mixing glass with ice
2. Add all ingredients
3. Shake
4. Strain into a rocks glass
5. Add ice

# F

## Fair and Warmer

1½ oz. light rum
1 tbsp. sweet vermouth
2 dashes curaçao

1. Fill mixing glass with ice
2. Add light rum, sweet vermouth and curaçao
3. Shake
4. Strain into a rocks glass filled with ice
5. Garnish with a lemon twist

## Fairbanks

1 oz. gin
1 oz. dry vermouth
1 oz. apricot brandy
dash grenadine
dash lemon juice

1. Fill mixing glass with ice
2. Add gin, dry vermouth, apricot brandy, grenadine and lemon juice
3. Shake
4. Strain into a cocktail glass
5. Garnish with a cherry

# Fallen Angel

2½ oz. gin
2½ oz. lemon juice
2 dashes crème de menthe
dash Angostura bitters

1. Fill mixing glass with ice
2. Add gin, lemon juice, crème de menthe and bitters
3. Shake
4. Strain into a rocks glass filled with ice


# Fans

2 oz. scotch
1 oz. Cointreau
1 oz. grapefruit juice (unsweetened)

1. Fill mixing glass with ice
2. Add scotch, Cointreau and grapefruit juice
3. Shake
4. Strain into a rocks glass filled with ice


# Fantasio

1½ oz. brandy
¾ oz. dry vermouth
1 tsp. white crème de cacao
1 tsp. maraschino liqueur

1. Fill mixing glass with ice
2. Add brandy, dry vermouth, white crème de cacao and maraschino liqueur
3. Shake
4. Strain into a rocks glass filled with ice

# Fare-Thee-Well

**1½ oz. gin**
**1½ oz. dry vermouth**
**2 dashes sweet vermouth**
**6 dashes curaçao**

1. Fill mixing glass with ice
2. Add gin, dry vermouth, sweet vermouth and curaçao
3. Shake
4. Strain into a cocktail glass

# Father Sherman

**1½ oz. brandy**
**½ oz. apricot brandy**
**2 tbs. orange juice**

1. Fill mixing glass with ice
2. Add brandy, apricot brandy and orange juice
3. Shake
4. Strain into a chilled cocktail glass

# Favorite

**¾ oz. gin**
**¾ oz. dry vermouth**
**¾ oz. apricot brandy**
**¼ tsp. lemon juice**

1. Fill mixing glass with ice
2. Add gin, dry vermouth, apricot brandy and lemon juice
3. Shake
4. Strain into a rocks glass filled with ice

# Fern Gully

1 oz. light rum
1 oz. dark rum
½ oz. cream of coconut
1 oz. orange juice
2 tsp. lime juice
½ oz. crème de noyaux (any almond-flavored liqueur may be substituted)

1. Fill mixing glass with ice
2. Add light rum, dark rum, cream of coconut, orange juice, lime juice and crème de noyaux
3. Shake
4. Strain into a goblet or large wineglass
5. Add ice

# Ferrari

2 oz. dry vermouth
1 oz. amaretto

1. Fill a rocks glass with ice
2. Add dry vermouth and amaretto
3. Stir
4. Garnish with a lemon twist

# Festival

¾ oz. dark crème de cacao
1 tbsp. apricot brandy
1 tsp. grenadine
¾ oz. heavy cream

1. Fill mixing glass with ice
2. Add dark crème de cacao, apricot brandy, grenadine and heavy cream
3. Shake
4. Strain into a rocks glass filled with ice

# Fifty-Fifty

1½ oz. gin
1½ oz. dry vermouth

1. Fill mixing glass with cracked ice
2. Add gin and dry vermouth
3. Stir
4. Strain into a chilled cocktail glass
5. Garnish with an olive

# '57 Chevy with a White License Plate

1 oz. white crème de cacao
1 oz. vodka

1. Fill a rocks glass with ice
2. Add white crème de cacao and vodka
3. Stir

# Fiji Fizz

1½ oz. dark rum
½ oz. bourbon
1 tsp. cherry brandy
3 dashes orange bitters
4 oz. cola

1. Fill mixing glass with ice
2. Add dark rum, bourbon, cherry brandy and orange bitters
3. Shake
4. Strain into a Collins glass
5. Add a few ice cubes
6. Fill with cola
7. Garnish with a lime slice

# Filby

**2 oz. gin**
**¾ oz. amaretto**
**½ oz. dry vermouth**
**½ oz. Campari**

1. Fill mixing glass with ice
2. Add gin, amaretto, dry vermouth and Campari
3. Stir
4. Strain into a cocktail glass
5. Garnish with an orange peel

# Fine and Dandy

**1½ oz. gin**
**¾ oz. Cointreau**
**¾ oz. lemon juice**
**dash Angostura bitters**

1. Fill mixing glass with ice
2. Add gin, Cointreau, lemon juice and bitters
3. Shake
4. Strain into a rocks glass filled with ice
5. Garnish with a cherry

# Fino

**1½ oz. fino sherry**
**1½ oz. sweet vermouth**

1. Fill mixing glass with ice
2. Add fino sherry and sweet vermouth
3. Shake
4. Strain into a rocks glass filled with ice
5. Garnish with a slice of lemon

# Fish House Punch

(This recipe has been around since 1732. It was originated at The Fish House, a men's club in Schuylkill, Pennsylvania. It packs a mean punch—even George Washington knew that!)

**2 cups lemon juice**
**6 oz. superfine granulated sugar**
**2 bottles Jamaican rum (750 ml. each)**
**1 bottle brandy or cognac (750 ml)**
**1 cup peach brandy or ½ cup peach liqueur**
**8 oz. club soda, chilled**

1. One day in advance, combine sugar and lemon juice in a bowl
2. Stir until sugar is dissolved
3. In a container with a cover, combine the sugar-lemon mixture, rum, brandy and peach brandy (or liqueur)
4. Stir
5. Cover and refrigerate
6. When ready to serve, place a block of ice in a punch bowl
7. Add club soda
8. Stir gently

# Fjord

**1 oz. brandy**
**½ oz. aquavit**
**1 oz. orange juice**
**½ oz. lime juice**
**1 tsp. grenadine**

1. Fill mixing glass with ice
2. Add brandy, aquavit, orange juice, lime juice and grenadine
3. Shake
4. Strain into a chilled cocktail glass

# Flamingo (1)

2 oz. gin
¾ oz. apricot brandy
¾ oz. lime juice
dash of grenadine

1. Fill mixing glass with ice
2. Add gin, apricot brandy, lime juice and grenadine
3. Shake
4. Strain into a cocktail glass

# Flamingo (2)

1¾ oz. añejo (aged) rum
juice of half a lime
2 oz. pineapple juice
½ oz. grenadine

1. Fill a mixing glass with ice
2. Add rum, lime juice, pineapple juice and grenadine
3. Shake vigorously
4. Strain into a stemmed cocktail glass

(This is a recipe that originated at La Floridita Bar in Havana in the 1920s. It has been resurrected by Dale DeGraff at the Rainbow Room in New York City.)

# Flim Flam

1½ oz. light rum
¾ oz. triple sec
½ oz. lemon juice
½ oz. orange juice

1. Fill mixing glass with ice
2. Add light rum, triple sec, lemon juice and orange juice
3. Shake
4. Strain into a chilled cocktail glass

# Florida

½ oz. gin
3 oz. orange juice
1 tsp. kirschwasser
1 tsp. triple sec
1 tsp. lemon juice

1. Fill mixing glass with ice
2. Add gin, orange juice, kirschwasser, triple sec and lemon juice
3. Shake
4. Strain into a Collins glass
5. Add ice
6. Garnish with an orange slice

# Florida Punch

1½ oz. Myers's dark rum
½ oz. brandy
1 oz. grapefruit juice
1 oz. orange juice

1. Fill mixing glass with ice
2. Add Myers's rum, brandy, grapefruit juice and orange juice
3. Shake
4. Strain into a highball glass filled with crushed ice
5. Garnish with an orange slice

# Flying Grasshopper

1½ oz. vodka
½ oz. green crème de menthe
½ oz. white crème de menthe

1. Fill mixing glass with ice
2. Add vodka, green crème de menthe and white crème de menthe
3. Shake
4. Strain into a rocks glass
5. Add ice, if desired

# Flying Scot

1 oz. scotch
1 oz. sweet vermouth
2–3 dashes sugar syrup
2–3 dashes Angostura bitters

1. Fill mixing glass with ice
2. Add scotch, sweet vermouth, sugar syrup and bitters
3. Shake
4. Strain into a rocks glass filled with ice

# Fogcutter

½ oz. brandy
½ oz. rum
½ oz. gin
3 oz. pineapple juice
1 oz. sour mix

1. Fill mixing glass with ice
2. Add brandy, rum, gin, pineapple juice and sour mix
3. Shake
4. Strain into a Collins glass filled with ice
5. Garnish with a lemon twist

# Foggy Day

1½ oz. gin
1 oz. Pernod

1. Fill mixing glass with ice
2. Add gin and Pernod
3. Shake
4. Strain into a rocks glass
5. Add ice
6. Garnish with a lemon twist

# Fog Horn

2½ oz. gin
ginger ale

1. Fill highball glass with ice
2. Add gin
3. Fill with ginger ale
4. Garnish with a lemon slice

# Forester

1 oz. bourbon
¾ oz. cherry liqueur
1 tsp. lemon juice

1. Fill mixing glass with ice
2. Add bourbon, cherry liqueur and lemon juice
3. Shake
4. Strain into a rocks glass filled with ice
5. Garnish with a cherry

# Foxhound

1½ oz. brandy
½ oz. cranberry juice cocktail
1 tsp. kummel
1 tsp. lemon juice

1. Fill mixing glass with ice
2. Add brandy, cranberry juice, kummel and lemon juice
3. Shake
4. Strain into a rocks glass filled with ice
5. Garnish with a lemon slice

# Fox River

1½ oz. rye whiskey
½ oz. dark crème de cacao
2 dashes orange bitters

1. Fill mixing glass with ice
2. Add rye, dark crème de cacao and bitters
3. Shake
4. Strain into a rocks glass filled with ice
5. Garnish with a lemon twist

# Foxtail

1. Fill a beer stein or a Collins glass with ice
2. Fill with beer
3. Garnish with a twist of lemon

# Fox Trot

1½ oz. light rum
½ oz. lemon juice (or lime juice)
2 dashes curaçao

1. Fill mixing glass with ice
2. Add rum, lemon juice and curaçao
3. Shake
4. Strain into a chilled cocktail glass

# Foxy Lady

½ oz. amaretto
½ oz. dark crème de cacao
2 oz. cream

1. Fill mixing glass with ice
2. Add amaretto, dark crème de cacao and cream
3. Shake
4. Strain into a chilled cocktail glass

# Frankenjack Cocktail

**1 oz. gin**
**½ oz. dry vermouth**
**½ oz. apricot brandy**
**½ oz. triple sec**

1. Fill mixing glass with ice
2. Add gin, dry vermouth, apricot brandy and triple sec
3. Shake
4. Strain into a rocks glass filled with ice

# Frappes

Use any liqueur
Pour 1½ oz. of that liqueur over crushed ice

# Freddy Fudpucker

**1 oz. tequila**
**½ oz. Galliano**
**orange juice**

1. Fill a Collins glass with ice
2. Add tequila
3. Fill with orange juice
4. Stir
5. Top with Galliano
6. Stir again

# French Connection

**2 oz. brandy**
**1 oz. amaretto**

1. Fill a rocks glass with ice
2. Add brandy and amaretto
3. Stir

# French Green Dragon

**1½ oz. cognac**
**1½ oz. green Chartreuse**

1. Fill mixing glass with ice
2. Add cognac and green Chartreuse
3. Shake
4. Strain into a rocks glass filled with ice

# French Lift

**3 oz. dry sparkling wine, chilled**
**½ oz. grenadine**
**2 oz. Perrier water**
**3 or 4 fresh blueberries**

1. Half fill a chilled champagne glass with sparkling wine
2. Add grenadine
3. Fill with Perrier
4. Drop blueberries into drink

# French Rose

**1 oz. gin**
**½ oz. cherry-flavored brandy**
**½ oz. cherry liqueur**

1. Fill mixing glass with ice
2. Add gin, cherry brandy and cherry liqueur
3. Shake
4. Strain into a chilled cocktail glass

# French 75

**1½ oz. cognac**
**½ oz. sugar syrup**
**juice of ½ lemon**
**brut champagne**

1. Fill mixing glass with cracked ice
2. Add cognac, sugar syrup and lemon juice
3. Shake
4. Pour into a highball glass
5. Fill with cold champagne
6. Garnish with a lemon twist

# The French Summer

**¾ oz. Chambord**
**3 oz. sparkling water (or club soda)**
**a few drops fresh lemon juice**

1. Fill a wineglass with ice
2. Add Chambord
3. Add sparkling water and lemon juice
4. Garnish with a slice of lemon and a slice of orange

# Friar Tuck

**2 oz. Frangelico**
**2 oz. lemon juice**
**1 tsp. grenadine**

1. Fill mixing glass with ice
2. Add Frangelico, lemon juice and grenadine
3. Shake
4. Strain into a rocks glass half filled with ice
5. Garnish with an orange slice

## Frisco Sour

**1½ oz. blended whiskey**
**¾ oz. Bénédictine**
**1 tsp. lime juice**
**1 tsp. lemon juice**

1. Fill mixing glass with ice
2. Add blended whiskey, Bénédictine, lime juice and lemon juice
3. Shake
4. Strain into a sour glass
5. Garnish with an orange slice

## Frobisher

**2 oz. gin**
**3 dashes Angostura bitters**
**chilled champagne**

1. Fill a highball glass with ice
2. Add gin and bitters
3. Stir
4. Fill with champagne
5. Add more ice, if desired
6. Garnish with a lemon twist

## Frostbite

**1½ oz. tequila (white)**
**½ oz. white crème de cacao**
**2–3 dashes blue curaçao (optional)**
**2 oz. cream**

1. Fill mixing glass with ice
2. Add tequila, white crème de cacao, blue curaçao (if desired) and cream
3. Shake
4. Strain into a frosted sour glass
5. Add ice

## Froth Blower

**1½ oz. gin**
**1 tsp. grenadine**
**½ egg white**

1. Fill mixing glass with ice
2. Add gin, grenadine and egg white
3. Shake
4. Strain into a chilled cocktail glass

## Froupe

**1½ oz. brandy**
**1½ oz. sweet vermouth**
**1 tsp. Bénédictine**

1. Fill mixing glass with ice
2. Add brandy, sweet vermouth and Bénédictine
3. Stir
4. Strain into a chilled cocktail glass

## Frozen Bikini

**2 oz. vodka**
**1 oz. peach schnapps**
**3 oz. peach nectar**
**2 oz. orange juice**
**splash fresh lemon juice**
**1 oz. chilled champagne**

1. In blender, combine all ingredients (except champagne) with 4 oz. crushed ice
2. Blend until smooth
3. Pour into a 12–16 oz. goblet
4. Top with champagne

(Courtesy of the Winter Garden Cafe in the World Financial Center, New York City)

## Frozen Daiquiri

**2 oz. light rum**
**1½ oz. lime juice**
**1 tsp. sugar**

1. Fill blender with approximately 4 oz. crushed ice
2. Add rum, lime juice and sugar
3. Blend at low speed for several seconds, until snowy in texture
4. Pour into a champagne saucer

## Frozen Fruit Daiquiri

**1½ oz. light rum**
**½ oz. sour mix**
**1 oz. appropriate fruit liqueur**
**1 oz. honey if fruit is unsweetened**
**½ oz. cream**
**lots of fresh fruit**

1. Fill blender with about 4 oz. of ice
2. Add all ingredients
3. Blend at medium speed for approximately 15 seconds, or until smooth
4. Pour into a large goblet or large wineglass

# Frozen Fruit Margarita

**1½ oz. tequila**
**½ oz. triple sec**
**½ oz. sour mix**
**fresh fruit to taste**
**1 oz. appropriate fruit liqueur**
**dash Rose's lime juice**

1. Fill blender with about 4 oz. of ice
2. Add all ingredients
3. Blend at medium speed for approximately 15 seconds, or until smooth
4. Pour into a large goblet or large wineglass
5. Garnish with a lime slice

# Frozen Margarita

**1½ oz. tequila**
**½ oz. triple sec**
**1 oz. sour mix**
**dash Rose's lime juice**

1. Fill blender with about 4 oz. of ice
2. Add tequila, triple sec, sour mix and lime juice
3. Blend at medium speed for approximately 15 seconds, or until smooth
4. Pour into a large goblet or large wineglass
5. Garnish with a lime slice

# Frozen Matador

1 oz. tequila
2 oz. pineapple juice
2 tsp. lime juice

1. Fill blender with about 3 oz. crushed ice
2. Add tequila, pineapple juice and lime juice
3. Blend at medium speed for approximately 15 seconds
4. Pour into a large goblet or a large wineglass
5. Garnish with a pineapple slice

# Frozen Mint Daiquiri

2½ oz. light rum
2 tsp. lime juice
1 tsp. sugar
6 mint leaves

1. Fill blender with about 6 oz. of ice
2. Add light rum, lime juice, sugar and mint leaves
3. Blend at medium speed for approximately 15 seconds, or until smooth
4. Pour into a large goblet or large wine glass

# Frozen Mint Julep

2 oz. bourbon
1 oz. lemon juice
1 oz. sugar syrup
5 or 6 small mint leaves

1. Muddle bourbon, lemon juice, sugar syrup and mint leaves in a glass
2. Pour mixture into a blender
3. Add 6 oz. crushed ice
4. Blend at high speed for 15 or 20 seconds
5. Pour into a chilled highball glass
6. Garnish with a mint sprig

# Fuzzy Fruit

1½ oz. peach schnapps
5 oz. grapefruit juice (unsweetened)

1. Fill highball glass with ice
2. Add peach schnapps and grapefruit juice
3. Stir

# Fuzzy Mother

1½ oz. gold tequila
151-proof rum

1. Pour tequila into a pony glass
2. Top with 151-proof rum
3. Ignite

# Fuzzy Navel

1½ oz. peach schnapps
6 oz. orange juice

1. Fill a highball glass with ice
2. Add peach schnapps and orange juice
3. Stir

# G

## Gasper

1½ oz. dry gin
1½ oz. apricot brandy

1. Fill mixing glass with ice
2. Add gin and apricot brandy
3. Shake
4. Strain into a chilled cocktail glass

## Gaugin

2 oz. light rum
1 tbsp. passion fruit syrup
1 tbsp. lime juice
1 tbsp. lemon juice

1. In blender, combine light rum, passion fruit syrup, lime juice and lemon juice with 3 oz. crushed ice
2. Blend at medium speed until smooth
3. Pour into a rocks glass
4. Garnish with a twist of lime

## Gazette

1½ oz. brandy
1 oz. sweet vermouth
1 tsp. lemon juice
1 tsp. sugar syrup

1. Fill mixing glass with ice
2. Add brandy, sweet vermouth, lemon juice and sugar syrup
3. Shake
4. Strain into a chilled cocktail glass

## Geisha

2 oz. bourbon
1 oz. sake
2 tsp. sugar syrup
1½ tsp. lemon juice

1. Fill mixing glass with ice
2. Add bourbon, sake, lemon juice and sugar syrup
3. Shake
4. Strain into a sour glass

## Genoa

1½ oz. vodka
¾ oz. Campari
2 oz. orange juice

1. Fill mixing glass with ice
2. Add vodka, Campari and orange juice
3. Shake
4. Strain into a rocks glass filled with ice

## Gentle Bull

1½ oz. tequila
¾ oz. Kahlúa
1 tbsp. heavy cream

1. Fill mixing glass with ice
2. Add tequila, Kahlúa and cream
3. Shake
4. Strain into a rocks glass filled with ice

# Georgia Peach Fizz

1½ oz. brandy
½ oz. peach brandy
½ oz. lemon juice
1 tsp. banana liqueur
1 tsp. sugar syrup
club soda

1. Fill mixing glass with ice
2. Add brandy, peach brandy, lemon juice, banana liqueur and sugar syrup
3. Shake
4. Strain into a Collins glass
5. Add ice
6. Top with club soda
7. Garnish with a fresh peach slice

# Gibson

2 oz. gin
½ oz. dry vermouth

1. Fill mixing glass with ice
2. Add gin and dry vermouth
3. Stir
4. Strain into a martini glass or a rocks glass filled with ice
5. Garnish with a pearl onion

(*Note:* A Gibson is a martini with a pearl onion garnish instead of an olive. Like a martini, the drier the Gibson, the less vermouth is used in proportion to the gin.)

# Gimlet

2 oz. gin
¼ oz. Rose's lime juice (½ oz. fresh lime juice may be substituted)

1. Fill mixing glass with ice
2. Add gin and lime juice
3. Shake
4. Strain into a chilled rocks glass
5. Add ice
6. Garnish with a lime slice

# Gin Alexander

½ oz. gin
½ oz. dark crème de cacao
½ oz. heavy cream
nutmeg or cinnamon

1. Fill mixing glass with ice
2. Add gin, dark crème de cacao and cream
3. Shake
4. Strain into a chilled cocktail glass
5. Sprinkle nutmeg or cinnamon on top

# Gin and Soda

1½ oz. gin
6 oz. club soda

1. Fill a highball glass with ice
2. Add gin and club soda
3. Stir
4. Garnish with a lemon twist

# Gin and Tonic

**2 oz. gin**
**tonic water**

1. Fill highball glass with ice
2. Add gin
3. Fill with tonic water
4. Stir
5. Garnish with a wedge of lime

# Gin Cassis

**1½ oz. gin**
**½ oz. crème de cassis**
**½ oz. lemon juice**

1. Fill shaker glass with ice
2. Add gin, crème de cassis and lemon juice
3. Shake
4. Strain into a rocks glass filled with ice

# Gin Daiquiri

**1½ oz. gin**
**½ oz. light rum**
**2 tsp. lime juice**
**1 tsp. sugar**

1. Fill mixing glass with ice
2. Add gin, light rum, lime juice and sugar
3. Shake
4. Strain into a rocks glass filled with ice
5. Garnish with a lime slice

# Gin Daisy

1½ oz. gin
½ tsp. sugar
juice of ½ lemon
1 tsp. grenadine
club soda

1. Fill mixing glass with ice
2. Add gin, sugar, lemon juice and grenadine
3. Shake
4. Strain into a highball glass over ice
5. Top with club soda
6. Garnish with a wedge of lemon

# Gin Fizz

1½ oz. dry gin
1 tbsp. powdered sugar
3 oz. sour mix
1 oz. club soda

1. Fill mixing glass with ice
2. Add gin, sugar and sour mix
3. Shake
4. Pour into a Collins glass over ice
5. Add club soda
6. Garnish with a cherry and an orange slice

# Ginger Breeze

1½ oz. light rum
1 tsp. cherry brandy
4 oz. orange juice
1 oz. ginger ale

1. Fill mixing glass with ice
2. Add rum, cherry brandy and orange juice
3. Shake
4. Strain into a highball glass
5. Add ice
6. Top with ginger ale

# Gin Rickey

**1½ oz. gin**
**juice of ½ lime**
**club soda**

1. Fill a highball glass with ice
2. Add gin and lime juice
3. Fill with club soda

# Gin Sour

**1½ oz. gin**
**4 oz. sour mix**

1. Fill mixing glass with ice
2. Add gin and sour mix
3. Shake
4. Strain into a sour glass
5. Add ice
6. Garnish with a cherry and an orange slice

# Girl Scout Cookie

**1½ oz. Kahlúa**
**1½ oz. cream**
**½ oz. peppermint schnapps**

1. Fill mixing glass with ice
2. Add Kahlúa, cream and peppermint schnapps
3. Shake
4. Strain into a rocks glass filled with ice

## Glad Eyes

1½ oz. Pernod
½ oz. peppermint schnapps

1. Fill mixing glass with ice
2. Add Pernod and peppermint schnapps
3. Shake
4. Strain into a chilled cocktail glass

## Glasgow

1½ oz. scotch
1 tsp. dry vermouth
1 tbsp. lemon juice
1 tsp. almond extract

1. Fill mixing glass with ice
2. Add scotch, dry vermouth, lemon juice and almond extract
3. Shake
4. Strain into a rocks glass filled with ice

## Gloom Chaser

1 oz. Grand Marnier
1 oz. curaçao
½ oz. lemon juice
1 tsp. grenadine

1. Fill mixing glass with ice
2. Add Grand Marnier, curaçao, lemon juice and grenadine
3. Shake
4. Strain into a chilled cocktail glass

# Gloom Lifter

2 oz. blended whiskey
½ oz. lemon juice
¼ oz. sugar syrup
½ egg white

1. Fill mixing glass with ice
2. Add blended whiskey, lemon juice, sugar syrup and egg white
3. Shake
4. Strain into a chilled cocktail glass

# Gluewein

6 oz. dry red wine
1 tsp. honey
2 whole cloves
1 cinnamon stick, broken into pieces
pinch ground nutmeg

1. Combine ingredients in a small saucepan
2. Heat without boiling
3. Stir until honey is dissolved
4. Pour into a warm mug

# Godchild

¾ oz. vodka
¾ oz. amaretto
¾ oz. heavy cream

1. Fill mixing glass with ice
2. Add vodka, amaretto and heavy cream
3. Shake
4. Strain into a champagne glass

# Godfather

**1½ oz. scotch**
**¾ oz. amaretto**

1. Fill rocks glass with ice
2. Add scotch and amaretto
3. Stir

# Godmother

**1½ oz. vodka**
**¾ oz. Kahlúa**

1. Fill a rocks glass with ice
2. Add vodka and Kahlúa
3. Stir

# Go-Go Juice

**½ oz. vodka**
**½ oz. gin**
**½ oz. light rum**
**½ oz. blue curaçao**
**½ oz. white tequila**
**½ oz. orange juice**
**1 oz. sour mix**
**7-Up**

1. Fill mixing glass with ice
2. Add all ingredients, except 7-Up
3. Shake
4. Strain into a Collins glass
5. Add ice
6. Top with 7-Up
7. Garnish with a lemon slice

# Golden Cadillac

**2 oz. Galliano**
**1 oz. white crème de cacao**
**1 oz. cream**

1. Fill mixing glass with ice
2. Add Galliano, crème de cacao and cream
3. Shake
4. Pour into a chilled highball glass
5. Add ice

# Golden Dawn

**1½ oz. gin**
**½ oz. orange juice**
**2 tsp. apricot brandy**

1. Fill mixing glass with ice
2. Add gin, orange juice and apricot brandy
3. Shake
4. Strain into a chilled cocktail glass

# Golden Daze

**1½ oz. gin**
**½ oz. apricot brandy**
**1 oz. orange juice**

1. Fill mixing glass with ice
2. Add gin, apricot brandy and orange juice
3. Shake
4. Strain into a chilled cocktail glass

# Golden Dream

2 oz. Galliano
1 oz. white crème de cacao
1 oz. cream
½ oz. orange juice
dash triple sec

1. Fill mixing glass with ice
2. Add Galliano, crème de cacao, cream, orange juice and triple sec
3. Shake
4. Pour into a chilled highball glass
5. Add ice

# Golden Fizz

1 oz. gin
2 oz. sour mix
1 egg yolk
1 oz. club soda

1. Fill mixing glass with ice
2. Add gin, sour mix and egg yolk
3. Shake
4. Strain into Collins glass filled with ice
5. Top with club soda

# Golden Gate

¾ oz. light rum
¾ oz. gin
½ oz. lemon juice
½ oz. white crème de cacao
1 tsp. 151-proof rum
dash Falernum

1. Fill mixing glass with ice
2. Add light rum, gin, lemon juice, white crème de cacao, 151-proof rum and Falernum
3. Shake
4. Strain into a rocks glass filled with ice
5. Garnish with an orange slice

# Golden Lemonade

½ cup sugar
1 cup fresh lemon juice
2 cups gold tequila

1. In a small saucepan, combine sugar with ½ cup water
2. Bring to a boil (over medium flame), stirring so that sugar is dissolved
3. Boil for one minute
4. Remove from heat
5. Add ½ cup cold water to mixture
6. Cool to room temperature
7. Stir in lemon juice
8. Combine lemon syrup and tequila in a pitcher
9. Stir well
10. Add ice
11. Serve in Collins glasses filled with ice

# Golden Margarita

2 oz. gold tequila
1 oz. curaçao
¾ oz. lime juice

1. Fill mixing glass with 2 oz. crushed ice, gold tequila, curaçao and lime juice
2. Shake
3. Pour into a rocks glass (rim may be frosted with salt, if desired, before pouring drink into glass)
4. Garnish with a slice of lime

# Golden Screw

1½ oz. vodka
dash Angostura bitters
orange juice

1. Fill a highball glass with ice
2. Add vodka and bitters
3. Fill with orange juice
4. Stir

# Golden Slipper

1 oz. apricot brandy
1 oz. yellow Chartreuse
1 egg yolk

1. Fill mixing glass with ice
2. Add apricot brandy, yellow Chartreuse and the egg yolk
3. Shake well
4. Strain into a chilled cocktail glass

# Golf

2 oz. gin
1 oz. dry vermouth
2 dashes Angostura bitters

1. Fill mixing glass with ice
2. Add gin, dry vermouth and bitters
3. Stir
4. Strain into a chilled cocktail glass
5. Garnish with an olive

# Good and Plenty

¾ oz. ouzo
¾ oz. anisette

Pour ouzo and anisette into a brandy snifter or a liqueur glass

# Gorilla Punch

1 oz. vodka
½ oz. blue curaçao
2 oz. orange juice
2 oz. pineapple juice

1. Fill mixing glass with ice
2. Add vodka, blue curaçao, orange juice and pineapple juice
3. Shake
4. Strain into a Collins glass filled with ice
5. Garnish with a cherry

# Gradeal Special

1½ oz. light rum
¾ oz. apricot brandy
¾ oz. gin
1 tsp. sugar syrup

1. Fill mixing glass with ice
2. Add light rum, apricot brandy, gin and sugar syrup
3. Shake
4. Strain into a chilled cocktail glass

# Grand Apple

1 oz. apple brandy
½ oz. cognac
½ oz. Grand Marnier

1. Fill mixing glass with ice
2. Add apple brandy, cognac and Grand Marnier
3. Stir
4. Strain into a rocks glass
5. Garnish with a lemon twist

# Grand Occasion

1½ oz. light rum
½ oz. Grand Marnier
½ oz. white crème de cacao
1 tbsp. lemon juice

1. Fill mixing glass with ice
2. Add light rum, Grand Marnier, white crème de cacao and lemon juice
3. Shake well
4. Strain into a chilled cocktail glass

# Grand Passion

2 oz. gin
1 oz. passion fruit nectar
2 dashes Angostura bitters

1. Fill mixing glass with ice
2. Add gin, passion fruit nectar and bitters
3. Shake well
4. Strain into a chilled cocktail glass

# Grand Slam

1½ oz. Swedish Punsch
¾ oz. dry vermouth
¾ oz. sweet vermouth

1. Fill mixing glass with ice
2. Add Swedish Punsch, dry vermouth and sweet vermouth
3. Stir
4. Strain into a chilled cocktail glass

# Grape Crush

1 oz. vodka
½ oz. Chambord
2 oz. sour mix
1 oz. cranberry juice cocktail
7-Up

1. Fill mixing glass with ice
2. Add vodka, Chambord, sour mix and cranberry juice
3. Shake
4. Strain into a highball glass filled with ice
5. Top with 7-Up

# Grapefruit Highball

1½ oz. light rum
6 oz. grapefruit juice

1. Fill highball glass with ice
2. Add light rum and grapefruit juice
3. Stir

# Grapeshot

**1½ oz. tequila**
**½ oz. curaçao**
**1 oz. grape juice**

1. Fill mixing glass with ice
2. Add tequila, curaçao and grape juice
3. Shake
4. Strain into a chilled cocktail glass

# Grape Vine

**1½ oz. gin**
**2 oz. grape juice**
**1 oz. lemon juice**
**dash grenadine**

1. Fill a rocks glass with ice
2. Add gin, grape juice, lemon juice and grenadine
3. Stir well

# Grasshopper

**1 oz. green crème de menthe**
**1 oz. white crème de cacao**
**1 oz. light cream**

1. Fill mixing glass with ice
2. Add green crème de menthe, white crème de cacao and cream
3. Shake
4. Strain into a chilled cocktail glass

# Grass Is Greener

1½ oz. light rum
¾ oz. green crème de menthe
¾ oz. lemon juice

1. Fill mixing glass with ice
2. Add light rum, green crème de menthe and lemon juice
3. Shake
4. Strain into a chilled champagne glass

# Great Dane

1 oz. aquavit
½ oz. Peter Heering (or other cherry brandy)
½ oz. cranberry juice cocktail
1 dash orange bitters

1. Fill mixing glass with ice
2. Add aquavit, Peter Heering (cherry brandy), cranberry juice and orange bitters
3. Shake
4. Strain into a chilled cocktail glass

# Great Secret

2 oz. gin
½ oz. Lillet
dash Angostura bitters

1. Fill mixing glass with ice
2. Add gin, Lillet and bitters
3. Shake
4. Strain into a chilled cocktail glass
5. Garnish with an orange slice

# Green Dragon

**2 oz. Russian vodka**
**1 oz. green Chartreuse**

1. Fill mixing glass with ice
2. Add vodka and green Chartreuse
3. Shake
4. Strain into a chilled cocktail glass

# Green Eye-Opener

**1½ oz. vodka**
**dash Rose's lime juice**
**2 oz. orange juice**
**dash blue curaçao**
**dash triple sec**

1. Fill mixing glass with ice
2. Add vodka, Rose's lime juice, orange juice, blue curaçao and triple sec
3. Shake
4. Pour into a highball glass
5. Garnish with a celery stalk, including the leafy part

(Courtesy of Sign of the Dove, New York City)

# Green Fire

**1½ oz. gin**
**2 tsp. green crème de menthe**
**2 tsp. kummel**

1. Fill mixing glass with ice
2. Add gin, green crème de menthe and kummel
3. Shake
4. Strain into a highball glass
5. Add ice

# Green Hornet

1½ oz. brandy
½ oz. green crème de menthe

1. Fill rocks glass with ice
2. Add brandy and crème de menthe
3. Stir

# Green Lizard (shooter)

1 oz. green Chartreuse
½ oz. 151-proof rum

1. Combine in a mixing glass filled with ice
2. Strain into a shot glass

# Green Room

1 oz. brandy
1½ oz. dry vermouth
2 dashes of curaçao

1. Fill mixing glass with ice
2. Add brandy, dry vermouth and curaçao
3. Shake
4. Strain into a chilled cocktail glass

# Grenadier

2 oz. brandy
1 oz. ginger brandy
dash ground ginger
1 tsp. sugar syrup

1. Fill mixing glass with ice
2. Add brandy, ginger brandy, ginger and sugar syrup

3. Stir
4. Strain into a chilled cocktail glass

# Greyhound

■_____■

**1½ oz. vodka**
**6 oz. grapefruit juice**

1. Fill a highball glass with ice
2. Add vodka and grapefruit juice
3. Stir

# Grog

■_____■

**2 oz. Jamaican rum**
**1 sugar cube**
**1 tbsp. lemon juice**
**3 cloves**
**1 cinnamon stick**

1. Combine all ingredients in a large mug
2. Add boiling water
3. Stir drink so that the sugar dissolves
4. Garnish with a lemon twist

# Ground Zero

■_____■

**¾ oz. peppermint schnapps**
**¾ oz. bourbon**
**¾ oz. vodka**
**½ oz. Kahlúa**

1. Fill mixing glass with ice
2. Add peppermint schnapps, bourbon, vodka and Kahlúa
3. Shake
4. Strain into a sour glass
5. Add ice

# Gypsy

2 oz. vodka
½ oz. Bénédictine
1 tsp. lemon juice
1 tsp. orange juice

1. Fill mixing glass with ice
2. Add vodka, Bénédictine, lemon juice and orange juice
3. Shake
4. Strain into a rocks glass filled with ice

# H

## Hairy Navel

¾ oz. peach schnapps
¾ oz. vodka
6 oz. orange juice

1. Fill a highball glass with ice
2. Add peach schnapps, vodka and orange juice
3. Stir

## Halley's Comfort

1½ oz. Southern Comfort
1½ oz. peach schnapps
club soda

1. Fill a rocks glass with ice
2. Add Southern Comfort and peach schnapps
3. Stir
4. Fill with club soda

## Hammerhead

1 oz. gold rum
1 oz. amaretto
1 oz. curaçao
1 or 2 dashes Southern Comfort

1. Fill mixing glass with ice
2. Add rum, amaretto, curaçao and Southern Comfort
3. Shake
4. Strain into a chilled cocktail glass

# Time Bomb

**1 oz. tequila**
**3 oz. cranberry juice cocktail**

1. Fill mixing glass with ice
2. Add tequila and cranberry juice
3. Stir
4. Strain into a sour glass
5. Add ice
6. Garnish with an orange peel

# The Happy Feller (shooter)

**3 oz. Finlandia or Absolut vodka**
**1 oz. Framboise**
**1 oz. Cointreau**
**dash Rose's lime juice**

1. Fill mixing glass with ice
2. Add vodka, Framboise, Cointreau and lime juice
3. Stir
4. Strain into shot glasses

(Makes approximately 3 shots)

# Harbor Light

**¾ oz. Metaxa**
**¾ oz. Galliano**

Pour Metaxa and Galliano into a brandy snifter or a liqueur glass

# Harlem Cocktail

1½ oz. gin
1 oz. pineapple juice
½ tsp. maraschino liqueur

1. Fill mixing glass with ice
2. Add gin, pineapple juice and maraschino liqueur
3. Shake
4. Strain into a chilled cocktail glass
5. Garnish with 2 pineapple chunks (skewer on a toothpick and balance across the rim of the glass)

# Harper's Ferry

1½ oz. dry vermouth
1 tbsp. Southern Comfort
1 tbsp. light rum
1 tbsp. curaçao

1. Fill mixing glass with ice
2. Add dry vermouth, Southern Comfort, light rum and curaçao
3. Shake
4. Strain into a chilled cocktail glass

# Harvard

1 oz. brandy
1 oz. sweet vermouth
¼ oz. lemon juice
dash sugar syrup
2 dashes Angostura bitters

1. Fill mixing glass with ice
2. Add brandy, sweet vermouth, lemon juice, sugar syrup and bitters
3. Shake
4. Strain into a chilled cocktail glass

# Harvey Wallbanger

1½ oz. vodka
4 oz. orange juice
½ oz. Galliano

1. Fill a Collins glass with ice
2. Add vodka and orange juice
3. Stir well
4. Float Galliano on top

# Havana Club

1½ oz. light rum
1 tbsp. dry vermouth

1. Fill mixing glass with ice
2. Add rum and dry vermouth
3. Shake
4. Strain into a chilled cocktail glass

# Hawaiian Cocktail

2 oz. gin
½ oz. triple sec
1 tbsp. pineapple juice

1. Fill mixing glass with ice
2. Add gin, triple sec and pineapple juice
3. Shake
4. Strain into a chilled cocktail glass

# Hawaiian Eye

1½ oz. bourbon
1 oz. Kahlúa

1 oz. heavy cream
½ oz. vodka
½ oz. banana liqueur
1 tsp. Pernod
1 egg white

1. In a blender, combine 3 oz. cracked ice with all ingredients
2. Blend at high speed for 15 seconds
3. Pour straight into a chilled highball glass
4. Garnish with a cherry and a pineapple slice

# Hawaiian Orange Blossom

1½ oz. gin
1 oz. curaçao
2 oz. orange juice
1 oz. pineapple juice

1. Fill mixing glass with ice
2. Add gin, curaçao, orange juice and pineapple juice
3. Shake
4. Strain into a sour glass
5. Garnish with an orange slice

# Hawaiian Punch (shooter)

¼ oz. crème de almond
¼ oz. Southern Comfort
¼ oz. Smirnoff 100-proof vodka
¼ oz. pineapple juice

1. Fill mixing glass with ice
2. Add crème de almond, Southern Comfort, Smirnoff vodka and pineapple juice
3. Shake
4. Strain into a rocks glass

# Henry Morgan's Grog

1½ oz. blended whiskey
1 oz. Pernod
½ oz. dark rum
1 oz. heavy cream
ground nutmeg

1. Half fill mixing glass with cracked ice
2. Add whiskey, Pernod, dark rum and heavy cream
3. Shake
4. Pour into a chilled rocks glass
5. Sprinkle top with ground nutmeg

# High Jamaican Wind

1½ oz. Myers's rum
½ oz. Kahlúa
cream

1. Fill a rocks glass with ice
2. Add Myers's dark rum and Kahlúa
3. Float cream on top

# Highland Fling

1½ oz. scotch
½ oz. sweet vermouth
2–3 dashes orange bitters

1. Fill mixing glass with ice
2. Add scotch, sweet vermouth and orange bitters
3. Shake
4. Strain into a chilled cocktail glass
5. Garnish with an olive

# High Roller

1½ oz. vodka
¾ oz. Grand Marnier
4 oz. orange juice
a few drops grenadine

1. Fill mixing glass with ice
2. Add vodka, Grand Marnier and orange juice
3. Shake
4. Strain into a rocks glass
5. Add ice
6. Add a few drops of grenadine to top

# Hoffman House

1½ oz. gin
½ oz. dry vermouth
2 dashes orange bitters

1. Fill mixing glass with ice
2. Add gin, dry vermouth and orange bitters
3. Shake
4. Strain into a chilled cocktail glass
5. Garnish with an olive

# Homecoming

1½ oz. amaretto
1½ oz. Bailey's Original Irish Cream

1. Fill mixing glass with ice
2. Add amaretto and Bailey's
3. Shake
4. Strain into a chilled cocktail glass

# Honey Bee

½ oz. honey
2½ oz. dark rum
½ oz. lemon juice

1. Fill mixing glass with ice
2. Add honey, dark rum and lemon juice
3. Shake
4. Strain into a chilled cocktail glass

# Honeymoon

¾ oz. apple brandy
¾ oz. Bénédictine
1 oz. lemon juice
2 dashes triple sec

1. Fill mixing glass with ice
2. Add apple brandy, Bénédictine, lemon juice and triple sec
3. Shake
4. Strain into a chilled cocktail glass

# Honolulu Lulu

1 oz. gin
1 oz. Bénédictine
1 oz. maraschino liqueur

1. Fill mixing glass with ice
2. Add gin, Bénédictine and maraschino liqueur
3. Stir
4. Strain into a chilled cocktail glass

# Hoopla

¾ oz. brandy
¾ oz. Cointreau

¾ oz. Lillet
¾ oz. lemon juice

1. Fill mixing glass with ice
2. Add brandy, Cointreau, Lillet and lemon juice
3. Shake
4. Strain into a chilled cocktail glass

# Hoot Mon

1½ oz. scotch
¾ oz. sweet vermouth
1 tsp. Bénédictine

1. Fill mixing glass with ice
2. Add scotch, sweet vermouth and Bénédictine
3. Stir
4. Strain into a chilled cocktail glass
5. Garnish with a twist of lemon

# Hop Toad

1 oz. light rum
1 oz. apricot brandy
1 oz. lime juice

1. Fill mixing glass with ice
2. Add light rum, apricot brandy and lime juice
3. Shake
4. Strain into a chilled cocktail glass

# Horse's Neck

2 oz. blended whiskey
ginger ale
1 lemon, peeled

1. Peel lemon in one strip, creating a spiral effect
2. Set peel aside
3. Pour blended whiskey into a Collins glass
4. Add ice
5. Drop in the lemon peel as a garnish
6. Top with ginger ale
7. Add a few drops of the fresh lemon juice

# Hot Apple Pie

1½ oz. Tuaca liqueur
hot apple cider

1. Pour Tuaca into a mug
2. Fill with hot apple cider

# Hot Buttered Rum

8 oz. apple cider
6 whole cloves
1 cinnamon stick
½ oz. lemon juice
2 oz. dark rum
1 tsp. butter

1. Pour apple cider, cloves, cinnamon stick and lemon juice into a small saucepan
2. Bring to a boil
3. Pour into a mug
4. Add rum
5. Top with butter

# Hot Coconut Coffee

1 oz. Malibu liqueur
hot coffee

1. Pour Malibu into a coffee mug
2. Fill with hot coffee
3. Top with whipped cream, if desired

# Hot Pants

**1½ oz. tequila**
**¾ oz. peppermint schnapps**
**1 tbsp. grapefruit juice**
**½ tsp. grenadine**

1. Fill mixing glass with ice
2. Add tequila, peppermint schnapps, grapefruit juice and grenadine
3. Shake
4. Pour into a rocks glass

(*Note:* You may frost the rim of the rocks glass with salt before pouring the drink in, if desired.)

# Hot Peppermint Patty

**1 oz. peppermint schnapps**
**½ oz. dark crème de cacao**
**1 tsp. green crème de menthe**
**1 packet instant hot chocolate mix**
**hot water**
**whipped cream**

1. Pour peppermint schnapps and crème de menthe into a coffee mug
2. Add hot chocolate mix
3. Stir until dissolved
4. Fill almost to the top with boiling water
5. Stir
6. Top with whipped cream and crème de menthe

# Hot Rum

**2 sugar cubes**
**4 oz. light rum**
**1½ tsp. lemon juice**
**hot water**

1. In a mug, dissolve the sugar cubes in a small amount of hot water
2. Add rum and lemon juice
3. Fill with hot water
4. Stir
5. Sprinkle cinnamon on top

# Hot Rum Toddy

**1½ oz. Jamaican dark rum**
**1 tsp. sugar**
**3 cloves**
**dash cinnamon**
**1 lemon slice**
**hot water**
**dash ground nutmeg**

1. Add rum, sugar, cloves, cinnamon and lemon slice to a large mug
2. Fill with hot water
3. Sprinkle top with nutmeg

# Hot Shots (shooter)

**½ oz. vodka**
**½ oz. peppermint schnapps**
**few drops Tabasco sauce**

1. Pour vodka and peppermint schnapps into a shot glass
2. Top with a few drops of Tabasco sauce

# Hot Toddy

1 oz. bourbon
4 oz. boiling water
1 tsp. sugar
3 whole cloves
1 cinnamon stick
1 lemon slice, thinly sliced

1. Put sugar, cloves, cinnamon stick and lemon slice into a heat-resistant mug
2. Add 1 oz. boiling water
3. Stir
4. Let stand for 5 minutes
5. Add bourbon and 3 oz. boiling water
6. Stir well
7. Sprinkle with ground nutmeg

# Houston Hurricane

1 oz. blended whiskey
1 oz. gin
1 oz. white crème de menthe
3 tbsp. lemon juice

1. Fill mixing glass with ice
2. Add blended whiskey, gin, white crème de menthe and lemon juice
3. Shake
4. Strain into a chilled cocktail glass

# Hudson Bay

1 oz. gin
½ oz. cherry brandy
1 tbsp. orange juice
1½ tsp. lime juice
1½ tsp. 151-proof rum

1. Fill mixing glass with ice
2. Add gin, cherry brandy, orange juice and lime juice and 151-proof rum
3. Shake
4. Strain into a chilled cocktail glass

# Hula-Hula

**2 oz. gin**
**1 oz. orange juice**
**dash curaçao**

1. Fill a rocks glass with ice
2. Add gin, orange juice and curaçao
3. Stir

# Hundred Percent

**1½ oz. Swedish Punsch**
**1 tsp. lemon juice**
**1 tsp. orange juice**
**dash of grenadine**

1. Fill mixing glass with ice
2. Add Swedish Punsch, lemon juice, orange juice and grenadine
3. Shake
4. Strain into a sour glass
5. Add ice

# Hunter's Cocktail

**1½ oz. rye whiskey**
**½ oz. cherry brandy**

1. Fill a rocks glass with ice
2. Add rye and cherry brandy
3. Stir
4. Garnish with a cherry

# Huntington Special

**1½ oz. gin**
**½ oz. lemon juice**
**1 tsp. grenadine**

1. Fill mixing glass with ice
2. Add gin, lemon juice and grenadine
3. Shake
4. Strain into a rocks glass filled with ice


# Huntress Cocktail

**¾ oz. bourbon**
**¾ oz. cherry liqueur**
**1 tsp. triple sec**
**1 oz. cream**

1. Fill mixing glass with ice
2. Add bourbon, cherry liqueur, triple sec and cream
3. Shake
4. Strain into a chilled cocktail glass


# Hurricane

**1 oz. light rum**
**1 oz. gold rum**
**½ oz. passion fruit syrup**
**½ oz. fresh lime juice**

1. Fill mixing glass with ice
2. Add light rum, gold rum, passion fruit syrup and lime juice
3. Shake
4. Strain into a chilled cocktail glass

# I

## Iceball

1½ oz. gin
¾ oz. white crème de menthe
¾ oz. Sambuca
2–3 tsp. cream

1. In a blender, add 3 oz. crushed ice, gin, white crème de menthe, Sambuca and cream
2. Blend at medium speed for about 15 seconds, until smooth
3. Pour into a goblet or a wineglass

## The Iceberg

2 oz. vodka
1 tsp. Pernod

1. Fill mixing glass with ice
2. Add vodka and Pernod
3. Shake
4. Strain into a chilled cocktail glass

## Ice Palace

1 oz. light rum
½ oz. Galliano
½ oz. apricot brandy
2 oz. pineapple juice
¼ oz. lemon juice

1. Fill mixing glass with ice
2. Add light rum, Galliano, apricot brandy, pineapple juice and lemon juice
3. Shake
4. Strain into a Collins glass
5. Add ice
6. Garnish with a cherry and an orange slice


# Ichbien

**2 oz. apple brandy**
**1 oz. curaçao**
**1 egg yolk**
**2 oz. milk or cream**

1. Fill mixing glass with ice
2. Add apple brandy, curaçao, egg yolk and cream
3. Shake
4. Strain into a chilled sour glass


# Ideal

**2 oz. gin**
**½ oz. sweet vermouth**
**1 tbsp. grapefruit juice**
**3 dashes maraschino liqueur**

1. Fill mixing glass with ice
2. Add gin, sweet vermouth, grapefruit juice and maraschino liqueur
3. Shake
4. Strain into a chilled cocktail glass

# Iguana

½ oz. vodka
½ oz. tequila
¼ oz. Kahlúa
1½ oz. sour mix

1. Fill mixing glass with ice
2. Add vodka, tequila, Kahlúa and sour mix
3. Shake
4. Strain into a chilled cocktail glass
5. Garnish with a lime slice

# Il Magnifico

1 oz. Tuaca
1 oz. curaçao
1 oz. cream

1. In a blender with 3 oz. cracked ice, add Tuaca, curaçao and cream
2. Blend at low speed for a few seconds, until smooth
3. Pour into a chilled cocktail glass

# Imperial Fizz

1 oz. bourbon
½ oz. lemon juice
½ tsp. sugar
chilled champagne

1. Fill mixing glass with ice
2. Add bourbon, lemon juice and sugar
3. Shake
4. Strain into a chilled champagne glass
5. Fill with chilled champagne

# Income Tax

1 oz. gin
1 tsp. dry vermouth
1 tsp. sweet vermouth
½ oz. orange juice
2–3 dashes Angostura bitters

1. Fill mixing glass with ice
2. Add gin, dry vermouth, sweet vermouth, orange juice and bitters
3. Shake
4. Strain into a rocks glass filled with ice

# Indian Summer (shooter)

1 oz. vodka
1 oz. Kahlúa
2 oz. pineapple juice

1. Fill a mixing glass with ice
2. Add vodka, Kahlúa and pineapple juice
3. Shake
4. Pour into shot glasses

(Will fill two 2-oz. shot glasses)

# Ink Street

1½ oz. blended whiskey
¾ oz. orange juice
¾ oz. lemon juice

1. Fill mixing glass with ice
2. Add blended whiskey, orange juice and lemon juice
3. Shake
4. Strain into a chilled cocktail glass
5. Garnish with an orange slice

# The International

1½ oz. cognac
1 tsp. vodka
2 tsp. anisette
2 tsp. Cointreau (any triple sec may be substituted)

1. Fill mixing glass with ice
2. Add cognac, vodka, anisette and Cointreau
3. Shake
4. Strain into a chilled cocktail glass

# International Stinger

1½ oz. Metaxa
½ oz. Galliano

1. Fill rocks glass with ice
2. Pour in Metaxa and Galliano
3. Stir

# Interplanetary Punch

24 oz. light rum
4 oz. dark rum
8 oz. peppermint schnapps
1 qt. mango nectar
12 oz. cream
1 qt. orange juice
8 mint sprigs
1 fresh mango, cut into pieces
1 small orange, thinly sliced

1. Combine light rum, dark rum, peppermint schnapps, mango nectar, cream and orange juice in a large punch bowl
2. Stir well
3. Add a block of ice

4. Float mint sprigs, mango chunks and orange slices on top
5. For best results, refrigerate for one hour before serving

# Invisible Man

**2 oz. gin**
**½ oz. brandy**
**½ oz. triple sec**
**2 dashes orange juice**
**ginger ale**

1. Fill a highball glass with ice
2. Add gin, brandy, triple sec and orange juice
3. Fill with ginger ale
4. Stir

# IRA Cocktail

**1½ oz. Jameson Irish Whiskey**
**1 oz. Bailey's Original Irish Cream**

1. Fill rocks glass with ice
2. Add Jameson whiskey and Bailey's
3. Stir

# Irish

**1½ oz. Irish whiskey**
**2 dashes curaçao**
**2 dashes Pernod**
**dash maraschino liqueur**

1. Fill mixing glass with ice
2. Add Irish whiskey, curaçao, Pernod and maraschino liqueur
3. Stir
4. Strain into a chilled cocktail glass
5. Garnish with a lemon twist

# Irish Coffee

1½ oz. Irish whiskey
hot coffee

1. Pour Irish whiskey into a coffee mug
2. Fill with hot coffee
3. Top with whipped cream, if desired

# Irish Cow

4½ oz. Bailey's Original Irish Cream
4½ oz. milk

1. Combine Bailey's and milk in a small saucepan
2. Warm at a low heat
3. Pour into a mug
4. Sprinkle nutmeg on top, if desired

# Irish Fix

2 oz. Irish whiskey
½ oz. Irish Mist
1 oz. pineapple juice
½ oz. lemon juice
½ tsp. sugar syrup

1. Fill mixing glass with ice
2. Add Irish whiskey, Irish Mist, pineapple juice, lemon juice and sugar syrup
3. Shake
4. Strain into a rocks glass filled with ice
5. Garnish with a lemon slice

# Irish Spring

1 oz. Irish whiskey
½ oz. peach brandy
1 oz. orange juice
1 oz. sour mix

1. Fill a Collins glass with ice
2. Add Irish whiskey, peach brandy, orange juice and sour mix
3. Stir well
4. Garnish with a cherry and an orange slice

# Irish Whiskey and Soda

1½ oz. Irish whiskey
6 oz. club soda

1. Fill a highball glass with ice
2. Add Irish whiskey and club soda
3. Stir gently

# Irish Whiskey Cocktail

2 oz. Irish whiskey
½ tsp. triple sec
½ tsp. anis
¼ tsp. maraschino liqueur
dash Angostura bitters

1. Fill mixing glass with ice
2. Add Irish whiskey, triple sec, anis, maraschino and bitters
3. Shake
4. Strain into a chilled cocktail glass
5. Garnish with an olive

# Israeli Coffee

**2 oz. Sabra liqueur**
**hot coffee**

1. Pour Sabra into a coffee mug
2. Fill with hot coffee
3. Top with whipped cream, if desired

# Italian Coffee

**1½ oz. Galliano**
**hot coffee**

1. Pour Galliano into a coffee mug
2. Fill with hot coffee
3. Top with whipped cream, if desired

# Italian Delight

**1 oz. amaretto**
**½ oz. orange juice**
**1½ oz. cream**

1. Fill mixing glass with ice
2. Add amaretto, orange juice and cream
3. Shake
4. Strain into a chilled cocktail glass
5. Garnish with a cherry

# Italian Stallion

**1½ oz. bourbon**
**½ oz. sweet vermouth**
**½ oz. Campari**
**1–2 dashes Angostura bitters**

1. Fill mixing glass with ice
2. Add bourbon, sweet vermouth, Campari and bitters
3. Stir
4. Strain into a chilled cocktail glass
5. Garnish with a lemon twist

# Italian Stinger

**1½ oz. brandy**
**½ oz. Galliano**

1. Fill mixing glass with ice
2. Add brandy and Galliano
3. Stir
4. Strain into a rocks glass filled with ice

# Ixtapa

**2 oz. Kahlúa**
**¾ oz. tequila**

1. Fill mixing glass with ice
2. Add Kahlúa and tequila
3. Stir
4. Strain into a chilled cocktail glass

# J

## Jack-in-the-Box

1½ oz. applejack
1 oz. pineapple juice
1½ tsp. lemon juice
3 dashes Angostura bitters

1. Fill mixing glass with ice
2. Add applejack, pineapple juice, lemon juice and bitters
3. Shake
4. Strain into a chilled cocktail glass

## Jack Rose

1½ oz. applejack
¾ oz. sour mix
½ oz. grenadine

1. Fill mixing glass with ice
2. Add applejack, sour mix and grenadine
3. Shake
4. Strain into a sour glass
5. Add ice

## Jack Withers

¾ oz. gin
¾ oz. dry vermouth
¾ oz. sweet vermouth
½ oz. orange juice

1. Fill mixing glass with ice
2. Add gin, dry vermouth, sweet vermouth and orange juice
3. Stir
4. Strain into a chilled cocktail glass

## Jade

**1½ oz. gold rum**
**½ oz. lime juice**
**½ tsp. green crème de menthe**
**1 tsp. sugar syrup**
**½ tsp. curaçao**

1. Fill mixing glass with ice
2. Add gold rum, lime juice, green crème de menthe, sugar syrup and curaçao
3. Shake
4. Strain into a rocks glass filled with ice
5. Garnish with a lime slice

## Jamaica Cooler

**2¼ oz. dark rum**
**1 tsp. superfine granulated sugar**
**½ oz. lemon juice**
**2 dashes orange bitters**
**7-Up**

1. In a goblet or large wineglass, dissolve the sugar in the dark rum
2. Add lemon juice and bitters
3. Add 4 or 5 ice cubes
4. Fill with 7-Up
5. Stir

# Jamaica Ginger

2 oz. dark rum
¾ oz. grenadine
3 dashes curaçao
3 dashes maraschino liqueur
dash Angostura bitters

1. Fill mixing glass with ice
2. Add dark rum, grenadine, curaçao, maraschino liqueur and bitters
3. Shake
4. Strain into a chilled cocktail glass

# Jamaican

1 oz. Jamaican rum
1 oz. Kahlúa
1 oz. lime juice
dash Angostura bitters
7-Up

1. Fill mixing glass with ice
2. Add rum, Kahlúa, lime juice and bitters
3. Shake
4. Strain into a Collins glass
5. Add ice
6. Top with 7-Up

# Jamaican Coffee

(see Calypso)

# Jamaican Milk Shake

2 oz. bourbon
1½ oz. Jamaican rum (dark)
1½ oz. milk or cream

1. Fill blender with 3 oz. cracked ice
2. Add bourbon, Jamaican rum and milk or cream
3. Blend at low speed, until smooth
4. Pour into a rocks glass

## Jamaican Wind

**1½ oz. Myers's dark rum**
**½ oz. Kahlúa**

1. Fill a rocks glass with ice
2. Add Myers's rum, then Kahlúa
3. Stir

## Janet Standard

**2 oz. brandy**
**dash Angostura bitters**
**1 tsp. orgeat syrup**

1. Put one ice cube in the bottom of a chilled cocktail glass
2. Add brandy, bitters and orgeat syrup
3. Stir
4. Garnish with a twist of lemon

## Japanese Fizz

**2 oz. blended whiskey**
**¾ oz. port**
**½ oz. lemon juice**
**1 tsp. sugar**
**club soda**

1. Fill mixing glass with ice
2. Add whiskey, port, lemon juice and sugar
3. Shake
4. Pour into a chilled highball glass

5. Add ice
6. Fill with club soda
7. Garnish with an orange slice

# Java Cooler

1 oz. gin
½ oz. lime juice
3 dashes bitters
tonic water

1. Fill a highball glass with ice
2. Add gin, lime juice and bitters
3. Stir
4. Fill with tonic water
5. Stir again

# Jell-O Shots (shooter)

cherry Jell-O brand gelatin
1 cup boiling water
1 cup vodka

or

lime Jell-O brand gelatin
1 cup boiling water
1 cup tequila
3–4 ounces lime juice

1. In a bowl, add liquor and boiling water to gelatin
2. Stir until gelatin has dissolved
3. Chill to set
4. Serve in paper soufflé cups

# Jelly Bean

**1 oz. anisette**
**1 oz. blackberry brandy**

1. Pour anisette and blackberry brandy into a cordial glass or a rocks glass
2. Stir
3. Add ice, if desired

# Jewel

**1 oz. gin**
**1 oz. sweet vermouth**
**1 tbsp. green Chartreuse**
**2 dashes orange bitters**

1. Fill mixing glass with ice
2. Add gin, sweet vermouth, green Chartreuse and orange bitters
3. Shake
4. Strain into a rocks glass filled with ice

# Joburg

**1½ oz. light rum**
**1½ oz. Dubonnet**
**3 dashes orange bitters**

1. Fill mixing glass with ice
2. Add rum, Dubonnet and orange bitters
3. Stir
4. Strain into a chilled cocktail glass
5. Garnish with a lemon twist

# Jockey Club

1½ oz. gin
½ oz. lemon juice
¼ tsp. white crème de cacao
dash of Angostura bitters

1. Fill mixing glass with ice
2. Add gin, lemon juice, white crème de cacao and bitters
3. Shake
4. Strain into a chilled cocktail glass

# Joe Collins

1½ oz. scotch
3 oz. sour mix
1 oz. club soda

1. Fill mixing glass with ice
2. Add scotch and sour mix
3. Shake
4. Strain into a Collins glass
5. Add ice
6. Top with club soda
7. Garnish with a cherry and an orange slice

# John Collins

2 oz. blended whiskey
3 oz. sour mix
1 oz. club soda

1. Fill mixing glass with ice
2. Add whiskey and sour mix
3. Shake
4. Strain into a Collins glass
5. Add ice

6. Top with club soda
7. Garnish with a cherry and an orange slice

# Johnnie's Cocktail

**2 oz. sloe gin**
**¾ oz. Cointreau**
**1 tsp. anisette**

1. Fill mixing glass with ice
2. Add sloe gin, Cointreau and anisette
3. Stir
4. Strain into a chilled cocktail glass

# Jolly Roger

**1 oz. dark rum**
**1 oz. banana liqueur**
**2 oz. lemon juice**

1. Fill mixing glass with ice
2. Add rum, banana liqueur and lemon juice
3. Shake
4. Strain into a goblet or large wineglass
5. Add ice

# Judge, Jr.

**1 oz. gin**
**1 oz. light rum**
**¾ oz. lemon juice**
**dash grenadine**

1. Fill mixing glass with ice
2. Add gin, rum, lemon juice and grenadine
3. Shake
4. Strain into a chilled cocktail glass

# Jungle Jim

**1 oz. vodka**
**1 oz. banana liqueur**
**1 oz. milk or cream**

1. Fill mixing glass with ice
2. Add vodka, banana liqueur and milk or cream
3. Shake
4. Strain into a rocks glass
5. Add ice, if desired

# Juniper Blend

**1 oz. cherry brandy**
**1 oz. gin**
**1 tsp. dry vermouth**

1. Fill mixing glass with ice
2. Add cherry brandy, gin and dry vermouth
3. Shake
4. Strain into a chilled cocktail glass

# Jupiter Cocktail

**1½ oz. gin**
**½ oz. dry vermouth**
**1 tsp. crème de violette**
**1 tsp. orange juice**

1. Fill mixing glass with ice
2. Add gin, dry vermouth, crème de violette and orange juice
3. Shake
4. Strain into a chilled cocktail glass

# K

## Kahlúa Egg Cream

1 oz. Kahlúa
2 oz. milk
club soda

1. Fill a rocks glass with ice
2. Add Kahlúa
3. Add milk
4. Top with club soda
5. Stir

## Kahlúa Toreador

2 oz. brandy
1 oz. Kahlúa
½ an egg white

1. Fill mixing glass with ice
2. Add brandy, Kahlúa and egg white
3. Shake
4. Strain into a rocks glass filled with ice

## Kamikaze

1 oz. vodka
1 oz. triple sec
1 oz. lime juice

1. Fill mixing glass with ice
2. Add vodka, triple sec and lime juice
3. Shake
4. Strain into a rocks glass filled with ice

# Kamikaze (shooter)

**2 oz. vodka**
**½ oz. triple sec**
**¼ oz. Rose's lime juice**

1. Fill mixing glass with ice
2. Add vodka, triple sec and lime juice
3. Shake
4. Strain into shot glasses

(Makes about 2 shots)

# Kangaroo

**1½ oz. vodka**
**1 oz. dry vermouth**

1. Fill mixing glass with cracked ice
2. Add vodka and dry vermouth
3. Stir
4. Strain into a chilled cocktail glass

# Kappa Colada

**1 oz. brandy**
**1 oz. cream of coconut**
**2 oz. pineapple juice syrup**

(*Note:* 3 oz. Pina Colada mix may be substituted for cream of coconut and pineapple syrup)

1. Fill mixing glass with ice
2. Add brandy, cream of coconut and pineapple syrup
3. Shake
4. Strain into a Collins glass
5. Add ice
6. Garnish with a cherry and an orange slice

# KCB

**1½ oz. gin**
**2 tsp. kirschwasser**
**3 drops apricot brandy**
**3 drops lemon juice**

1. Fill mixing glass with ice
2. Add gin, kirschwasser, apricot brandy and lemon juice
3. Shake
4. Strain into a chilled cocktail glass

# Kentucky Cocktail

**2 oz. bourbon**
**1 oz. pineapple juice**

1. Fill mixing glass with ice
2. Add bourbon and pineapple juice
3. Shake
4. Strain into a chilled cocktail glass

# Kentucky Coffee

**1½ oz. Kentucky bourbon**
**hot coffee**

1. Pour Kentucky bourbon into a coffee mug
2. Fill with hot coffee
3. Top with whipped cream, if desired

# Kentucky Colonel

**1½ oz. bourbon**
**½ oz. Bénédictine**

1. Fill mixing glass with ice
2. Add bourbon and Bénédictine
3. Shake
4. Strain into a rocks glass
5. Add ice
6. Garnish with a twist of lemon

# Kentucky Cooler

**1½ oz. bourbon**
**½ oz. rum**
**¼ oz. orange juice**
**¼ oz. lemon juice**
**dash grenadine**

1. Fill mixing glass with ice
2. Add bourbon, rum, orange juice, lemon juice and grenadine
3. Shake
4. Strain into a chilled cocktail glass

# Kentucky Orange Blossom

**1½ oz. bourbon**
**½ oz. triple sec**
**1 oz. orange juice**

1. Fill mixing glass with ice
2. Add bourbon, triple sec and orange juice
3. Shake
4. Strain into a rocks glass filled with ice
5. Garnish with a twist of lemon

# Kerry Cooler

**2 oz. Irish whiskey**
**1½ oz. sherry**
**1 oz. orgeat syrup**
**1½ oz. lemon juice**
**1 oz. club soda**

1. Fill mixing glass with ice
2. Add Irish whiskey, sherry, orgeat syrup and lemon juice
3. Shake
4. Strain into a highball glass
5. Add ice
6. Top with club soda
7. Garnish with a slice of lemon

# Kialoa

**1 oz. Kahlúa**
**1 oz. cream**
**½ oz. Mount Gay rum**

1. Fill mixing glass with ice
2. Add Kahlúa, cream and Mount Gay rum
3. Strain into a rocks glass
4. Add ice

# Killer Kool-Aid

**1½ oz. vodka**
**½ oz. peach schnapps**
**½ oz. amaretto**
**3 oz. cranberry juice cocktail**

1. Fill highball glass with ice
2. Layer ingredients
3. Do not stir

# King Alphonse

**2 oz. Kahlúa**
**1 oz. cream**

1. Pour Kahlúa into a cordial glass
2. Float cream on top

# Kingdom Come

**¾ oz. gin**
**1½ oz. dry vermouth**
**1 tsp. white crème de menthe**
**1 tbsp. grapefruit juice**

1. Fill shaker glass with ice
2. Add gin, dry vermouth, white crème de menthe and grapefruit juice
3. Shake
4. Strain into a rocks glass filled with about 4 oz. crushed ice

# King's Peg

**2½ oz. cognac**
**chilled brut champagne**

1. Put several ice cubes into a wineglass
2. Add cognac
3. Fill with chilled champagne

# Kingston

1½ oz. Jamaican rum
1 oz. gin
½ oz. lemon juice
½ oz. sugar syrup

1. Fill mixing glass with ice
2. Add Jamaican rum, gin, lemon juice and sugar syrup
3. Shake
4. Strain into a chilled cocktail glass

# Kioki Coffee

¾ oz. brandy
¾ oz. Kahlúa
hot coffee

1. Pour brandy and Kahlúa into a coffee mug
2. Fill with hot coffee
3. Top with whipped cream, if desired

# Kir

white wine
crème de cassis

1. Fill wineglass ¾ with chilled white wine
2. Add a few drops of crème de cassis
3. Garnish with a twist of lemon

(*Note:* Depending on the size of the wineglass, exact number of ounces may vary. In general, the proportion is 7 parts wine to 1 part crème de cassis.)

# Kir Royale

**chilled champagne**
**Framboise (crème de cassis may be substituted)**

1. Fill wineglass ¾ with chilled champagne
2. Add a few drops of Framboise or crème de cassis
3. Garnish with a twist of lemon

(*Note:* Depending on the size of the wineglass, exact number of ounces may vary. In general, the proportion is 7 parts champagne to 1 part Framboise or crème de cassis.)


# The Kiss

**1½ oz. vodka**
**½ oz. chocolate liqueur**
**¼ oz. cherry liqueur**
**¾ oz. heavy cream**

1. Fill mixing glass with ice
2. Add vodka, chocolate liqueur, cherry liqueur and cream
3. Shake
4. Strain into a chilled cocktail glass


# Kiss in the Dark

**¾ oz. gin**
**¾ oz. cherry brandy**
**¼ oz. dry vermouth**

1. Fill mixing glass with ice
2. Add gin, cherry brandy and dry vermouth
3. Shake
4. Strain into a chilled cocktail glass

# Kiss Me Quick

2 oz. Pernod
1 tsp. Cointreau
2–3 dashes Angostura bitters
1 oz. club soda

1. Fill rocks glass with ice
2. Add Pernod, Cointreau and bitters
3. Stir
4. Top with club soda

# Kiss the Boys Goodbye

1 oz. sloe gin
1 oz. brandy
¼ oz. lemon juice
½ egg white

1. Fill mixing glass with ice
2. Add sloe gin, brandy, lemon juice and egg white
3. Shake
4. Strain into a chilled cocktail glass

# Klondike Cooler

1½ oz. blended whiskey
2 tbsp. orange rind
2–3 oz. fresh orange juice
ginger ale

1. Fill a highball glass with ice
2. Add whiskey, orange rind and orange juice
3. Stir
4. Top with ginger ale

# Knickerbocker

2 oz. gin
½ oz. dry vermouth
1 tsp. sweet vermouth

1. Fill mixing glass with ice
2. Add gin, dry vermouth and sweet vermouth
3. Shake
4. Strain into a chilled cocktail glass

# Knockout

¾ oz. Southern Comfort
¾ oz. apricot brandy
¾ oz. sloe gin
¾ oz. orange juice

1. Fill a rocks glass with ice
2. Add Southern Comfort, apricot brandy, sloe gin and orange juice
3. Stir well

# Kremlin Cocktail

1 oz. vodka
1 oz. white crème de cacao
1 oz. cream

1. Fill mixing glass with ice
2. Add vodka, white crème de cacao and cream
3. Shake
4. Strain into a rocks glass filled with ice

# Kretchma

1 oz. vodka
1 oz. white crème de cacao
1 tsp. lemon juice
3 drops grenadine

1. Fill mixing glass with ice
2. Add vodka, white crème de cacao, lemon juice and grenadine
3. Shake
4. Strain into a rocks glass filled with ice

# Kyoto

1½ oz. gin
½ oz. dry vermouth
½ oz. apricot brandy
½ oz. triple sec

1. Fill mixing glass with ice
2. Add gin, dry vermouth, apricot brandy and triple sec
3. Shake
4. Strain into a rocks glass filled with ice
5. Garnish with a cherry

# L

## Ladies

2 oz. Canadian whiskey
2 dashes Pernod
2 dashes Angostura bitters
2 dashes anisette

1. Fill mixing glass with ice
2. Add Canadian whiskey, Pernod, bitters and anisette
3. Shake
4. Strain into a chilled cocktail glass

## Lady Be Good

1½ oz. brandy
¾ oz. white crème de menthe
¾ oz. sweet vermouth

1. Fill mixing glass with ice
2. Add brandy, white crème de menthe and sweet vermouth
3. Shake
4. Strain into a chilled cocktail glass

## Ladyfinger

1½ oz. gin
¾ oz. kirschwasser
¾ oz. cherry brandy

1. Fill mixing glass with ice
2. Add gin, kirschwasser and cherry brandy
3. Shake
4. Strain into a chilled cocktail glass

## Lager 'N' Lime

½ oz. Rose's lime juice
beer (preferably draft)

1. Pour cold beer into a beer glass or a beer mug
2. Add Rose's lime juice

## La Jolla

1½ oz. brandy
½ oz. banana liqueur
1 tsp. orange juice
2 tsp. lemon juice

1. Fill mixing glass with ice
2. Add brandy, banana liqueur, orange juice and lemon juice
3. Shake
4. Strain into a chilled cocktail glass

## Lallah Rookh

1½ oz. light rum
¾ oz. cognac
2 tsp. vanilla extract
1 tsp. sugar syrup
whipped cream

1. Fill mixing glass with cracked ice
2. Add light rum, cognac, vanilla extract and sugar syrup
3. Shake
4. Pour into a goblet or large wineglass
5. Top with whipped cream

# Lasky

¾ oz. gin
¾ oz. Swedish Punsch
1 tbsp. grape juice

1. Fill mixing glass with ice
2. Add gin, Swedish Punsch and grape juice
3. Shake
4. Strain into a rocks glass filled with ice

# Last Round

1 oz. gin
1 oz. dry vermouth
2 dashes brandy
2 dashes Pernod

1. Fill mixing glass with ice
2. Add gin, dry vermouth, brandy and Pernod
3. Shake
4. Strain into a chilled cocktail glass

# The Laura

1½ oz. bourbon
1 oz. sweet vermouth
½ oz. dry vermouth
½ oz. Campari
½ oz. Galliano

1. Fill mixing glass with ice
2. Add bourbon, sweet vermouth, dry vermouth, Campari and Galliano
3. Shake
4. Strain into a chilled cocktail glass
5. Garnish with a cherry

272

# Lawhill

1½ oz. blended whiskey
¼ oz. dry vermouth
2 tsp. orange juice
3 drops Pernod
3 drops maraschino liqueur
3 dashes Angostura bitters

1. Fill mixing glass with ice
2. Add blended whiskey, dry vermouth, orange juice, Pernod, maraschino and bitters
3. Shake
4. Strain into a rocks glass filled with ice

# Leap Frog

1½ oz. gin
½ oz. lemon juice
ginger ale

1. Fill a highball glass with ice
2. Add gin and lemon juice
3. Stir
4. Fill with ginger ale

# Leap Year

1½ oz. gin
½ oz. Grand Marnier
½ oz. sweet vermouth
1 tsp. lemon juice

1. Fill mixing glass with ice
2. Add gin, Grand Marnier, sweet vermouth and lemon juice
3. Stir
4. Strain into a chilled cocktail glass

## Leave It to Me

1 oz. gin
½ oz. apricot brandy
½ oz. dry vermouth
3 dashes lemon juice
3 dashes grenadine

1. Fill mixing glass with ice
2. Add gin, apricot brandy, dry vermouth, lemon juice and grenadine
3. Shake
4. Strain into a chilled cocktail glass

## Lectric Lemonade

½ oz. vodka
½ oz. gin
½ oz. light rum
½ oz. triple sec
½ oz. tequila
2–3 oz. sour mix
7-Up

1. Fill mixing glass with ice
2. Add vodka, gin, light rum, triple sec, tequila and sour mix
3. Shake
4. Pour into a Collins glass
5. Top with 7-Up

## Lemonade (modern)

1½ oz. sloe gin
1½ oz. sherry
2 oz. lemon juice
1 oz. sugar syrup
club soda

1. Fill mixing glass with ice
2. Add sloe gin, sherry, lemon juice and sugar syrup
3. Shake
4. Pour into a highball glass
5. Top with club soda
6. Garnish with a slice of lemon

# Lemon Drop (shooter)

**½ oz. tequila, chilled**
**½ oz. vodka, chilled**

1. Coat the inside of a shot glass with sugar (use a lemon slice to moisten the glass first)
2. Pour in tequila and vodka (preferably premium brands)

# Leprechaun

**2 oz. Irish whiskey**
**tonic water**

1. Fill a rocks glass with ice
2. Add Irish whiskey
3. Fill with tonic water
4. Stir
5. Garnish with a twist of lemon

# Leprechaun's Libation

**1 oz. green crème de menthe**
**2½ oz. Old Bushmills Irish whiskey**

1. Fill blender with 3½ oz. cracked ice
2. Add green crème de menthe and Old Bushmills Irish whiskey
3. Blend
4. Pour into a goblet or large wine glass

(Courtesy of Beach Grill, Westminster, Colorado)

# Liberty Cocktail

1½ oz. apple brandy
¾ oz. light rum
¼ tsp. sugar syrup

1. Fill mixing glass with ice
2. Add apple brandy, light rum and sugar syrup
3. Stir
4. Strain into a chilled cocktail glass


# Liebfraumilch

1 oz. white crème de cacao
1 oz. cream
½ oz. lime juice

1. Fill mixing glass with ice
2. Add white crème de cacao, cream and lime juice
3. Shake
4. Strain into a chilled cocktail glass


# Lillet Noyaux

1½ oz. Lillet
½ oz. gin
1 tsp. crème de noyaux

1. Fill mixing glass with ice
2. Add Lillet, gin and crème de noyaux
3. Shake
4. Strain into a chilled cocktail glass
5. Garnish with a twist of orange

# Limbo

2 oz. light rum
½ oz. banana liqueur
1 oz. orange juice

1. Fill mixing glass with ice
2. Add light rum, banana liqueur and orange juice
3. Shake
4. Strain into a chilled cocktail glass

# Lime Rickey

1½ oz. gin
½ oz. lime juice
club soda

1. Fill a highball glass with ice
2. Add gin, then lime juice
3. Fill with club soda
4. Stir gently
5. Garnish with a slice of lime

# Linstead

1½ oz. blended whiskey
1½ oz. pineapple juice
3 drops Pernod
4–5 drops lemon juice
3 dashes Angostura bitters

1. Fill mixing glass with ice
2. Add blended whiskey, pineapple juice, Pernod, lemon juice and bitters
3. Shake
4. Strain into a rocks glass filled with ice
5. Garnish with a twist of lemon

# Lion Tamer (shooter)

¾ oz. Southern Comfort
¼ oz. lime juice

1. Fill mixing glass with ice
2. Add Southern Comfort and lime juice
3. Stir
4. Strain into a chilled shot glass

# Little Devil

1 oz. gin
1 oz. gold rum
½ oz. triple sec
½ oz. lemon juice

1. Fill mixing glass with ice
2. Add gin, gold rum, triple sec and lemon juice
3. Stir
4. Strain into a chilled cocktail glass

# Little Princess

1½ oz. light rum
1½ oz. sweet vermouth

1. Fill mixing glass with ice
2. Add light rum and sweet vermouth
3. Shake
4. Strain into a rocks glass filled with ice

# Little Purple Men

1 oz. sambuca
1 oz. Chambord

Pour sambuca and Chambord into a brandy snifter

(*Note:* It has been reported that after consuming two of these drinks you'll start seeing little purple men.)

# Live Bait's Blue Bijou

1¼ oz. light rum
1 oz. blue curaçao
3 oz. orange juice
3 oz. pineapple juice
3–4 drops Rose's lime juice

1. In blender, combine light rum, blue curaçao, orange juice, pineapple juice and Rose's lime juice with 3 oz. cracked ice
2. Blend until well mixed
3. Pour into a goblet or Collins glass
4. Garnish with a pineapple chunk

(Courtesy of Live Bait, New York City)

# Loch Lomond

1½ oz. scotch
½ oz. sugar syrup
several dashes Angostura bitters

1. Fill mixing glass with ice
2. Add scotch, sugar syrup and bitters
3. Shake
4. Strain into a rocks glass filled with ice

# Lolita

1½ oz. tequila
¼ oz. lime juice
1 tsp. honey
3–4 dashes Angostura bitters

1. Fill mixing glass with ice
2. Add tequila, lime juice, honey and bitters
3. Shake
4. Strain into a rocks glass filled with ice

# Lollipop

¾ oz. Cointreau
¾ oz. kirschwasser
1 tbsp. green Chartreuse
2–3 drops maraschino liqueur

1. Fill mixing glass with ice
2. Add Cointreau, kirschwasser, green Chartreuse and maraschino liqueur
3. Shake
4. Strain into a rocks glass filled with ice

# London

1½ oz. gin
2 dashes Pernod
2 dashes orange bitters
1 tsp. powdered sugar

1. Fill mixing glass with ice
2. Add gin, Pernod, orange bitters and powdered sugar
3. Shake
4. Strain into a chilled cocktail glass

# London Special

1 sugar cube
2 dashes Angostura bitters
chilled champagne

1. In a chilled champagne glass, place a large twist of orange, sugar cube and bitters
2. Fill with chilled champagne
3. Stir


# Lone Tree

¾ oz. gin
¾ oz. dry vermouth
¾ oz. sweet vermouth
3 dashes orange bitters

1. Fill mixing glass with ice
2. Add gin, dry vermouth, sweet vermouth and orange bitters
3. Stir
4. Strain into a chilled cocktail glass
5. Garnish with an olive


# Long Beach Ice Tea

½ oz. vodka
½ oz. gin
½ rum
½ oz. triple sec
½ oz. tequila
1 oz. sour mix
cranberry juice cocktail

1. Fill mixing glass with ice
2. Add vodka, gin, rum, triple sec, tequila and sour mix
3. Shake
4. Pour into a Collins glass
5. Add more ice, if necessary
6. Top with cranberry juice
7. Garnish with a lemon slice

# Long Hot Night

**2 oz. bourbon**
**3 oz. pineapple juice**
**3 oz. cranberry juice cocktail**

1. Place 4 or 5 ice cubes in a highball glass
2. Pour in bourbon
3. Stir
4. Add pineapple juice and cranberry juice
5. Stir again

# Long Island Ice Tea

**½ oz. vodka**
**½ oz. gin**
**½ oz. rum**
**½ oz. triple sec**
**½ oz. tequila**
**1 oz. sour mix**
**cola**

1. Fill mixing glass with ice
2. Add vodka, gin, rum, triple sec, tequila and sour mix
3. Shake
4. Pour into a Collins glass
5. Add more ice, if necessary
6. Top with cola
7. Garnish with a lemon slice

# Look Out Below

**1½ oz. 151-proof rum**
**2 tsp. lime juice**
**1 tsp. grenadine**

1. Fill mixing glass with ice
2. Add 151-proof rum, lime juice and grenadine

3. Shake
4. Strain into a rocks glass filled with ice

# Lord Rodney

1½ oz. blended whiskey
¾ oz. dark rum
1 tsp. coconut syrup
3–4 drops white crème de cacao

1. Fill mixing glass with ice
2. Add blended whiskey, dark rum, coconut syrup and crème de cacao
3. Shake
4. Strain into a chilled cocktail glass

# Los Angeles Cocktail

4 oz. blended whiskey
1 oz. lemon juice
2 oz. sugar syrup
4 dashes sweet vermouth
1 egg

1. Fill mixing glass with cracked ice
2. Add blended whiskey, lemon juice, sugar syrup, sweet vermouth and egg
3. Shake
4. Pour into two chilled rocks glasses

(This recipe serves two)

# Loud-Hailer

¾ oz. gin
¾ oz. dry vermouth
dash of Cointreau

1 tsp. grenadine
1 oz. orange juice

1. Fill mixing glass with ice
2. Add gin, dry vermouth, Cointreau, grenadine and orange juice
3. Shake
4. Strain into a chilled cocktail glass

## Loudspeaker

1 oz. brandy
1 oz. gin
1 tsp. Cointreau
2 tsp. lemon juice

1. Fill mixing glass with ice
2. Add brandy, gin, Cointreau and lemon juice
3. Stir
4. Strain into a chilled cocktail glass

## Louisiana Lullaby

1½ oz. dark rum
2 tsp. Dubonnet
3 drops Grand Marnier

1. Fill mixing glass with ice
2. Add dark rum, Dubonnet and Grand Marnier
3. Shake
4. Strain into a chilled cocktail glass
5. Garnish with a twist of lemon

## Love

2 oz. sloe gin
1 egg white

½ oz. lemon juice
**several drops raspberry syrup**

1. Fill mixing glass with ice
2. Add sloe gin, egg white, lemon juice and raspberry syrup
3. Shake
4. Strain into a chilled cocktail glass

# Lover's Delight

¾ oz. Cointreau
¾ oz. **Forbidden Fruit**
¾ oz. **brandy**

1. Fill mixing glass with ice
2. Add Cointreau, Forbidden Fruit and brandy
3. Shake
4. Strain into a rocks glass filled with ice

# Lube Job

**1 oz. Bailey's Irish Cream**
**1 oz. vodka**

1. Fill a rocks glass with ice
2. Add Bailey's and vodka
3. Stir

# Lugger

**1 oz. brandy**
**1 oz. apple brandy**
**1 oz. apricot brandy**

1. Fill mixing glass with ice
2. Add brandy, apple brandy and apricot brandy
3. Shake
4. Strain into a chilled cocktail glass

# M

## Madeira Cocktail

1½ oz. blended whiskey
1½ oz. madeira
1 tsp. grenadine
dash lemon juice

1. Fill mixing glass with cracked ice
2. Add blended whiskey, madeira, grenadine and lemon juice
3. Shake
4. Pour into a rocks glass
5. Garnish with a slice of orange

## Magpie

1 oz. melon liqueur (Midori)
1 oz. vodka
½ oz. white crème de cacao
1 oz. cream

1. Fill mixing glass with ice
2. Add melon liqueur, vodka, white crème de cacao and cream
3. Shake
4. Strain into a rocks glass filled with ice

## Mah-Jonng

1 oz. gin
½ oz. dark rum
½ oz. Cointreau

1. Fill mixing glass with ice
2. Add gin, dark rum and Cointreau
3. Shake
4. Strain into a chilled cocktail glass

## Maiden's Blush

**1 oz. gin**
**4 dashes curaçao**
**4 dashes grenadine**
**2 dashes lemon juice**

1. Fill mixing glass with ice
2. Add gin, curaçao, grenadine and lemon juice
3. Shake
4. Strain into a chilled cocktail glass

## Maiden's Prayer

**1 oz. gin**
**1 oz. triple sec**
**2 tbsp. lemon juice**
**½ tsp. orange juice**

1. Fill mixing glass with ice
2. Add gin, triple sec, lemon juice and orange juice
3. Stir
4. Strain into a chilled cocktail glass

## Mainbrace

**1½ oz. gin**
**¾ oz. triple sec**
**1 tbsp. grape juice**

1. Fill mixing glass with ice
2. Add gin, triple sec and grape juice
3. Shake
4. Strain into a chilled cocktail glass

# Mai Tai

**1 oz. light rum**
**½ oz. orgeat syrup**
**½ oz. triple sec**
**1½ oz. sour mix**

1. Fill mixing glass with ice
2. Add light rum, orgeat syrup, triple sec and sour mix
3. Shake
4. Strain into a Collins glass filled with ice
5. Garnish with a cherry and an orange slice

# Malibu Monsoon

**1½ oz. Bacardi light rum**
**¾ oz. Malibu liqueur**
**splash Grand Marnier**
**1 oz. pineapple juice**
**splash cranberry juice cocktail**
**a few drops grenadine**

1. Fill mixing glass with ice
2. Add Bacardi light rum, Malibu liqueur, Grand Marnier, pineapple juice and cranberry juice
3. Shake
4. Pour into a large wineglass or goblet
5. Add a few drops of grenadine
6. Garnish with a cherry and a slice of orange

(Courtesy of Michael Benz at Ciaobella, New York City)

# Malibu Wave

1 oz. tequila
½ oz. triple sec
1 tsp. blue curaçao
1½ oz. sour mix

1. Fill mixing glass with ice
2. Add tequila, triple sec, blue curaçao and sour mix
3. Shake
4. Strain into a chilled cocktail glass
5. Garnish with a lime slice

# Mamie Taylor

3 oz. scotch
½ oz. lime juice
ginger ale

1. Fill a Collins glass with ice
2. Add scotch and lime juice
3. Stir
4. Fill with ginger ale
5. Stir again
6. Garnish with a slice of lemon

# Mandarine Colada

1½ oz. light rum
1 oz. Mandarine Napoléon liqueur
2 oz. pineapple juice
1 oz. cream of coconut
2 orange slices

1. Fill blender with 3 oz. ice, light rum, Mandarine Napoléon liqueur, pineapple juice, cream of coconut and 1 orange slice
2. Blend until smooth

3. Pour into a 16-oz. soda glass
4. Garnish with other orange slice

(Courtesy of Sugar Reef, New York City)

# Manhasset

1½ oz. blended whiskey
½ oz. lemon juice
1 tsp. dry vermouth
1 tsp. sweet vermouth

1. Fill mixing glass with ice
2. Add whiskey, lemon juice, dry vermouth and sweet vermouth
3. Shake
4. Strain into a rocks glass filled with ice
5. Garnish with a twist of lemon

# Manhattan

1½ oz. blended whiskey
½ oz. sweet vermouth

1. Fill mixing glass with ice
2. Add whiskey and sweet vermouth
3. Stir
4. Strain into a chilled cocktail glass
5. Garnish with a cherry

(*Note:* If serving "on the rocks," stir in a rocks glass filled with ice, garnish and serve.)

# Manhattan (dry)

1½ oz. blended whiskey
¼ oz. dry vermouth

1. Fill mixing glass with ice
2. Add whiskey and dry vermouth
3. Stir
4. Strain into a chilled cocktail glass
5. Garnish with an olive

(*Note:* If serving "on the rocks," stir in a rocks glass filled with ice, garnish and serve.)

# Manhattan (perfect)

**1½ oz. blended whiskey**
**⅛ oz. dry vermouth**
**⅛ oz. sweet vermouth**

1. Fill mixing glass with ice
2. Add whiskey, dry vermouth and sweet vermouth
3. Stir
4. Strain into a chilled cocktail glass
5. Garnish with a twist of lemon

(*Note:* If serving "on the rocks," stir in a rocks glass filled with ice, garnish and serve.)

# Manhattan South

**1 oz. gin**
**½ oz. dry vermouth**
**½ oz. Southern Comfort**
**dash Angostura bitters**

1. Fill mixing glass with ice
2. Add gin, dry vermouth, Southern Comfort and bitters
3. Stir
4. Strain into a chilled cocktail glass

# Maple Leaf

**1 oz. Canadian whiskey**
**¼ oz. lemon juice**
**1 tsp. maple syrup**

1. Fill mixing glass with ice
2. Add Canadian whiskey, lemon juice and maple syrup
3. Shake
4. Strain into a chilled cocktail glass

# Marconi Wireless

**1½ oz. apple brandy**
**½ oz. sweet vermouth**
**2 dashes orange bitters**

1. Fill mixing glass with ice
2  Add apple brandy, sweet vermouth and orange bitters
3. Shake
4. Strain into a chilled cocktail glass

# Margarita

**1½ oz. tequila**
**½ oz. triple sec**
**1½ oz. sour mix**
**several dashes lime juice**

1. Fill mixing glass with ice
2. Add tequila, triple sec, sour mix and lime juice
3. Shake
4. Strain into a chilled cocktail glass or a rocks glass filled with ice
5. Garnish with a slice of lime

(*Note:* If drink is requested "with salt," frost the rim of the glass with salt before pouring in drink. To do so, moisten the rim of the glass with a wedge of lime, and dip into a plate of salt.)

# Margarita, My Honey

1½ oz. Cuervo Especial gold tequila
¾ oz. Cointreau
juice of ½ lime
juice of ½ lemon
2 drops honey
drop orange juice

1. Fill mixing glass with ice
2. Add Cuervo gold, Cointreau, lime juice, lemon juice, honey and orange juice
3. Shake well
4. Salt the rim of a chilled cocktail glass, if desired
5. Strain drink into chilled cocktail glass
6. Garnish with a lime slice

# Marlon Brando

1½ oz. scotch
½ oz. amaretto
cream

1. Fill a rocks glass with ice
2. Add scotch and amaretto
3. Float cream on top

# Marmalade

1½ oz. curaçao
tonic water

1. Fill a highball glass with ice
2. Add curaçao
3. Fill with tonic water
4. Stir
5. Garnish with a slice of orange

# Martinez

**2 oz. gin (preferably Old Tom)**
**3 oz. dry vermouth**
**3–4 drops maraschino liqueur**
**3–4 drops Angostura bitters**

1. Fill mixing glass with ice
2. Add gin, dry vermouth, maraschino liqueur and bitters
3. Shake
4. Strain into a rocks glass filled with ice

# Martini

**1½ oz. gin**
**dash (approx. ⅛ oz.) dry vermouth**

1. Fill mixing glass with ice
2. Add gin and dry vermouth
3. Stir
4. Strain into a martini glass
5. Garnish with an olive

(*Note:* If serving "on the rocks," stir in a rocks glass filled with ice, garnish and serve.)

# Martini (dry)

**1½ oz. gin**
**drop (approx. ¹/₁₀ oz.) dry vermouth**

1. Fill mixing glass with ice
2. Add gin and dry vermouth
3. Stir
4. Strain into a martini glass
5. Garnish with an olive

(*Note:* If serving "on the rocks," stir in a rocks glass filled with ice, garnish and serve.)

# Martini (very dry)

1½ oz. gin
approx. ¹⁄₁₂ oz. dry vermouth

1. Fill mixing glass with ice
2. Add dry vermouth (In actuality, almost no dry vermouth is used. Let vermouth barely touch side of mixing glass)
3. Add gin
4. Stir
5. Strain into a martini glass
6. Garnish with an olive

(*Note:* If serving "on the rocks," stir in a rocks glass filled with ice, garnish and serve.)

# Martini (extremely dry)

2 oz. gin

Follow directions for other martini recipes. No vermouth is used. This translates to "gin straight up" or "gin on the rocks."

# Mary Garden

1½ oz. Dubonnet
¾ oz. dry vermouth

1. Fill mixing glass with ice
2. Add Dubonnet and dry vermouth
3. Shake
4. Strain into a rocks glass filled with ice

# Mary Pickford

1½ oz. light rum
½ oz. pineapple juice
3 dashes grenadine

1. Fill mixing glass with ice
2. Add light rum, pineapple juice and grenadine
3. Shake
4. Strain into a chilled cocktail glass

# Mashed Old-Fashioned

1 maraschino cherry
1 piece orange
1 cube sugar
2 dashes bitters
dash club soda
1 oz. bourbon

1. In a rocks glass, place cherry, piece of orange, sugar cube, bitters and club soda
2. Mash with muddler or with the back of a spoon
3. Fill the glass with ice
4. Add bourbon
5. Garnish with a cherry and an orange slice

# Matador

1 oz. tequila
1½ oz. pineapple juice
½ oz. lime juice

1. Fill mixing glass with ice
2. Add tequila, pineapple juice and lime juice
3. Shake
4. Strain into a chilled cocktail glass

# Maurice

**1 oz. gin**
**½ oz. sweet vermouth**
**½ oz. dry vermouth**
**½ oz. orange juice**
**dash Angostura bitters**

1. Fill mixing glass with ice
2. Add gin, sweet vermouth, dry vermouth, orange juice and bitters
3. Shake
4. Strain into a chilled cocktail glass

# Maxim

**1½ oz. gin**
**1 oz. dry vermouth**
**dash white crème de cacao**

1. Fill mixing glass with ice
2. Add gin, dry vermouth and white crème de cacao
3. Shake
4. Strain into a chilled cocktail glass

# May Blossom Fizz

**1½ oz. Swedish Punsch**
**1½ oz. lemon juice**
**1 tsp. grenadine**
**club soda**

1. Fill mixing glass with ice
2. Add Swedish Punsch, lemon juice and grenadine
3. Shake
4. Strain into a highball glass
5. Add ice
6. Top with club soda

# McClelland

2 oz. sloe gin
1 oz. curaçao
3 dashes orange bitters

1. Fill mixing glass with ice
2. Add sloe gin, curaçao and orange bitters
3. Shake
4. Strain into a chilled cocktail glass

# Melon Ball

1 oz. vodka
½ oz. Midori melon liqueur
5 oz. orange juice

1. Fill a highball glass with ice
2. Add vodka and Midori
3. Fill with orange juice
4. Stir

# Melon Ball Sunrise

1 oz. vodka
½ oz. Midori melon liqueur
orange juice
grenadine

1. Fill a highball glass with ice
2. Pour in vodka and Midori
3. Fill with orange juice
4. Stir
5: Pour in a drop of grenadine over the back of a spoon, allowing
   it to rise from the bottom

# Melon Cocktail

**2 oz. gin**
**3 drops lemon juice**
**3 drops maraschino liqueur**

1. Fill mixing glass with ice
2. Add gin, lemon juice and maraschino liqueur
3. Shake
4. Strain into a chilled cocktail glass

# Melon Colada

**1½ oz. light rum**
**½ oz. Midori (or other melon liqueur)**
**1 oz. cream of coconut**
**3 oz. pineapple juice**
**splash cream**
**½ oz. dark rum (optional)**

1. Fill blender with 3 oz. crushed ice, light rum, Midori, cream of coconut, pineapple juice, cream and dark rum (if desired)
2. Blend at medium speed for approximately 15 seconds, until smooth
3. Pour into a goblet or a large wineglass
4. Garnish with a pineapple slice or spear

# Meltdown (shooter)

**1 oz. Stolichnaya (chilled)**
**½ oz. peach schnapps**

1. Pour chilled Stolichnaya into a shot glass
2. Top with peach schnapps

# Memphis Belle Cocktail

**1½ oz. brandy**
**¾ oz. Southern Comfort**
**½ oz. lemon juice**
**3–4 dashes orange bitters**

1. Fill mixing glass with ice
2. Add brandy, Southern Comfort, lemon juice and orange bitters
3. Shake
4. Strain into a chilled cocktail glass

# Merry Widow

**1½ oz. cherry brandy**
**1½ oz. maraschino liqueur**

1. Fill mixing glass with ice
2. Add cherry brandy and maraschino liqueur
3. Shake
4. Strain into a chilled cocktail glass

# Mexican Coffee

**½ oz. tequila**
**½ oz. Kahlúa**
**hot coffee**

1. Pour tequila and Kahlúa into a coffee mug
2. Fill with hot coffee
3. Top with whipped cream, if desired

# Mexican Flag (shooter)

**½ oz. sloe gin**
**½ oz. vodka**
**½ oz. Midori melon liqueur**

1. Pour sloe gin into a shot glass
2. Float vodka on top, and then float Midori on top of vodka

# Mexican Missile (shooter)

¾ oz. tequila
¾ oz. green Chartreuse
dash Tabasco

1. Combine tequila and green Chartreuse in a shot glass
2. Add dash of Tabasco to season

(Courtesy of Soapy Smith's Eagle Bar, Denver, Colorado)

# Mexicano

2 oz. light rum
2 tsp. orange juice
2 tsp. kummel
3–4 dashes Angostura bitters

1. Fill mixing glass with ice
2. Add light rum, orange juice, kummel and bitters
3. Shake
4. Strain into a rocks glass filled with ice

# Miami Beach

1½ oz. scotch
1½ oz. dry vermouth
1 oz. grapefruit juice

1. Fill mixing glass with ice
2. Add scotch, dry vermouth and grapefruit juice
3. Stir
4. Strain into a chilled cocktail glass

# Midnight Sun

**2½ oz. vodka**
**½ oz. grenadine**

1. In a mixing glass, combine 3 or 4 ice cubes, vodka and grenadine
2. Stir
3. Strain into a chilled cocktail glass

# Midori Sour

**2 oz. Midori (or other melon liqueur)**
**1 oz. lemon juice**
**1 tsp. sugar syrup**

1. Fill mixing glass with ice
2. Add Midori, lemon juice and sugar syrup
3. Shake
4. Strain into a chilled sour glass filled with ice

# Millionaire

**1½ oz. bourbon**
**½ oz. Pernod**
**2–3 dashes curaçao**
**2–3 dashes grenadine**
**½ egg white**

1. Fill mixing glass with ice
2. Add bourbon, Pernod, curaçao, grenadine and egg white
3. Shake
4. Strain into a chilled cocktail glass

# Millionaire's Coffee

½ oz. **Kahlúa**
½ oz. **Bailey's Original Irish Cream**
½ oz. **Grand Marnier**
½ oz. **Frangelico**
**hot coffee**

1. Pour Kahlúa, Bailey's, Grand Marnier and Frangelico into a coffee mug or a hot drink glass
2. Fill with hot coffee
3. Top with whipped cream

# Mimosa

**3 oz. orange juice**
**3 oz. chilled champagne**
**dash Cointreau or triple sec (optional)**

1. Pour orange juice into a large, chilled wineglass
2. Fill with chilled champagne
3. Top with Cointreau or triple sec (if desired)
4. Stir gently

(*Note:* The proportion of orange juice to champagne may be changed to suit personal taste.)

# Mind Eraser

¾ oz. **Kahlúa**
1¼ oz. **vodka**
**1 oz. tonic water**

1. Fill a rocks glass with ice
2. Add Kahlúa and vodka
3. Top with tonic
4. Stir lightly
5. Drink through a straw in one shot

# Mint Cooler

**2 oz. scotch**
**3 dashes white crème de menthe**
**club soda**

1. Fill a Collins glass with ice
2. Add scotch and white crème de menthe
3. Stir
4. Fill with club soda
5. Stir gently

# Mint Julep

**2 oz. bourbon**
**6 mint leaves**
**½ oz. sugar syrup**

1. In a Collins glass, place the 6 mint leaves and sugar syrup
2. Mash leaves
3. Add 1 oz. of the bourbon
4. Fill glass with crushed ice
5. Add the rest of the bourbon
6. Stir well
7. Garnish with a mint sprig

# Mission Accomplished (shooter)

**2 oz. vodka**
**½ oz. triple sec**
**¼ oz. Rose's lime juice**
**dash of grenadine**

1. Fill mixing glass with ice
2. Add vodka, triple sec, lime juice and grenadine
3. Shake
4. Strain into shot glasses

(Makes about 2 shots)

# Mississippi Mule

**1½ oz. gin**
**1 tsp. crème de cassis**
**1 tsp. lemon juice**

1. Fill mixing glass with ice
2. Add gin, crème de cassis and lemon juice
3. Shake
4. Strain into a rocks glass with ice

# Mocha Mint

**1 oz. Kahlúa**
**1 oz. white crème de menthe**
**1 oz. white crème de cacao**

1. Fill mixing glass with ice
2. Add Kahlúa, white crème de menthe and white crème de cacao
3. Shake
4. Strain into a chilled cocktail glass

# Mockingbird

**1½ oz. tequila**
**2 tsp. white crème de menthe**
**1 oz. lime juice**

1. Fill mixing glass with ice
2. Add tequila, white crème de menthe and lime juice
3. Shake
4. Strain into a chilled cocktail glass

# Modern (1)

1½ oz. sloe gin
¾ oz. scotch
2–3 drops Pernod
2–3 drops grenadine
2 dashes orange bitters

1. Fill mixing glass with some ice
2. Add sloe gin, scotch, Pernod, grenadine and bitters
3. Shake
4. Pour into a rocks glass

# Modern (2)

3 oz. scotch
3 dashes dark rum
3 dashes Pernod
3 dashes lemon juice
3 dashes orange bitters

1. Fill mixing glass with some ice
2. Add scotch, dark rum, Pernod, lemon juice and bitters
3. Shake
4. Pour into a rocks glass
5. Garnish with a cherry

# Moll

1 oz. gin
1 oz. sloe gin
1 oz. dry vermouth
dash orange bitters
½ tsp. sugar

1. Fill mixing glass with ice
2. Add gin, sloe gin, dry vermouth, orange bitters and sugar
3. Shake
4. Pour into a chilled cocktail glass

# Monkey Wrench

**3 oz. light rum**
**4 oz. grapefruit juice**

1. Fill a highball glass with ice
2. Pour in light rum and grapefruit juice
3. Stir

# Montana

**1½ oz. brandy**
**2 tsp. dry vermouth**
**2 tsp. port**

1. Fill a rocks glass with ice
2. Add brandy, dry vermouth and port
3. Stir

# Monte Carlo

**1½ oz. rye whiskey**
**½ oz. Bénédictine**
**3–4 dashes Angostura bitters**

1. Fill mixing glass with ice
2. Add rye, Bénédictine and bitters
3. Shake
4. Pour into a chilled cocktail glass

# Montmarte Cocktail

**1½ oz. gin**
**½ oz. sweet vermouth**
**½ oz. triple sec**

1. Fill mixing glass with ice
2. Add gin, sweet vermouth and triple sec
3. Shake
4. Pour into a rocks glass filled with ice

# Montreal Club Bouncer

**1½ oz. gin**
**1½ oz. Pernod**

1. Fill a rocks glass with ice
2. Add gin and Pernod
3. Stir

# Moonlight

**2½ oz. apple brandy**
**3 tsp. lemon juice**
**2 tsp. sugar syrup**
**club soda**

1. Fill mixing glass with ice
2. Add apple brandy, lemon juice and sugar syrup
3. Shake
4. Pour into a rocks glass filled with ice
5. Top with club soda
6. Garnish with a slice of lemon

# Moonshine Cocktail

**½ oz. white Dubonnet**
**dash Pernod**
**½ oz. brandy**
**½ oz. peach brandy**

1. Fill mixing glass with ice
2. Add Dubonnet, Pernod, brandy and peach brandy
3. Shake
4. Strain into a chilled cocktail glass

# Morning

1 oz. brandy
1 oz. dry vermouth
3 drops Pernod
3 drops curaçao
3 drops maraschino liqueur
2 dashes orange bitters

1. Fill mixing glass with ice
2. Add brandy, dry vermouth, Pernod, curaçao, maraschino liqueur and orange bitters
3. Shake
4. Strain into a rocks glass filled with ice
5. Garnish with a cherry

# Morning Becomes Electric

2 oz. dry vermouth
1 oz. brandy
2 tsp. port
dash curaçao

1. Fill mixing glass with ice
2. Add dry vermouth, brandy, port and curaçao
3. Stir well
4. Strain into a chilled cocktail glass

# Morning Glory

1 oz. scotch
1 oz. brandy
3 drops curaçao
dash Pernod
2 dashes Angostura bitters
½ tsp. sugar syrup
club soda

1. Fill mixing glass with ice
2. Add scotch, brandy, curaçao, Pernod, bitters and sugar syrup
3. Shake
4. Strain into a Collins glass filled with ice
5. Top with club soda
6. Stir with a wet bar spoon coated with powdered sugar

## Moscow Mimosa

**3 oz. chilled champagne**
**3 oz. chilled orange juice**
**½ oz. vodka**

1. Pour champagne, orange juice and vodka into a wineglass
2. Stir gently

## Moscow Mule

**¾ oz. lime juice**
**1½ oz. vodka**
**ginger ale**

1. Half fill a Collins glass with ice
2. Add lime juice and a slice of lime
3. Pour in the vodka
4. Top with ginger ale
5. Stir

## Mother Sherman

**1½ oz. apricot brandy**
**1 oz. orange juice**
**3–4 dashes orange bitters**

1. Fill mixing glass with ice
2. Add apricot brandy, orange juice and orange bitters

3. Shake
4. Strain into a rocks glass filled with ice

# Moulin Rouge

1½ oz. sloe gin
½ oz. sweet vermouth
3 dashes Angostura bitters

1. Fill mixing glass with ice
2. Add sloe gin, sweet vermouth and bitters
3. Shake
4. Strain into a chilled cocktail glass

# Mountain Red Punch

3 bottles chilled red wine (preferably California wine)
4½ oz. amaretto
4½ oz. brandy
4½ oz. cherry-flavored brandy
16 oz. ginger ale

1. Pour red wine, amaretto, brandy and cherry-flavored brandy over a block of ice in a large punch bowl
2. Place in refrigerator for one hour
3. When ready to serve, pour in ginger ale
4. Stir lightly
5. Garnish with toasted almonds, chopped julienne style

# Mount Fuji

1½ oz. gin
½ oz. lemon juice
½ oz. heavy cream
1 tsp. pineapple juice
1 egg white
3 dashes cherry brandy

1. Fill mixing glass with ice
2. Add gin, lemon juice, heavy cream, pineapple juice, egg white and cherry brandy
3. Shake
4. Strain into a rocks glass filled with ice

## Mudslide

1 oz. vodka
1 oz. Kahlúa
1 oz. Bailey's Original Irish Cream

1. Fill mixing glass with ice
2. Add vodka, Kahlúa and Bailey's
3. Shake
4. Strain into a chilled cocktail glass

## Mule's Hind Leg

½ oz. gin
½ oz. apple brandy
2 tsp. Bénédictine
2 tsp. apricot brandy
2 tsp. maple syrup (or to taste)

1. Fill mixing glass with ice
2. Add gin, apple brandy, Bénédictine, apricot brandy and maple syrup
3. Shake
4. Strain into a rocks glass filled with ice

# N

## Napoli

1 oz. Campari
1 oz. vodka
½ oz. dry vermouth
¼ oz. sweet vermouth
club soda

1. Fill a Collins glass with ice
2. Add Campari, vodka, dry vermouth and sweet vermouth
3. Stir well
4. Fill with club soda
5. Garnish with a twist of orange

## Narragansett

1½ oz. bourbon
1 oz. sweet vermouth
dash anisette

1. Fill a rocks glass with ice
2. Add bourbon, sweet vermouth and anisette
3. Stir
4. Garnish with a twist of lemon

## Navy Grog

½ oz. light rum
½ oz. dark rum
¼ oz. Falernum

½ oz. guava nectar
½ oz. pineapple juice
½ oz. orange juice
1 oz. sour mix

1. Fill mixing glass with ice
2. Add all ingredients
3. Shake
4. Pour into a chilled highball glass or a chilled double rocks glass
5. Garnish with a lime slice and a sprig of mint (optional)

(*Note:* This drink may also be prepared in an electric blender.)

# Negroni

1 oz. gin
1 oz. Campari
1 oz. sweet vermouth

1. Fill mixing glass with ice
2. Add gin, Campari and sweet vermouth
3. Stir
4. Strain into a chilled cocktail glass
5. Garnish with a twist of lemon

# Negroni Cooler

1½ oz. Campari
1½ oz. sweet vermouth
½ oz. gin
club soda

1. Fill mixing glass with ice
2. Add Campari, sweet vermouth and gin
3. Shake
4. Strain into a highball glass filled with ice
5. Top with club soda
6. Garnish with a twist of lemon

# Netherland

1 oz. brandy
1 oz. triple sec
dash orange bitters

1. Fill mixing glass with ice
2. Add brandy, triple sec and orange bitters
3. Shake
4. Strain into a rocks glass filled with ice

# Nevins

1½ oz. bourbon
2 tsp. grapefruit juice
1 tsp. lemon juice
1 tsp. apricot brandy
3 dashes Angostura bitters

1. Fill mixing glass with ice
2. Add bourbon, grapefruit juice, lemon juice, apricot brandy and
   bitters
3. Shake
4. Strain into a highball glass filled with ice

# Newbury

1 oz. gin
1 oz. sweet vermouth
3 dashes curaçao

1. Fill mixing glass with ice
2. Add gin, sweet vermouth and curaçao
3. Stir
4. Strain into a chilled cocktail glass
5. Garnish with a twist of lemon and a twist of orange

# New Orleans

**1½ oz. bourbon**
**½ oz. Pernod**
**3–4 dashes Angostura bitters**
**dash orange bitters**
**dash anisette**
**½ tsp. sugar syrup, or to taste**

1. Fill mixing glass with cracked ice
2. Add bourbon, Pernod, Angostura bitters, orange bitters, anisette and sugar syrup
3. Shake
4. Pour into a chilled rocks glass
5. Garnish with a twist of lemon

# Newton's Special

**2 oz. brandy**
**¾ oz. Cointreau**
**dash Angostura bitters**

1. Fill mixing glass with ice
2. Add brandy, Cointreau and bitters
3. Stir
4. Strain into a chilled cocktail glass

# New World

**1½ oz. blended whiskey**
**½ oz. lime juice**
**1 tsp. grenadine**

1. Fill mixing glass with ice
2. Add blended whiskey, lime juice and grenadine
3. Shake
4. Pour into a chilled rocks glass
5. Garnish with a twist of lime

# New York Cocktail

**1½ oz. whiskey**
**½ tsp. powdered sugar**
**½ oz. lime juice**
**dash grenadine**

1. Fill mixing glass with cracked ice
2. Add whiskey, powdered sugar, lime juice and grenadine
3. Shake
4. Pour into a chilled cocktail glass
5. Garnish with a twist of orange

# Night Cap

**¾ oz. brandy**
**¾ oz. curaçao**
**¾ oz. anisette**
**1 egg yolk**

1. Fill a mixing glass with ice
2. Add brandy, curaçao, anisette and egg yolk
3. Shake
4. Pour into a chilled cocktail glass

# Nightingale

**1 oz. banana liqueur**
**½ oz. curaçao**
**1 oz. cream**
**½ egg white**

1. Fill mixing glass with ice
2. Add banana liqueur, curaçao, cream and egg white
3. Shake
4. Pour into a chilled cocktail glass

# Nineteen

2 oz. dry vermouth
½ oz. gin
½ oz. kirschwasser
dash Pernod
4 dashes sugar syrup

1. Fill mixing glass with ice
2. Add dry vermouth, gin, kirschwasser, Pernod and sugar syrup
3. Stir well
4. Strain into a chilled cocktail glass

# Nineteen Pick-Me-Up

1½ oz. Pernod
¾ oz. gin
3–4 dashes sugar syrup
3–4 dashes Angostura bitters
3–4 dashes orange bitters
club soda

1. Fill mixing glass with ice
2. Add Pernod, gin, sugar syrup, Angostura bitters and orange bitters
3. Shake
4. Pour into a chilled highball glass
5. Fill with club soda

# Ninja Turtle

1½ oz. Tanqueray gin
½ oz. blue curaçao
orange juice

1. Fill a highball glass with ice
2. Add gin and blue curaçao

3. Fill with orange juice
4. Stir

# Ninotchka

1½ oz. vodka
1 tsp. lemon juice
2 tsp. white crème de cacao

1. Fill mixing glass with ice
2. Add vodka, lemon juice and white crème de cacao
3. Shake
4. Pour into a chilled cocktail glass

# Nocturnal

2 oz. bourbon
1 oz. dark crème de cacao
½ oz. cream

1. Fill mixing glass with ice
2. Add bourbon, dark crème de cacao and cream
3. Shake
4. Strain into a rocks glass filled with 2 oz. crushed ice

# Nutty Colada

2 oz. amaretto
1 oz. gold rum
1½ oz. cream of coconut
2 oz. pineapple juice

1. Fill blender with 3 oz. cracked ice
2. Add amaretto, gold rum, cream of coconut and pineapple juice
3. Blend at low speed for approximately 10–15 seconds, or until smooth
4. Pour into a chilled Collins glass
5. Garnish with a slice of pineapple

# Nutty Irishman

½ oz. **Frangelico**
½ oz. **Irish whiskey**
2 oz. **cream**

1. Fill mixing glass with ice
2. Add Frangelico, Irish whiskey and cream
3. Shake
4. Strain into a rocks glass filled with ice

# Nutty Irishman (shooter)

½ oz. **Frangelico**
½ oz. **Bailey's Original Irish Cream**

Layer Frangelico and Bailey's in a shot glass

# Nutty Stinger

1½ oz. **amaretto**
1 oz. **white crème de menthe**

1. Fill mixing glass with ice
2. Add amaretto and white crème de menthe
3. Shake
4. Strain into a chilled cocktail glass

# O

## Odd McIntyre

1 oz. brandy
1 oz. triple sec
1 oz. Lillet
½ oz. lemon juice

1. Fill mixing glass with ice
2. Add brandy, triple sec, Lillet and lemon juice
3. Shake
4. Strain into a chilled cocktail glass

## Odéon Casino

3 oz. peach juice
3 oz. chilled champagne
dash peach schnapps (optional)

1. Pour peach juice into a large chilled wineglass
2. Fill with chilled champagne
3. Top with peach schnapps (if desired)
4. Stir gently

(*Note:* The proportion of peach juice to champagne may be changed to suit personal taste.)

## Oh, Henry!

1½ oz. blended whiskey
¼ oz. Bénédictine
3 oz. ginger ale

1. Fill a rocks glass with ice
2. Add blended whiskey, Bénédictine and ginger ale
3. Stir
4. Garnish with a slice of lemon

## Oil Slick

**1 oz. vodka**
**1 oz. white crème de cacao**
**1 oz. milk**
**float of dark rum**

1. Fill a small rocks glass with ice
2. Layer vodka, white crème de cacao and milk
3. Float dark rum on top

(Courtesy of The Cowgirl Hall of Fame, New York City)

## Old Etonian

**1 oz. gin**
**1 oz. Lillet**
**2 dashes crème de noyaux**
**2 dashes orange bitters**

1. Fill mixing glass with ice
2. Add gin, Lillet, crème de noyaux and orange bitters
3. Stir
4. Strain into a chilled cocktail glass

## Old-Fashioned

**See Bourbon Old-Fashioned**

# Old Pale

1 oz. peppermint schnapps
1½ oz. vodka
1 tsp. strawberry liqueur

1. In a mixing glass, combine several ice cubes with peppermint schnapps, vodka and strawberry liqueur
2. Stir
3. Pour into a chilled cocktail glass

# Olympic

¾ oz. brandy
¾ oz. curaçao
½ oz. orange juice

1. Fill mixing glass with ice
2. Add brandy, curaçao and orange juice
3. Shake
4. Strain into a rocks glass filled with ice

# Oom Paul

1 oz. apple brandy
1 oz. Dubonnet
3 dashes Angostura bitters

1. Fill mixing glass with ice
2. Add apple brandy, Dubonnet and bitters
3. Shake
4. Strain into a rocks glass filled with ice

# Opening

2 oz. whiskey
1 oz. sweet vermouth
1 tsp. grenadine

1. Fill mixing glass with ice
2. Add whiskey, sweet vermouth and grenadine
3. Stir
4. Strain into a chilled cocktail glass

## Opera (1)

**1½ oz. gin**
**½ oz. Dubonnet**
**½ oz. cherry liqueur**

1. Fill mixing glass with ice
2. Add gin, Dubonnet and cherry liqueur
3. Stir
4. Strain into a chilled cocktail glass
5. Garnish with a twist of orange

## Opera (2)

**¾ oz. gin**
**¾ oz. Dubonnet**
**¾ oz. Grand Marnier**
**½ oz. orange juice**

1. Fill mixing glass with ice
2. Add gin, Dubonnet, Grand Marnier and orange juice
3. Shake
4. Strain into a chilled cocktail glass

## Orange Bloom

**1 oz. gin**
**½ oz. sweet vermouth**
**½ oz. Cointreau**

1. Fill mixing glass with ice
2. Add gin, sweet vermouth and Cointreau

3. Stir
4. Strain into a chilled cocktail glass
5. Garnish with a cherry

# Orange Blossom

1 oz. gin
½ oz. sugar syrup (triple sec may be substituted)
1½ oz. orange juice

1. Fill mixing glass with ice
2. Add gin, sugar syrup (or triple sec) and orange juice
3. Shake
4. Strain into a chilled cocktail glass

(*Note:* If desired, frost rim of cocktail glass with sugar before pouring drink into it.)

# Orange Buck

1½ oz. gin
1 oz. orange juice
1 tbsp. lime juice
ginger ale

1. Fill mixing glass with ice
2. Add gin, orange juice and lime juice
3. Shake
4. Strain into a highball glass filled with ice
5. Top with ginger ale

# Orange Comfort

1½ oz. Southern Comfort
2 tsp. anisette
1 tbsp. orange juice
2 tsp. lemon juice

1. Fill mixing glass with ice
2. Add Southern Comfort, anisette, orange juice and lemon juice
3. Shake
4. Strain into a chilled rocks glass
5. Garnish with a slice of orange

# Orange Fizz

**2½ oz. gin**
**1½ oz. orange juice**
**½ oz. lemon juice**
**2 tsp. triple sec**
**1 tsp. sugar**
**2 dashes orange bitters**
**club soda**

1. Fill mixing glass with ice
2. Add gin, orange juice, lemon juice, triple sec, sugar and orange bitters
3. Shake
4. Strain into a highball glass filled with ice
5. Top with club soda
6. Garnish with a slice of orange

# Orange Gimlet

**1½ oz. gin**
**1 oz. Lillet**
**2 dashes orange bitters**

1. Fill mixing glass with ice
2. Add gin, Lillet and orange bitters
3. Shake
4. Strain into a chilled cocktail glass

# Orange Oasis

1½ oz. gin
½ oz. cherry brandy
4 oz. orange juice
ginger ale

1. Fill a highball glass with ice
2. Add gin, cherry brandy and orange juice
3. Stir
4. Top with ginger ale

# Orgasm

½ oz. white crème de cacao
½ oz. amaretto
½ oz. triple sec
½ oz. vodka
1 oz. cream

1. Fill mixing glass with ice
2. Add white crème de cacao, amaretto, triple sec, vodka and cream
3. Shake
4. Strain into a rocks glass filled with ice

# Oriental

1 oz. rye whiskey
¼ oz. sweet vermouth
¼ oz. Cointreau
½ oz. lime juice

1. Fill mixing glass with ice
2. Add rye, sweet vermouth, Cointreau and lime juice
3. Shake
4. Strain into a chilled cocktail glass

# Ostend Fizz

1 oz. kirschwasser
1 oz. crème de cassis
club soda

1. Fill a highball glass with ice
2. Add kirschwasser and crème de cassis
3. Stir
4. Fill with club soda
5. Garnish with a twist of lemon

# Out of the Blue

¼ oz. Absolut vodka
¼ oz. blueberry schnapps
¼ oz. blue curaçao
splash sour mix
¼ oz. club soda

1. Fill mixing glass with ice
2. Add Absolut vodka, blueberry schnapps, blue curaçao and sour mix
3. Shake
4. Pour into a rocks glass
5. Top with club soda

# Oxbend

1 oz. Southern Comfort
½ oz. tequila
6 oz. orange juice
dash of grenadine

1. Fill a highball glass with ice
2. Add Southern Comfort, tequila, orange juice and grenadine
3. Stir

# P

## Pacific Pacifier

1 oz. Cointreau
½ oz. banana liqueur
½ oz. cream

1. Fill mixing glass with ice
2. Add Cointreau, banana liqueur and cream
3. Shake
4. Strain into a rocks glass filled with ice

## Paddy Cocktail

1½ oz. Irish whiskey
¾ oz. sweet vermouth
3 dashes Angostura bitters

1. Fill mixing glass with ice
2. Add Irish whiskey, sweet vermouth and bitters
3. Shake
4. Strain into a chilled cocktail glass

## Pago Pago

1½ oz. gold rum
½ oz. pineapple juice
½ oz. lime juice
2–3 drops green Chartreuse
2–3 drops white crème de cacao

1. Fill mixing glass with ice
2. Add gold rum, pineapple juice, lime juice, green Chartreuse and white crème de cacao
3. Shake
4. Strain into a rocks glass filled with ice

# Paisley Martini

**2 oz. gin**
**1 tsp. dry vermouth**
**½ tsp. scotch**

1. Fill mixing glass with ice
2. Add gin, dry vermouth and scotch
3. Shake
4. Strain into a rocks glass filled with ice

# Pall Mall

**¾ oz. gin**
**¾ oz. dry vermouth**
**¾ oz. sweet vermouth**
**1 tsp. white crème de menthe**
**dash orange bitters**

1. Fill a rocks glass with ice
2. Add all ingredients
3. Stir

# Palmetto

**1½ oz. light rum**
**½ oz. sweet vermouth**
**2 dashes orange bitters**

1. Fill a rocks glass with ice
2. Add light rum, sweet vermouth and orange bitters

3. Stir
4. Garnish with a twist of lemon

## Panama

**1 oz. Myers's dark rum**
**½ oz. white crème de cacao**
**½ oz. cream**

1. Fill a mixing glass with ice
2. Add Myers's rum, crème de cacao and cream
3. Shake
4. Strain into a rocks glass filled with ice
5. Sprinkle nutmeg on top

## Pancho Villa

**1 oz. light rum**
**1 oz. gin**
**½ oz. apricot brandy**
**1 tsp. cherry brandy**
**1 tsp. pineapple juice**

1. Fill mixing glass with ice
2. Add light rum, gin, apricot brandy, cherry brandy and pineapple juice
3. Shake
4. Strain into a rocks glass filled with ice

## Pancho Villa (shooter)

**½ oz. crème de almond**
**½ oz. Cuervo white tequila**
**½ oz. 151-proof rum**

1. Layer crème de almond and tequila in a shot glass
2. Top with float of 151-proof rum

(Courtesy of Soapy Smith's Eagle Bar, Denver, Colorado)

# Panda Bear

1 oz. amaretto
½ oz. white crème de cacao
½ oz. dark crème de cacao
5 oz. vanilla ice cream
¼ oz. chocolate syrup
2–3 dashes vanilla extract

1. Fill blender with amaretto, both crèmes de cacao, vanilla ice cream, chocolate syrup and vanilla extract
2. Blend until smooth
3. Pour into a chilled goblet


# Panther

1½ oz. tequila
½ oz. sour mix

1. Fill mixing glass with ice
2. Add tequila and sour mix
3. Shake
4. Strain into a rocks glass filled with ice


# Pantomime

1½ oz. dry vermouth
3 drops orgeat syrup
3 drops grenadine
1 egg white

1. Fill mixing glass with ice
2. Add dry vermouth, orgeat syrup, grenadine and egg white
3. Shake
4. Strain into a chilled cocktail glass

# Paradise

1 oz. gin
1 oz. apricot brandy
1 oz. orange juice

1. Fill mixing glass with ice
2. Add gin, apricot brandy and orange juice
3. Stir
4. Strain into a chilled cocktail glass

# Parisian

¾ oz. gin
¾ oz. dry vermouth
¾ oz. crème de cassis

1. Fill mixing glass with ice
2. Add gin, dry vermouth and crème de cassis
3. Shake
4. Strain into a chilled cocktail glass

# Parisian Blonde

1 oz. light rum
1 oz. curaçao
1 oz. heavy cream
½ tsp. powdered sugar

1. Fill mixing glass with ice
2. Add light rum, curaçao, heavy cream and powdered sugar
3. Shake
4. Strain into a chilled cocktail glass

# Park Avenue

2 oz. gin
½ oz. sweet vermouth
1 oz. pineapple juice
2–3 drops curaçao

1. Fill mixing glass with ice
2. Add gin, sweet vermouth, pineapple juice and curaçao
3. Shake
4. Strain into a chilled cocktail glass

# Pavarotti

1½ oz. amaretto
½ oz. brandy
½ oz. white crème de cacao

1. Fill mixing glass with ice
2. Add amaretto, brandy and white crème de cacao
3. Shake
4. Strain into a rocks glass filled with ice

# Peach Alexander

½ peach, pared, pitted and chopped
1½ oz. half-and-half
1 oz. peach schnapps
½ oz. white crème de cacao

1. Combine peach, half-and-half, peach schnapps, white crème de cacao and 3 oz. crushed ice in a blender
2. Blend until smooth
3. Pour into an 8-oz. glass
4. Garnish with a slice of fresh peach

# Peach Blow Fizz

2 oz. gin
1 oz. lemon juice
1 oz. heavy cream
1 tsp. sugar syrup
2 tsp. strawberry liqueur
club soda

1. Fill mixing glass with ice
2. Add gin, lemon juice, heavy cream, sugar syrup and strawberry liqueur
3. Shake
4. Strain into a sour glass
5. Add ice
6. Fill with club soda
7. Garnish with a strawberry

# Peach Buck

1¼ oz. vodka
½ oz. peach brandy
½ oz. lemon juice
ginger ale

1. Fill mixing glass with cracked ice
2. Add vodka, peach brandy and lemon juice
3. Shake
4. Pour into a highball glass
5. Fill with ginger ale

# Peach Coconut Flip

1 peach, pared and pitted
1½ oz. light rum
2 oz. coconut cream
2 oz. milk

1. Fill blender with 3 oz. crushed ice, peach, light rum, coconut cream and milk
2. Blend until smooth
3. Pour into a goblet
4. Garnish with a slice of fresh peach

## Peach Treat

1 oz. peach brandy
2 oz. orange juice
chilled champagne

1. Fill mixing glass with ice
2. Add peach brandy and orange juice
3. Shake
4. Strain into a Collins glass filled with ice
5. Fill with champagne
6. Garnish with a peach slice

## Peach Velvet

1½ oz. peach brandy
½ oz. white crème de cacao
½ oz. heavy cream

1. Fill blender with 4 oz. cracked ice
2. Add peach brandy, white crème de cacao and heavy cream
3. Blend at medium speed for 10 seconds, or until smooth
4. Pour into a rocks glass
5. Garnish with a slice of fresh peach

## Peachy Keen Freeze

1½ oz. amaretto
2 oz. heavy cream or half-and-half
1 tbsp. sugar
½ fresh peach, pared

1. Combine amaretto, cream, sugar and peach with 3 oz. crushed ice in a blender
2. Blend until smooth
3. Pour into a goblet

## Pearl Harbor

1 oz. vodka
½ oz. Midori melon liqueur
pineapple juice

1. Fill a highball glass with ice
2. Add vodka and Midori
3. Fill with pineapple juice
4. Stir

## Pear Tequila Supreme

1½ oz. white tequila
1 oz. triple sec
¼ cup undiluted frozen limeade concentrate
¾ cup fresh pear (Bartlett), pared, cored and diced
½ egg white

1. In a blender, combine tequila, triple sec, limeade, pear and egg white
2. Blend until smooth
3. Pour into goblets

(Makes 2 servings)

## Pegu Club

1½ oz. gin
¾ oz. orange curaçao
1 tsp. lime juice
dash Angostura bitters
dash orange bitters

1. Fill mixing glass with ice
2. Add gin, orange curaçao, lime juice, Angostura and orange bitters
3. Shake
4. Strain into a chilled cocktail glass

## Pendennis Cocktail

**1½ oz. gin**
**1 tbs. apricot brandy**
**½ oz. lime juice**
**2 dashes Peychaud's bitters**

1. Fill mixing glass with ice
2. Add gin, apricot brandy, lime juice, and bitters
3. Shake
4. Strain into a chilled cocktail glass

## Pensacola

**1½ oz. light rum**
**½ oz. guava nectar**
**½ oz. orange juice**
**½ oz. lemon juice**

1. Fill blender with 3 oz. cracked ice
2. Add light rum, guava nectar, orange juice and lemon juice
3. Blend at medium speed for 10–15 seconds, or until smooth
4. Pour into large wineglass

## Peppar Martini

**2 oz. Absolut Peppar vodka**
**½ oz. dry vermouth (or to taste)**

1. Fill mixing glass with ice
2. Add Absolut Peppar and dry vermouth

3. Stir
4. Strain into a chilled martini glass or a rocks glass filled with ice
5. Garnish with a jalapeño pepper

# Peppermint Patty

½ oz. peppermint schnapps
½ oz. dark crème de cacao
1 oz. cream

1. Fill a rocks glass with ice
2. Add peppermint schnapps and dark crème de cacao
3. Add cream
4. Stir

# Peppermint Stinger

1½ oz. brandy
1 oz. peppermint schnapps

1. Fill blender with 4 oz. cracked ice
2. Add brandy and peppermint schnapps
3. Blend at low speed for 5 seconds, or until smooth
4. Pour into a rocks glass

# Perfect Manhattan

See Manhattan (perfect)

# Perfect Rob Roy

See Rob Roy (perfect)

# Pernod Cocktail

**2 oz. Pernod**
**½ oz. water**
**3 dashes sugar syrup**
**3 dashes Angostura bitters**

1. Fill mixing glass with ice
2. Add Pernod, water, sugar syrup and bitters
3. Shake
4. Strain into a chilled cocktail glass

# Pernod Flip

**1 oz. Pernod**
**½ oz. Cointreau**
**½ oz. lemon juice**
**1½ tsp. sugar syrup**
**1 egg**

1. Fill mixing glass with ice
2. Add Pernod, Cointreau, lemon juice, sugar syrup and egg
3. Shake
4. Strain into a rocks glass filled with ice

# Pernod Frappe

**1½ oz. Pernod**
**½ oz. anisette**
**3 dashes Angostura bitters**

1. Fill mixing glass with ice
2. Add Pernod, anisette and bitters
3. Shake
4. Strain into a chilled cocktail glass

# Philadelphia Scotchman

**1 oz. apple brandy**
**1 oz. port**
**1 oz. orange juice**
**club soda**

1. Fill mixing glass with ice
2. Add apple brandy, port and orange juice
3. Shake
4. Strain into a highball glass filled with ice
5. Fill with club soda

# Phoebe Snow

**1½ oz. brandy**
**1½ oz. Dubonnet**
**3 drops Pernod**

1. Fill mixing glass with ice
2. Add brandy, Dubonnet and Pernod
3. Shake
4. Strain into a rocks glass filled with ice

# Picon

**1 oz. Amer Picon**
**1 oz. dry vermouth**

1. Fill mixing glass with ice
2. Add Amer Picon and dry vermouth
3. Shake
4. Strain into a chilled cocktail glass

# Picon Fizz

**1½ oz. Amer Picon**
**1 tbsp. grenadine**
**club soda**
**2 tbsp. cognac**

1. Pour Amer Picon and grenadine into a highball glass
2. Add 4 or 5 ice cubes
3. Stir
4. Fill with chilled club soda
5. Float cognac on top

# Picon Orange

**1½ oz. Amer Picon**
**1½ oz. orange juice**
**club soda**

1. Fill mixing glass with ice
2. Add Amer Picon and orange juice
3. Shake
4. Strain into a rocks glass filled with ice
5. Fill with club soda

# Picon Sour

**1½ oz. Amer Picon**
**1½ oz. sour mix**
**½ tsp. sugar (if desired)**

1. Fill mixing glass with ice
2. Add Amer Picon, sour mix and sugar (if desired)
3. Shake
4. Strain into a chilled sour glass filled with ice

# Pilot Boat

1½ oz. dark rum
1 oz. banana liqueur
2 oz. fresh lime juice or fresh lemon juice

1. Fill mixing glass with ice
2. Add dark rum, banana liqueur and fresh lime or lemon juice
3. Shake
4. Strain into a chilled cocktail glass

# Pimm's Cup

1½ oz. Pimm's No. 1
1 lemon slice
7-Up

1. Fill a highball glass with ice
2. Pour in Pimm's
3. Add lemon slice
4. Fill with 7-Up
5. Garnish with a slice of cucumber

# Piña

1½ oz. tequila
3 oz. pineapple juice
1 oz. lime juice
1 tsp. sugar syrup

1. Fill mixing glass with ice
2. Add tequila, pineapple juice, lime juice and sugar syrup
3. Shake
4. Strain into a rocks glass filled with ice

# Piña Colada

1½ oz. light rum
1 oz. cream of coconut
2 oz. canned pineapple chunks
2 oz. pineapple juice
splash of cream

1. In a blender, combine light rum, cream of coconut, canned pineapple chunks, cream and 3 oz. crushed ice
2. Blend at medium speed for 10–15 seconds, or until smooth
3. Pour into a goblet or a large wineglass
4. Garnish with a cherry and an orange slice or a pineapple spear

# Piñata

1 oz. tequila
1 tbsp. banana liqueur
1 oz. lime juice

1. Fill mixing glass with ice
2. Add tequila, banana liqueur and lime juice
3. Shake
4. Strain into a rocks glass filled with ice

# Pineapple Bomber

1 oz. Captain Morgan rum
1 oz. Southern Comfort
½ oz. amaretto
3 oz. pineapple juice

1. Fill mixing glass with ice
2. Add Captain Morgan rum, Southern Comfort, amaretto and pineapple juice
3. Shake
4. Pour into a Collins glass filled with ice

# Pineapple Bomber (shooter)

¾ oz. Captain Morgan rum
¾ oz. Southern Comfort
½ oz. amaretto
1 oz. pineapple juice

1. Fill mixing glass with ice
2. Add Captain Morgan rum, Southern Comfort, amaretto and pineapple juice
3. Stir well
4. Strain into shot glasses

(Makes 2 shots)

# Pineapple Francine

½ oz. light rum
½ oz. apricot brandy
1 oz. pineapple juice
1 oz. cream
1 oz. canned pineapple chunks, crushed

1. Fill blender with 3 oz. ice
2. Add light rum, apricot brandy, pineapple juice, cream and pineapple
3. Blend for 10–15 seconds, or until smooth
4. Pour into a goblet or a large wineglass

# Pineapple Gimlet

1½ oz. gin
½ oz. Rose's lime juice
pineapple juice

1. Fill a rocks glass with ice
2. Add gin and lime juice
3. Stir well
4. Top with pineapple juice

# Pineapple Vodka

**premium vodka**
**fresh pineapple slices**

1. Fill a large clean jar with fresh pineapple
2. Add a premium vodka
3. Cover and let stand for 3 days, turning the jar several times daily
4. Remove most of the fruit and refrigerate
5. Serve the vodka over ice in a wineglass or rocks glass

# Pine Tree

**1 oz. triple sec**
**lemonade (from a mix)**

1. Fill a highball glass with crushed ice
2. Add triple sec
3. Fill with lemonade
4. Stir
5. Garnish with a mint leaf

# Pink Almond

**1 oz. blended whiskey**
**½ oz. crème de noyaux**
**½ oz. amaretto**
**½ oz. kirschwasser**
**½ oz. lemon juice**

1. Fill mixing glass with ice
2. Add blended whiskey, crème de noyaux, amaretto, kirschwasser and lemon juice
3. Shake
4. Pour into a chilled sour glass
5. Garnish with a slice of lemon

# Pink and Tan

**1½ oz. Malibu coconut rum**
**diet cola (with Nutrasweet)**

1. Fill a highball glass with ice
2. Add Malibu
3. Fill with diet cola
4. Stir

(Courtesy of Michael Salatto, New York, New York)


# Pink Gin

**2 oz. gin**
**2 dashes Angostura bitters**

1. Fill mixing glass with ice
2. Add gin and bitters
3. Stir
4. Strain into a rocks glass filled with ice


# Pink Lady

**1 oz. gin**
**½ oz. grenadine**
**1½ oz. cream**

1. Fill mixing glass with ice
2. Add gin, grenadine and cream
3. Shake
4. Strain into a chilled cocktail glass

# Pink Lemonade

1½ oz. vodka
1 oz. cranberry juice cocktail
2 oz. sour mix
7-Up

1. Fill mixing glass with ice
2. Add vodka, cranberry juice and sour mix
3. Shake
4. Pour into a highball glass or a Collins glass
5. Top with 7-Up
6. Garnish with a slice of lemon

# Pink Lemonade (shooter)

1 oz. vodka
1 oz. cranberry juice cocktail
1 oz. sour mix

1. Fill mixing glass with ice
2. Add vodka, cranberry juice and sour mix
3. Shake
4. Strain into shot glasses

(Makes 2 shots)

# Pink Panther

¾ oz. gin
¾ oz. dry vermouth
½ oz. crème de cassis
½ oz. orange juice
1 egg white

1. Fill mixing glass with ice
2. Add gin, dry vermouth, crème de cassis, orange juice and egg white

3. Shake
4. Strain into a chilled cocktail glass

## Pink Pussycat

1½ oz. gin
¾ oz. grenadine
1 egg white

1. Fill mixing glass with ice
2. Add gin, grenadine and egg white
3. Shake well
4. Strain into a chilled cocktail glass

## Pink Rose

1½ oz. gin
1 tsp. lemon juice
1 tsp. heavy cream
1 egg white
3–4 dashes grenadine

1. Fill mixing glass with ice
2. Add gin, lemon juice, heavy cream, egg white and grenadine
3. Shake
4. Strain into a chilled cocktail glass

## Pink Squirrel

½ oz. white crème de cacao
½ oz. crème de noyaux
2 oz. cream

1. Fill mixing glass with ice
2. Add white crème de cacao, crème de noyaux and cream
3. Shake
4. Strain into a chilled cocktail glass

# Pink Veranda

1 oz. gold rum
½ oz. dark rum
1½ oz. cranberry juice
½ oz. lime juice
1 tsp. sugar
½ egg white

1. Fill mixing glass with ice
2. Add gold rum, dark rum, cranberry juice, lime juice, sugar and egg white
3. Shake
4. Pour into a rocks glass

# Pink Whiskers

1 oz. apricot brandy
½ oz. dry vermouth
1 oz. orange juice
1 tsp. grenadine
3 dashes white crème de menthe
1 oz. port

1. Fill mixing glass with ice
2. Add apricot brandy, dry vermouth, orange juice, grenadine and white crème de menthe
3. Shake
4. Strain into a rocks glass filled with ice
5. Float port on top

# Pirate Cocktail

1½ oz. Jamaican rum
½ oz. sweet vermouth
2 dashes Angostura bitters

1. Fill mixing glass with ice
2. Add rum, sweet vermouth and bitters
3. Shake
4. Strain into a large glass
5. Add ice

# Pisco Punch

**3 oz. brandy**
**1 tsp. lime juice**
**1 tsp. pineapple juice**
**cold water**
**2 or 3 pineapple cubes**

1. Pour brandy, lime juice, pineapple juice and pineapple cubes into a brandy snifter
2. Fill with cold water
3. Stir

# Pisco Sour

**2 oz. brandy (Pisco)**
**1½ oz. sour mix**
**1 tsp. lime juice**
**½ egg white**
**2 dashes Angostura bitters**

1. Fill mixing glass with ice
2. Add brandy, sour mix, lime juice and egg white
3. Shake
4. Strain into a sour glass
5. Add ice
6. Top with Angostura bitters

# Planter's Punch

1½–2 oz. Myers's dark rum
3 oz. orange juice
juice of ½ lemon or lime
1 tsp. superfine granulated sugar
dash grenadine

1. Fill mixing glass with cracked ice
2. Add Myers's rum, orange juice, lemon or lime juice, sugar and grenadine
3. Shake
4. Pour into a chilled Collins glass
5. Garnish with a cherry and an orange slice

# Plaza

1 oz. gin
1 oz. dry vermouth
1 oz. sweet vermouth
1 tbsp. pineapple juice

1. Fill mixing glass with ice
2. Add gin, dry vermouth, sweet vermouth and pineapple juice
3. Shake
4. Strain into a chilled cocktail glass

# Poinsettia

4 oz. chilled champagne
2 oz. cranberry juice cocktail

1. Pour chilled champagne into a champagne flute or tulip glass
2. Add cranberry juice

# Poker

**1½ oz. gold rum**
**1½ oz. dry vermouth**

1. Fill mixing glass with ice
2. Add gold rum and dry vermouth
3. Shake
4. Strain into a chilled cocktail glass

# Pollyanna

**1½ oz. gin**
**2 tsp. sweet vermouth**
**2 tsp. grenadine**

1. Fill mixing glass with ice
2. Add gin, sweet vermouth and grenadine
3. Shake
4. Strain into a rocks glass filled with ice
5. Garnish with a slice of pineapple and a slice of orange

# Polly's Special

**1½ oz. scotch**
**½ oz. triple sec**
**½ oz. grapefruit juice**

1. Fill mixing glass with ice
2. Add scotch, triple sec and grapefruit juice
3. Shake
4. Strain into a rocks glass filled with ice

# Polo

1½ oz. gin
2 tsp. orange juice
2 tsp. grapefruit juice

1. Fill rocks glass with ice
2. Add gin, orange juice and grapefruit juice
3. Stir

# Polynesian Cocktail

1½ oz. vodka
¾ oz. cherry brandy
3 tbsp. lime juice

1. Frost the rim of a cocktail glass with powdered sugar
2. Fill a mixing glass with ice
3. Add vodka, cherry brandy and lime juice
4. Shake
5. Strain into a chilled cocktail glass

# Polynesian Punch

12 oz. light rum
12 oz. dark rum
6 oz. cream of coconut
8 oz. sloe gin
4 oz. peppermint schnapps
½ oz. grenadine
1 qt., 1 pt. unsweetened pineapple juice
8 oz. lemon juice
8 oz. chilled club soda

1. Pour light rum, dark rum, cream of coconut, sloe gin, peppermint schnapps, grenadine, pineapple juice and lemon juice into a punch bowl over a block of ice

2. Stir
3. Garnish with thin slices of fresh pineapple and orange
4. Refrigerate for 1 hour
5. When ready to serve, add club soda and stir gently

# Poop Deck

**1 oz. blackberry brandy**
**½ oz. port**
**½ oz. brandy**

1. Fill mixing glass with ice
2. Add blackberry brandy, port and brandy
3. Shake
4. Strain into a chilled cocktail glass

# Poppy Cocktail

**1½ oz. gin**
**¾ oz. white crème de cacao**

1. Fill mixing glass with ice
2. Add gin and white crème de cacao
3. Shake
4. Strain into a chilled cocktail glass

# Popsicle

**1 oz. amaretto**
**orange juice**
**cream**

1. Fill a highball glass with ice
2. Add amaretto
3. Fill glass half with orange juice, half with cream
4. Stir well

# Port Antonio

**1 oz. gold rum**
**½ oz. dark rum**
**½ oz. lime juice**
**½ oz. Tia Maria**
**1 tsp. Falernum**

1. Fill mixing glass with ice
2. Add gold rum, dark rum, lime juice, Tia Maria and Falernum
3. Shake
4. Strain into a highball glass
5. Fill with ice
6. Garnish with a slice of lime

# Port Sangaree

**½ tsp. powdered sugar**
**1 oz. water**
**2 oz. port**
**club soda**
**1 tbsp. brandy (optional)**

1. In a sour glass, dissolve powdered sugar in water
2. Fill with ice cubes
3. Pour in port
4. Fill with club soda
5. Top with brandy (if desired)

# Port Wine Cocktail

**2½ oz. port**
**½ tsp. brandy**

1. Fill mixing glass with ice
2. Add port and brandy
3. Stir
4. Strain into a chilled cocktail glass

# Pousse-Café (1)

⅓ oz. banana liqueur
½ oz. cherry brandy
⅓ oz. cognac

1. Pour banana liqueur into a liqueur glass
2. Float the cherry brandy on top
3. Float the cognac on top of that

# Pousse-Café (2)

½ oz. green crème de menthe
½ oz. Galliano
½ oz. blackberry liqueur

1. Pour green crème de menthe into a liqueur glass
2. Float the Galliano on top
3. Float the blackberry liqueur on top of that

# Prado

1½ oz. tequila
½ oz. cherry liqueur
¾ oz. lime juice
½ egg white
1 tsp. grenadine

1. Fill mixing glass with cracked ice
2. Add tequila, cherry liqueur, lime juice, egg white and grenadine
3. Shake
4. Pour into a sour glass
5. Garnish with a cherry

# Prairie Fire (shooter)

1½ oz. Cuervo gold tequila, chilled
dash of Tabasco sauce

1. Fill shot glass with chilled Cuervo gold tequila
2. Add a dash of Tabasco

# Preakness

1½ oz. blended whiskey
¼ oz. Bénédictine
¼ oz. sweet vermouth
dash Angostura bitters

1. Fill mixing glass with ice
2. Add blended whiskey, Bénédictine, sweet vermouth and bitters
3. Shake
4. Strain into a chilled cocktail glass

# Presbyterian

1 oz. whiskey
club soda
ginger ale

1. Fill a highball glass with ice
2. Add whiskey
3. Fill glass half with club soda, half with ginger ale
4. Stir well
5. Garnish with a twist of lemon

# Presidente

1½ oz. light rum
½ oz. dry vermouth
1 tbsp. curaçao
dash grenadine

1. Fill mixing glass with ice
2. Add light rum, dry vermouth, curaçao and grenadine
3. Shake
4. Strain into a chilled cocktail glass
5. Garnish with a twist of lemon

# Prince

1½ oz. blended whiskey
2 dashes orange bitters
3 drops white crème de menthe

1. Fill mixing glass with ice
2. Add blended whiskey and orange bitters
3. Shake
4. Strain into a rocks glass filled with ice
5. Top with a few drops of white crème de menthe

# Prince Edward

1½ oz. scotch
½ oz. Lillet
1 tbsp. Drambuie

1. Fill mixing glass with ice
2. Add scotch, Lillet and Drambuie
3. Shake
4. Strain into a rocks glass filled with ice
5. Garnish with a slice of orange

# Prince of Wales

1 oz. madeira
1 oz. brandy
3–4 drops curaçao
2 dashes Angostura bitters
chilled champagne

1. Fill mixing glass with ice
2. Add madeira, brandy, curaçao and bitters
3. Shake
4. Strain into a chilled champagne glass
5. Fill with champagne
6. Garnish with a slice of orange

# Princess Mary's Pride

1½ oz. apple brandy
2 tbsp. Dubonnet (rouge)
1 tbsp. dry vermouth

1. Fill mixing glass with ice
2. Add apple brandy, Dubonnet and dry vermouth
3. Shake
4. Strain into a rocks glass filled with ice

# Prince's Smile

1 oz. gin
½ oz. apricot brandy
½ oz. apple brandy
dash lemon juice

1. Fill mixing glass with ice
2. Add gin, apricot brandy, apple brandy and lemon juice
3. Shake
4. Strain into a chilled cocktail glass

# Princeton

**1½ oz. gin**
**¾ oz. port**
**3–4 dashes orange bitters**

1. Fill mixing glass with ice
2. Add gin, port and orange bitters
3. Shake
4. Strain into a chilled cocktail glass
5. Garnish with a twist of lemon

# Prohibition

**1 oz. gin**
**1 oz. Lillet**
**2 dashes orange juice**
**dash apricot brandy**

1. Fill mixing glass with ice
2. Add gin, Lillet, orange juice and apricot brandy
3. Shake
4. Strain into a chilled cocktail glass
5. Garnish with a twist of lemon

# Punt e Mes Negroni

**½ oz. gin**
**½ oz. Punt e Mes**
**½ oz. sweet vermouth**

1. Fill mixing glass with ice
2. Add gin, Punt e Mes and sweet vermouth
3. Shake
4. Strain into a chilled cocktail glass
5. Garnish with a twist of orange

(*Note:* This drink may also be made with vodka instead of gin.)

# The Purple Hooter Shooter

**3 oz. Absolut vodka**
**1 oz. Rose's lime juice**
**dash Chambord (for color)**

1. Fill mixing glass with ice
2. Add Absolut, lime juice and Chambord
3. Stir
4. Strain into shot glasses

(Makes approximately 2 shots)

(Originated by Coleen Patrick, New York City)

# Purple Passion

**1½ oz. vodka**
**grape juice**

1. Fill a highball glass with ice
2. Add vodka
3. Fill with grape juice
4. Stir

# Q

## Quaker

1 oz. brandy
¾ oz. light rum
½ oz. lemon juice
½ oz. raspberry syrup

1. Fill mixing glass with ice
2. Add brandy, light rum, lemon juice and raspberry syrup
3. Shake
4. Strain into a chilled cocktail glass
5. Garnish with a twist of lemon

## Quarter Deck

1½ oz. light rum
1 tbsp. sherry
1 tsp. lime juice

1. Fill mixing glass with ice
2. Add light rum, sherry and lime juice
3. Shake
4. Strain into a rocks glass filled with ice

## Quebec Cocktail

1½ oz. Canadian whiskey
½ oz. Amer Picon
½ oz. dry vermouth
½ oz. cherry liqueur

363

1. Fill mixing glass with ice
2. Add whiskey, Amer Picon, dry vermouth and cherry liqueur
3. Shake
4. Strain into a chilled cocktail glass

## Queen

**several pineapple chunks**
**1½ oz. gin**
**¾ oz. sweet vermouth**

1. In a mixing glass, muddle the pineapple chunks
2. Add ice, gin and sweet vermouth
3. Stir well
4. Strain into a rocks glass filled with ice

## Queen Elizabeth

**1½ oz. gin**
**½ oz. Cointreau**
**½ oz. lemon juice**
**1 tsp. Pernod**

1. Fill a mixing glass with ice
2. Add gin, Cointreau, lemon juice and Pernod
3. Stir well
4. Strain into a chilled cocktail glass

## Queen Elizabeth Wine

**1½ oz. Bénédictine**
**¾ oz. dry vermouth**
**¾ oz. lemon juice**

1. Fill a mixing glass with ice
2. Add Bénédictine, dry vermouth and lemon juice

3. Stir well
4. Strain into a chilled cocktail glass

# Quelle Vie

1½ oz. brandy
¾ oz. kummel

1. Fill mixing glass with ice
2. Add brandy and kummel
3. Stir
4. Strain into a chilled cocktail glass

# Quickie

1 oz. bourbon
1 oz. light rum
¼ oz. triple sec

1. Fill a mixing glass with ice
2. Add bourbon, light rum and triple sec
3. Stir well
4. Strain into a chilled cocktail glass

# R

## Racquet Club

1½ oz. gin
¾ oz. dry vermouth
dash orange bitters

1. Fill mixing glass with ice
2. Add gin, dry vermouth and orange bitters
3. Stir
4. Strain into a chilled cocktail glass

## Rainbow Pousse-Café

½ oz. dark crème de cacao
½ oz. crème de violette
½ oz. yellow Chartreuse
½ oz. maraschino liqueur
½ oz. Bénédictine
½ oz. green Chartreuse
½ oz. cognac

1. Pour dark crème de cacao into pousse-café glass
2. Float each of the other ingredients, one on top of the other, in the order indicated

## Ramos Fizz

1 oz. gin
½ oz. cream
1½ oz. sour mix

**2 dashes orange juice**
**1 egg white**
**club soda**

1. Fill mixing glass with ice
2. Add gin, cream, sour mix, orange juice and egg white
3. Shake
4. Strain into a chilled Collins glass
5. Fill with club soda


# Raspberry Smash

**1 oz. Absolut vodka**
**½ oz. Chambord**
**2 oz. pineapple juice**

1. Fill mixing glass with ice
2. Add Absolut, Chambord and pineapple juice
3. Shake
4. Strain into a rocks glass filled with ice


# Raspberry Vodka

**1 liter premium vodka (1000 ml)**
**2 cups sugar**
**1 lb. fresh raspberries**

1. In a container, combine vodka, sugar and raspberries
2. Cover tightly
3. Store container in a cool, dark place for approximately 8 weeks (Every week or so, open container and stir mixture)
4. Using a sieve, strain mixture into a glass jar
5. Refrigerate or store in freezer
6. Serve straight up or on the rocks

# Rattlesnake

1½ oz. blended whiskey
1 tsp. lemon juice
1 tsp. sugar
1 egg white
¼ tsp. Pernod

1. Fill mixing glass with ice
2. Add blended whiskey, lemon juice, sugar, egg white and Pernod
3. Shake
4. Strain into a rocks glass filled with ice

# Red Apple

1 oz. 100-proof vodka
1 oz. apple juice
½ oz. lemon juice
3–4 dashes grenadine
1–2 dashes orange bitters (optional)

1. Fill mixing glass with ice
2. Add vodka, apple juice, lemon juice, grenadine and orange bitters
3. Shake
4. Strain into a rocks glass filled with ice

# Red Baron

2 oz. gin
½ oz. sour mix
½ oz. orange juice
dash grenadine

1. Fill mixing glass with ice
2. Add gin, sour mix, orange juice and grenadine
3. Shake
4. Strain into a chilled cocktail glass

# Red Cloud

1½ oz. gin
½ oz. apricot liqueur
½ oz. lemon juice
3 dashes grenadine
2 dashes Angostura bitters

1. Fill mixing glass with ice
2. Add gin, apricot liqueur, lemon juice, grenadine and bitters
3. Shake
4. Strain into a rocks glass filled with ice

# Red Devil

½ oz. sloe gin
½ oz. vodka
½ oz. Southern Comfort
½ oz. triple sec
½ oz. banana liqueur
2 tbsp. Rose's lime juice
2 oz. orange juice

1. Fill mixing glass with ice
2. Add all ingredients
3. Shake well
4. Pour into a Collins glass

# Red Lion Cocktail

1 oz. gin
1 oz. Grand Marnier
½ oz. orange juice
½ oz. lemon juice

1. Fill mixing glass with ice
2. Add gin, Grand Marnier, orange juice and lemon juice
3. Shake
4. Strain into a chilled cocktail glass

# Red Snapper

1 oz. gin
Bloody Mary mix (packaged or from scratch—see Bloody
  Mary)

1. Fill a highball glass with ice
2. Add gin
3. Fill with Bloody Mary mix
4. Stir well
5. Garnish with lime slice or celery stalk

# Reform

1½ oz. dry sherry
¾ oz. dry vermouth
dash orange bitters

1. Fill a mixing glass with ice
2. Add dry sherry, dry vermouth and orange bitters
3. Strain into a chilled cocktail glass

# Renaissance Cocktail

1½ oz. gin
½ oz. dry sherry
1 tbsp. cream

1. Fill mixing glass with ice
2. Add gin, dry sherry and cream
3. Shake
4. Strain into a chilled cocktail glass
5. Garnish with a sprinkle of nutmeg

# Rendezvous

1½ oz. gin
½ oz. kirschwasser
½ oz. Campari

1. Fill mixing glass with ice
2. Add gin, kirschwasser and Campari
3. Shake
4. Strain into a chilled cocktail glass
5. Garnish with a lemon twist

# Resolute

1½ oz. gin
1 tbsp. apricot brandy
½ oz. lemon juice

1. Fill mixing glass with ice
2. Add gin, apricot brandy and lemon juice
3. Shake
4. Strain into a rocks glass filled with ice

# Rhett Butler

1 oz. Southern Comfort
½ oz. lime juice
½ oz. lemon juice
1 tsp. curaçao
½ tsp. sugar

1. Fill mixing glass with ice
2. Add Southern Comfort, lime juice, lemon juice, curaçao and sugar
3. Shake
4. Strain into a rocks glass filled with ice

# Rickey

1½ oz. liquor (of choice)
club soda

1. Fill a highball glass with ice
2. Add liquor
3. Fill with club soda
4. Garnish with a twist of lime

# Roasted Toasted Almond

¾ oz. vodka
¾ oz. Kahlúa
¾ oz. amaretto
¾ oz. cream

1. Fill mixing glass with ice
2. Add vodka, Kahlúa, amaretto and cream
3. Shake
4. Strain into a chilled cocktail glass

# Rob Roy

¼ oz. sweet vermouth
1½ oz. scotch

1. Fill a rocks glass with ice
2. Pour in sweet vermouth, then scotch
3. Stir
4. Garnish with a cherry

(*Note:* If serving "straight up," mix scotch and vermouth in a mixing glass and strain into a martini glass.)

# Rob Roy (dry)

¼ oz. dry vermouth
1½ oz. scotch

1. Fill a rocks glass with ice
2. Pour in dry vermouth, then scotch
3. Stir
4. Garnish with an olive

(*Note:* If serving "straight up," mix scotch and vermouth in a mixing glass and strain into a martini glass.)

# Rob Roy (perfect)

⅛ oz. dry vermouth
⅛ oz. sweet vermouth
1½ oz. scotch

1. Fill a rocks glass with ice
2. Pour in dry vermouth and sweet vermouth, then scotch
3. Stir
4. Garnish with a twist of lemon

(*Note:* If serving "straight up," mix scotch and vermouths in a mixing glass and strain into a martini glass.)

# Robson

1½ oz. Jamaican rum
1 tbsp. orange juice
1 tsp. grenadine
1 tsp. lemon juice

1. Fill mixing glass with ice
2. Add Jamaican rum, orange juice, grenadine and lemon juice
3. Shake
4. Strain into a rocks glass filled with ice

# Rockaway Beach

1½ oz. light rum
½ oz. dark rum
½ oz. tequila
1 oz. orange juice
½ oz. pineapple juice
½ oz. cranberry juice cocktail
1 tsp. crème de noyaux

1. Fill mixing glass with 4 oz. cracked ice
2. Add light rum, dark rum, tequila, orange juice, pineapple juice, cranberry juice and crème de noyaux
3. Shake
4. Strain into a chilled Collins glass
5. Add ice
6. Garnish with a cherry

# Rocky Green Dragon

1½ oz. gin
½ oz. green Chartreuse
½ oz. cognac

1. Fill mixing glass with ice
2. Add gin, green Chartreuse and cognac
3. Shake
4. Strain into a rocks glass filled with ice

# Rolls Royce

1½ oz. gin
½ oz. dry vermouth
½ oz. sweet vermouth
3–4 dashes Bénédictine

1. Fill mixing glass with ice
2. Add gin, dry vermouth, sweet vermouth and Bénédictine
3. Stir
4. Strain into a chilled cocktail glass

## Roman Stinger

1½ oz. brandy
¾ oz. sambuca
¾ oz. white crème de menthe

1. Fill mixing glass with ice
2. Add brandy, sambuca and white crème de menthe
3. Shake
4. Strain into a chilled cocktail glass

## Rose Hall

1½ oz. Jamaican rum
½ oz. banana liqueur
1 oz. orange juice
1 tsp. Rose's lime juice

1. Fill mixing glass with ice
2. Add rum, banana liqueur, orange juice and lime juice
3. Shake
4. Strain into a chilled cocktail glass
5. Garnish with a slice of lime

## Rouffy Party Punch Cooler

1 liter vodka
1 6-oz. can frozen lemonade concentrate, defrosted
1 6-oz. can frozen orange juice concentrate, defrosted
1 cup water
7-Up

1. In a large bowl, combine vodka, frozen juice concentrates and water
2. Stir well
3. Place in freezer until frozen
4. When ready to serve, use an ice-cream scooper to shave off some of the concoction into highball glasses
5. Fill with 7-Up

# Royal Fizz

1 oz. gin
2 oz. sour mix
1 egg
club soda

1. Fill mixing glass with ice
2. Add gin, sour mix and egg
3. Shake
4. Strain into a chilled Collins glass
5. Fill with club soda

# Royal Gin Fizz

2 oz. gin
½ oz. Grand Marnier
1 oz. sour mix
1 egg
club soda

1. Fill mixing glass with ice
2. Add gin, Grand Marnier, sour mix and egg
3. Shake
4. Strain into a chilled sour glass
5. Fill with club soda
   Garnish with a slice of lemon

# Royal Peach Freeze

1½ oz. champagne
2 oz. peach schnapps
2 oz. orange juice
½ oz. Rose's lime juice

1. In blender, combine champagne, peach schnapps, orange juice and Rose's lime juice with 3 oz. crushed ice
2. Blend until smooth
3. Pour into a goblet

# Royal Screw

2 oz. cognac
2 oz. orange juice, chilled
champagne

1. Pour cognac into a champagne glass
2. Add orange juice
3. Stir gently
4. Fill with champagne

# Royal Smile

1½ oz. gin
1 oz. grenadine
3–4 drops lemon juice

1. Fill mixing glass with ice
2. Add gin, grenadine and lemon juice
3. Shake
4. Strain into a chilled cocktail glass

# Ruby Fizz

**2 oz. sloe gin**
**½ oz. lemon juice**
**1 tsp. sugar**
**1 tsp. grenadine**
**1 egg white**
**club soda**

1. Fill mixing glass with ice
2. Add sloe gin, lemon juice, sugar, grenadine and egg white
3. Shake
4. Strain into a chilled highball glass
5. Add ice
6. Fill with club soda

# Rum and Orange Juice

**1½ oz. rum (usually dark rum)**
**orange juice**

1. Fill a highball glass with ice
2. Add rum
3. Fill with orange juice
4. Stir

# Rum and Tonic

**1½ oz. rum (light or dark, depending on taste)**
**tonic water**

1. Fill a highball glass with ice
2. Add rum
3. Fill with tonic water
4. Stir
5. Garnish with a slice of lime (optional)

# Rum Collins

2 oz. light rum
1 tsp. sugar syrup
½ oz. lime juice
club soda

1. Fill a Collins glass with ice
2. Add light rum, sugar syrup and lime juice
3. Stir well
4. Fill with club soda
5. Garnish with a slice of lime

# Rum Curaçao Cooler

1½ oz. dark rum
1½ oz. curaçao
½ oz. lime juice
club soda

1. Fill mixing glass with ice
2. Add dark rum, curaçao and lime juice
3. Shake
4. Strain into a highball glass filled with ice
5. Fill with club soda
6. Garnish with a slice of orange

# Rum Rickey

1½ oz. light rum
½ oz. lime juice
1 tsp. sugar syrup (optional)
club soda

1. Fill mixing glass with ice
2. Add light rum and lime juice (and sugar syrup, if desired)
3. Shake

4. Strain into a Collins glass filled with ice
5. Fill with club soda
6. Garnish with a wedge of lime

# Rum Sour

**2 oz. light rum (dark rum may be used instead)**
**1 tsp. lime juice**
**1 oz. sour mix**
**dash orange juice**

1. Fill mixing glass with ice
2. Add rum, lime juice, sour mix and orange juice
3. Shake
4. Strain into a sour glass
5. Fill with ice
6. Garnish with a cherry and an orange slice

# Ruptured Duck

**1 oz. banana liqueur**
**1 oz. crème de noyaux**
**1 oz. cream**

1. Fill mixing glass with ice
2. Add banana liqueur, crème de noyaux and cream
3. Shake
4. Strain into a chilled cocktail glass

# Russian

**1 oz. gin**
**1 oz. vodka**
**1 oz. white crème de cacao**

1. Fill mixing glass with ice
2. Add gin, vodka and white crème de cacao

3. Shake
4. Strain into a chilled cocktail glass

# Russian Banana

¾ oz. vodka
¾ oz. banana liqueur
¾ oz. dark crème de cacao
1 oz. cream

1. Fill mixing glass with ice
2. Add vodka, banana liqueur, dark crème de cacao and cream
3. Shake
4. Strain into a chilled cocktail glass

# Russian Bear

1 oz. vodka
1 oz. dark crème de cacao
1 oz. heavy cream

1. Fill mixing glass with ice
2. Add vodka, dark crème de cacao and heavy cream
3. Shake
4. Strain into a chilled cocktail glass

# Russian Coffee

¾ oz. vodka
¾ oz. coffee liqueur
¾ oz. heavy cream

1. Fill blender with 3 oz. cracked ice
2. Add vodka, coffee liqueur and heavy cream
3. Blend for 5 seconds, or until smooth
4. Pour into a cocktail glass

# Russian Quaalude

⅓ oz. Frangelico
⅓ oz. Bailey's Original Irish Cream
⅓ oz. vodka

1. Layer Frangelico, Bailey's and vodka in a rocks glass without ice

# Russian Rose

2 oz. vodka
2 tbsp. grenadine
dash orange bitters

1. Fill mixing glass with ice
2. Add vodka, grenadine and orange bitters
3. Shake
4. Strain into a chilled cocktail glass

# Russian Turkey

2 oz. vodka
2 oz. cranberry juice cocktail

1. Fill a rocks glass with ice
2. Add vodka and cranberry juice
3. Stir

# Rusty Nail

2 oz. scotch
1 oz. Drambuie

1. Fill a rocks glass with ice
2. Add scotch and Drambuie
3. Stir

# S

## St. Patrick's Day Mocha Java

¾ oz. Bailey's Irish Cream
¾ oz. Kahlúa
hot coffee
whipped cream

1. Pour Bailey's and Kahlúa into a mug
2. Fill with hot coffee
3. Top with whipped cream

(Courtesy of Carrow's, Santa Barbara, California)

## Saketini

2½ oz. gin
½ oz. sake

1. Fill mixing glass with ice
2. Add gin and sake
3. Stir
4. Strain into a chilled cocktail glass or a rocks glass filled with ice
5. Garnish with a twist of lemon

## Salty Dog

1½ oz. vodka
grapefruit juice

1. Salt the rim of a highball glass
2. Fill with ice
3. Add vodka
4. Fill with grapefruit juice
5. Stir

## Sambuca-Gin Shake

**2 oz. gin**
**½ oz. sambuca**
**1 egg white**
**½ oz. cream**

1. Half-fill mixing glass with crushed ice
2. Add gin, sambuca, egg white and cream
3. Shake
4. Pour into a rocks glass

## Sanctuary

**1½ oz. Dubonnet (rouge)**
**¾ oz. Amer Picon**
**¾ oz. Cointreau**

1. Fill mixing glass with ice
2. Add Dubonnet, Amer Picon and Cointreau
3. Shake
4. Strain into a rocks glass filled with ice

## San Francisco

**¾ oz. sloe gin**
**½ oz. dry vermouth**
**½ oz. sweet vermouth**
**dash Angostura bitters**
**dash orange bitters**

1. Fill mixing glass with ice
2. Add sloe gin, dry vermouth, sweet vermouth, Angostura bitters and orange bitters
3. Shake
4. Strain into a rocks glass filled with ice
5. Garnish with a cherry

# Sangria

1 bottle dry red wine
1 oz. brandy (optional)
1 oz. triple sec or curaçao (optional)
1 tbsp. sugar or to taste
club soda, very cold
orange slices
lime slices
lemon slice
several pineapple chunks

1. In a large pitcher, combine red wine, brandy, triple sec, sugar and fruit
2. Refrigerate overnight
3. When ready to serve, add club soda and more sugar (if desired)
4. Stir

(For a white sangria, substitute white wine for red wine.)

# Sangria Especiale

2 bottles red wine
1 bottle champagne
4 oz. gin
4 oz. cognac
sugar, to taste
juice of 2 oranges
juice of 2 lemons

1. Add all ingredients to a punch bowl
2. Stir
3. Add ice
4. Garnish with slices of oranges and lemons

# Sangria Shabbabe

1 tbsp. sugar
1 tbsp. lemon juice
2 oz. red wine
1 oz. white wine
1 oz. orange juice
7-Up
fresh orange and lemon slices

1. In a bottle or large wineglass, dissolve sugar in lemon juice
2. Fill the bottle or glass with ice
3. Pour in red wine, white wine and orange juice
4. Stir well
5. Fill with 7-Up
6. Garnish with orange and lemon slices

# San Juan

1½ oz. Puerto Rican rum
1 oz. grapefruit juice
1 oz. lime juice
½ oz. cream of coconut
2–3 dashes 151-proof rum

1. In a blender, combine 3 oz. crushed ice, Puerto Rican rum, grapefruit juice, lime juice and cream of coconut
2. Blend for 10 seconds at medium speed, or until smooth
3. Pour into a goblet or large wineglass
4. Top with 151-proof rum

# San Sebastian

1 oz. gin
1½ tsp. light rum
1½ tsp. triple sec

**1 tbsp. grapefruit juice**
**1 tbsp. lemon juice**

1. Fill mixing glass with ice
2. Add gin, light rum, triple sec, grapefruit juice and lemon juice
3. Shake
4. Strain into a chilled cocktail glass

# Sapphire Martini

**¼ oz. Chambraise**
**1½ oz. Bombay Sapphire gin**

1. Fill mixing glass with ice
2. Add Chambraise and Bombay Sapphire gin
3. Stir
4. Strain into a chilled cocktail glass or a rocks glass filled with ice
5. Garnish with a fresh strawberry

(Courtesy of Oscar Taylor's, Phoenix, Arizona)

# Saratoga

**2 oz. brandy**
**1 oz. crushed pineapple**
**2 dashes maraschino liqueur**
**2 dashes Angostura bitters**

1. Fill mixing glass with ice
2. Add brandy, crushed pineapple, maraschino liqueur and bitters
3. Shake
4. Strain into a chilled cocktail glass

# Saucy Sue

2 oz. apple brandy
½ tsp. apricot brandy
½ tsp. Pernod

1. Fill mixing glass with ice
2. Add apple brandy, apricot brandy and Pernod
3. Stir
4. Strain into a chilled cocktail glass

# Save the Planet

1 oz. vodka
1 oz. Midori melon liqueur
½ oz. blue curaçao
1–2 dashes green Chartreuse

1. Fill shaker glass with ice
2. Add vodka, Midori and blue curaçao
3. Shake
4. Strain into a chilled cocktail glass
5. Float green Chartreuse on top

# Savoy Hotel

½ oz. white crème de cacao
½ oz. Bénédictine
½ oz. brandy

Slowly layer ingredients, beginning with white crème de cacao, into a pony glass

# Savoy Springtime

¼ oz. gin
¼ oz. Cointreau
¼ oz. fresh orange juice
chilled champagne

1. Pour gin, Cointreau and orange juice into a champagne glass
2. Fill with chilled champagne
3. Stir very gently

(From the Savoy Hotel, London, England)

# Savoy Tango

1½ oz. apple brandy
1 oz. sloe gin

1. Fill mixing glass with ice
2. Add apple brandy and sloe gin
3. Stir
4. Strain into a chilled cocktail glass

# Sazerac

2 oz. bourbon
1 tsp. superfine granulated sugar
2 dashes Angostura bitters
3 dashes Pernod

1. Pour bourbon into a mixing glass
2. Add sugar and bitters
3. Stir until sugar is dissolved
4. Put Pernod into a rocks glass
5. Strain mixture into rocks glass
6. Fill with ice

# Scarlet O'Hara

**1½ oz. Southern Comfort**
**cranberry juice cocktail**

1. Fill a highball glass with ice
2. Add Southern Comfort
3. Fill with cranberry juice (grenadine may be substituted)

# Scorpion

**2 oz. light rum**
**1 oz. brandy**
**2 oz. orange juice**
**½ oz. lemon juice**
**½ oz. crème de noyaux**

1. Fill blender with 3 oz. crushed ice, light rum, brandy, orange juice, lemon juice and crème de noyaux
2. Blend until smooth
3. Pour into a highball glass
4. Garnish with a slice of orange

# Scotch and Soda

**1½ oz. scotch**
**club soda**

1. Fill a highball glass with ice
2. Add scotch
3. Fill with club soda
4. Stir gently

# Scotch Mist

**1½ oz. scotch**

1. Fill a rocks glass with crushed ice
2. Add scotch
3. Garnish with a twist of lemon

# Scotch Stone Sour

**1½ oz. scotch whiskey**
**¾ oz. lemon juice**
**1 tsp. sugar**
**1½ oz. orange juice**

1. Fill mixing glass with ice
2. Add scotch, lemon juice, sugar and orange juice
3. Shake
4. Strain into a sour glass or a rocks glass filled with ice
5. Garnish with a cherry and a slice of orange

# Scottish Coffee

**1½ oz. Drambuie**
**hot coffee**
**whipped cream**

1. Pour Drambuie into a coffee mug
2. Fill with hot coffee
3. Top with whipped cream

# Screwdriver

**1½ oz. vodka**
**orange juice**

1. Fill a highball glass with ice
2. Add vodka
3. Fill with orange juice
4. Stir

# Sea Breeze

**1½ oz. vodka**
**3 oz. cranberry juice cocktail**
**3 oz. grapefruit juice**

1. Fill highball glass with ice
2. Add vodka, cranberry juice and grapefruit juice
3. Stir

(*Note:* In general, people usually like a bit more cranberry juice than grapefruit juice, but it is purely a matter of taste.)

# Self-Starter

**1 oz. gin**
**½ oz. Lillet**
**1 tsp. apricot brandy**
**2–3 drops Pernod**

1. Fill mixing glass with ice
2. Add gin, Lillet, apricot brandy and Pernod
3. Shake
4. Strain into a chilled cocktail glass

# Separator
## (also called a Dirty Mother)

**1½ oz. brandy**
**¾ oz. Kahlúa**

1. Fill a rocks glass with ice
2. Add brandy and Kahlúa
3. Stir

# September Morn

**2½ oz. light rum**
**½ oz. lime juice**
**1 tsp. grenadine**
**1 egg white**

1. Fill mixing glass with ice
2. Add light rum, lime juice, grenadine and egg white
3. Shake
4. Strain into a chilled highball glass

# 7 & 7

**1½ oz. Seagram's 7 blended whiskey**
**7-Up**

1. Fill a highball glass with ice
2. Add Seagram's 7
3. Fill with 7-Up
4. Garnish with cherry and an orange slice (optional) or a twist of lemon (optional)

# Seventh Heaven

**1 oz. Seagram's 7 whiskey**
**¼ oz. amaretto**
**orange juice**

1. Fill a highball glass with ice
2. Add Seagram's 7 and amaretto
3. Fill with orange juice
4. Stir

# Sevilla

**1 oz. dark Jamaican rum**
**1 oz. sweet vermouth**

1. Fill mixing glass with ice
2. Add dark Jamaican rum and sweet vermouth
3. Shake
4. Strain into a rocks glass filled with ice
5. Garnish with a twist of orange

# Seville

**1½ oz. gin**
**½ oz. fino sherry**
**½ oz. lemon juice**
**½ oz. orange juice**
**2 tsp. sugar syrup**

1. Half-fill mixing glass with ice
2. Add gin, fino sherry, lemon juice, orange juice and sugar syrup
3. Shake
4. Pour into a rocks glass

# Sex on the Beach

¾ oz. peach schnapps
¾ oz. vodka
3 oz. pineapple juice (grapefruit juice may be substituted)
3 oz. cranberry juice cocktail

1. Fill a highball glass with ice
2. Add peach schnapps and vodka
3. Fill with pineapple juice (or grapefruit juice) and cranberry juice
4. Stir

## Sex on the Beach (the original)

1 oz. vodka
½ oz. Midori melon liqueur
½ oz. Chambord (or other raspberry liqueur)
1½ oz. pineapple juice
1½ oz. cranberry juice cocktail

1. Fill mixing glass with ice
2. Add vodka, Midori, Chambord, pineapple juice and cranberry juice
3. Shake
4. Pour into a highball glass

(*Note:* This can also be made into a shooter. This recipe will yield approximately 3 shots. You may want to cut down on the juices a bit.)

## Sex on the Beach in Winter

¾ oz. peach schnapps
¾ oz. vodka
3 oz. pineapple juice (grapefruit juice may be substituted)
3 oz. cranberry juice cocktail
½ tsp. cream of coconut

1. Fill blender with 3 oz. ice, peach schnapps, vodka, pineapple juice (or grapefruit juice) and cranberry juice
2. Blend until smooth
3. Pour into a goblet or Collins glass

## Shandy

**cold beer**
**1 oz. 7-Up**

1. Fill beer mug with cold beer (preferably draft beer)
2. Top with 7-Up

## Shanghai

**1½ oz. dark rum**
**1 oz. sambuca**
**½ oz. lemon juice**
**3 drops grenadine**

1. Fill mixing glass with ice
2. Add dark rum, sambuca, lemon juice and grenadine
3. Shake
4. Strain into a chilled cocktail glass

## Shark Bite

**1½ oz. Myers's dark rum**
**3 oz. orange juice**
**½ oz. sour mix**
**¾ oz. grenadine**

1. Combine Myers's rum, orange juice, sour mix and grenadine with 3 oz. ice in a blender
2. Blend until smooth
3. Pour into a goblet
4. Add a couple of straws and watch the pinks separate

(Courtesy of The Shark Bar, New York City)

# Shark's Tooth

1½ oz. dark Jamaican rum
½ oz. lime juice
½ oz. lemon juice
¼ oz. grenadine
club soda

1. Fill mixing glass with ice
2. Add rum, lime juice, lemon juice and grenadine
3. Shake
4. Strain into a highball glass filled with ice
5. Fill with club soda

# Sharky Punch

1½ oz. apple brandy
½ oz. rye whiskey
1 tsp. sugar syrup
club soda

1. Fill mixing glass with ice
2. Add apple brandy, rye whiskey and sugar syrup
3. Shake
4. Strain into a rocks glass filled with ice
5. Fill with club soda

# Sherry Cocktail

2½ oz. cream sherry
1 dash Angostura bitters

1. Fill mixing glass with ice
2. Add cream sherry and bitters
3. Stir
4. Strain into a chilled cocktail glass

# Sherry Eggnog

3 oz. sherry
1 egg
1 tsp. powdered sugar
1 cup milk

1. In a blender, combine 3 oz. crushed ice, sherry, egg, sugar and milk
2. Blend
3. Pour into a chilled goblet or Collins glass
4. Garnish with a pinch of nutmeg

# Sherry Twist

3 oz. sherry
1 oz. brandy
1 oz. dry vermouth
½ oz. curaçao
2–3 dashes lemon juice

1. Fill mixing glass with ice
2. Add sherry, brandy, dry vermouth, curaçao and lemon juice
3. Shake
4. Strain into a chilled sour glass
5. Add ice, if desired
6. Garnish with a pinch of ground cinnamon

# Sicilian Kiss

1½ oz. Southern Comfort
½ oz. amaretto

1. Fill a rocks glass with ice
2. Add Southern Comfort and amaretto
3. Stir

# Sidecar

1½ oz. brandy
¾ oz. triple sec
¾ oz. sour mix

1. Fill mixing glass with ice
2. Add brandy, triple sec and sour mix
3. Shake
4. Strain into a chilled cocktail glass

# Silk Panties (shooter)

¾ oz. peach schnapps
¾ oz. sambuca

1. Fill mixing glass with ice
2. Add peach schnapps and sambuca
3. Stir
4. Strain into a shot glass

# Silver Fizz

1 oz. gin
2 oz. sour mix
1 egg white
club soda

1. Fill mixing glass with ice
2. Add gin, sour mix and egg white
3. Shake
4. Strain into a chilled Collins glass
5. Fill with club soda

# Silver King

**1 oz. gin**
**1 oz. lemon juice**
**1 egg white**
**2–3 drops sugar syrup**
**2 dashes orange bitters**

1. Fill mixing glass with ice
2. Add gin, lemon juice, egg white, sugar syrup and orange bitters
3. Shake
4. Strain into a highball glass
5. Fill with ice

# Silver Nipple

**1½ oz. sambuca**
**1 oz. vodka**

1. Fill a rocks glass with ice
2. Add sambuca and vodka
3. Stir

# Singapore Sling

**1 oz. gin**
**2 oz. sour mix**
**½ oz. grenadine**
**club soda**
**1 dash cherry brandy**

1. Fill mixing glass with ice
2. Add gin, sour mix and grenadine
3. Shake
4. Strain into a Collins glass filled with ice
5. Fill with club soda
6. Top with cherry brandy

## Sink or Swim

1½ oz. brandy
½ oz. sweet vermouth
2–3 dashes Angostura bitters

1. Fill mixing glass with ice
2. Add brandy, sweet vermouth and bitters
3. Shake
4. Strain into a rocks glass filled with ice

## Sir Walter

1½ oz. brandy
¾ oz. light rum
1 tsp. curaçao
1 tsp. grenadine
1 tsp. lime juice

1. Fill mixing glass with ice
2. Add brandy, light rum, curaçao, grenadine and lime juice
3. Shake
4. Strain into a rocks glass filled with ice

## Skip and Go Naked

1 oz. gin
2 oz. sour mix
beer

1. Fill a Collins glass with ice
2. Add gin and sour mix
3. Fill with beer
4. Stir

# Sledgehammer

**¾ oz. brandy**
**¾ oz. gold rum**
**¾ oz. apple brandy**
**1 dash Pernod**

1. Fill mixing glass with ice
2. Add brandy, gold rum, apple brandy and Pernod
3. Shake
4. Strain into a chilled cocktail glass

# Sleepyhead

**3 oz. brandy**
**ginger ale**

1. Fill a rocks glass with ice
2. Add brandy
3. Top with ginger ale
4. Garnish with a twist of orange

# Slimeball (shooter)

**½ cup Midori melon liqueur**
**1 cup boiling water**
**lime Jell-O brand gelatin**
**½ cup vodka**

1. Add Midori and boiling water to lime Jell-O
2. Add vodka
3. Chill to set
4. Serve in paper soufflé cups

(The Slimeball is a variation of the Jell-O Shot.)

# Slippery Nipple

2 oz. sambuca
1½ oz. Bailey's Original Irish Cream
drop grenadine

1. Pour sambuca into a cocktail glass
2. Float Bailey's on top
3. Put a drop of grenadine right in the center

# Sloe Brandy

2 oz. brandy
½ oz. sloe gin
1 tsp. lemon juice

1. Fill mixing glass with ice
2. Add brandy, sloe gin and lemon juice
3. Shake
4. Strain into a chilled cocktail glass

# Sloe Comfortable Screw

½ oz. vodka
½ oz. sloe gin
½ oz. Southern Comfort
orange juice

1. Fill a highball glass with ice
2. Add vodka, sloe gin and Southern Comfort
3. Fill with orange juice
4. Stir

# Sloe Gin Fizz

1 oz. sloe gin
2 oz. sour mix
club soda

1. Fill mixing glass with ice
2. Add sloe gin and sour mix
3. Shake
4. Strain into a chilled Collins glass
5. Fill with club soda
6. Garnish with a cherry

# Sloe Screw

¾ oz. vodka
¾ oz. sloe gin
orange juice

1. Fill a highball glass with ice
2. Add vodka and sloe gin
3. Fill with orange juice
4. Stir

# Sloe Tequila

2 oz. tequila
½ oz. sloe gin
1 tsp. lime juice

1. Fill mixing glass with ice
2. Add tequila, sloe gin and lime juice
3. Shake
4. Strain into a chilled cocktail glass

# Sloppy Joe

½ oz. light rum
½ oz. dry vermouth
1 oz. lime juice
2–3 drops triple sec
2–3 drops grenadine

1. Fill mixing glass with ice
2. Add light rum, dry vermouth, lime juice, triple sec and grenadine
3. Shake
4. Strain into a rocks glass filled with ice

## Smith and Kerns

1½ oz. Kahlúa
1 oz. cream
club soda

1. Fill a highball glass with ice
2. Add Kahlúa and cream
3. Stir
4. Fill with club soda
5. Stir again, gently

## Snowball

1 oz. gin
¼ oz. white crème de menthe
¼ oz. Pernod
¼ oz. crème d'Yvette
¼ oz. cream

1. Fill mixing glass with ice
2. Add gin, white crème de menthe, Pernod, crème d'Yvette and cream
3. Shake
4. Strain into a chilled cocktail glass or champagne saucer

## Snow Cap (shooter)

½ oz. tequila
½ oz. Bailey's Original Irish Cream

Layer tequila and Bailey's in a shot glass

# Snow Shoe

1½ oz. 101-proof Wild Turkey bourbon
½ oz. peppermint schnapps

1. Fill a rocks glass with ice
2. Add Wild Turkey and peppermint schnapps
3. Stir

# Snuggler

1½ oz. peppermint schnapps
hot chocolate

1. Pour peppermint schnapps into a mug
2. Fill with hot chocolate
3. Top with whipped cream, if desired

# S.O.B. Shooter (shooter)

⅓ oz. Cointreau
⅓ oz. brandy
⅓ oz. 151-proof rum

Pour all ingredients into a shot glass

# Sombrero

1½ oz. Kahlúa
½ oz. cream

1. Fill a rocks glass with ice
2. Add Kahlúa
3. Top with cream
4. Stir

# Soul Kiss

**1 oz. whiskey**
**1 oz. dry vermouth**
**½ oz. Dubonnet**
**¾ oz. orange juice**

1. Fill mixing glass with ice
2. Add whiskey, dry vermouth, Dubonnet and orange juice
3. Stir
4. Strain into a rocks glass filled with ice

# Sour Grapes (shooter)

**2 oz. vodka**
**2 oz. Chambord**
**2 oz. sour mix**

1. Fill mixing glass with ice
2. Add vodka, Chambord and sour mix
3. Shake
4. Strain into shot glasses

(Makes about 4 shots)

# Southern Bride

**1½ oz. gin**
**1 oz. grapefruit juice**
**1 dash maraschino liqueur**

1. Fill a mixing glass with ice
2. Add gin, grapefruit juice and maraschino liqueur
3. Shake
4. Strain into a chilled cocktail glass

# Southern Gin

2½ oz. gin
2 dashes orange bitters
3–4 drops curaçao

1. Fill mixing glass with ice
2. Add gin, orange bitters and curaçao
3. Shake
4. Strain into a chilled cocktail glass

# Soviet Cocktail

1½ oz. vodka
½ oz. amontillado sherry
½ oz. dry vermouth

1. Fill mixing glass with ice
2. Add vodka, amontillado sherry and dry vermouth
3. Shake
4. Strain into a chilled cocktail glass

# Spanish Coffee

¾ oz. brandy
¾ oz. Tia Maria
hot coffee

1. Pour brandy and Tia Maria into a coffee mug
2. Fill with hot coffee
3. Top with whipped cream, if desired

# Spanish Moss

**1½ oz. tequila**
**1 oz. coffee liqueur**
**3 drops green crème de menthe**

1. Fill mixing glass with ice
2. Add tequila and coffee liqueur
3. Shake
4. Strain into a chilled cocktail glass
5. Add a few drops of green crème de menthe to top

# Spanish Town

**1½ oz. light rum**
**2 dashes triple sec**

1. Fill mixing glass with ice
2. Add light rum and triple sec
3. Stir
4. Strain into a chilled cocktail glass

# Sparkling Wine Julep

**2 sprigs of mint**
**1 tbsp. sugar syrup**
**1½ oz. brandy**
**3 oz. chilled dry sparkling wine**

1. In a champagne glass, put 1 sprig of mint and sugar syrup
2. Crush mint in sugar syrup

3. Fill glass with crushed ice
4. Add brandy
5. Fill with sparkling wine
6. Stir gently
7. Garnish with the other sprig of mint

# Sparkling Wine Polonaise

**1 tsp. blackberry liqueur**
**1 tsp. blackberry brandy**
**½ tsp. cognac**
**3 oz. chilled dry sparkling wine**

1. Moisten the rim of a chilled champagne glass with blackberry liqueur and sugar-frost the rim
2. Pour in blackberry brandy, cognac and sparkling wine
3. Stir very gently two or three times

# Special Rough

**1 oz. apple brandy**
**1 oz. brandy**
**dash Pernod**

1. Fill mixing glass with ice
2. Add apple brandy, brandy and Pernod
3. Stir
4. Strain into a chilled cocktail glass

# Sphinx

**2 oz. gin**
**2 tsp. sweet vermouth**
**2 tsp. dry vermouth**

1. Fill mixing glass with ice
2. Add gin, sweet vermouth and dry vermouth
3. Stir
4. Strain into a chilled cocktail glass
5. Garnish with a slice of lemon

## Star

**1½ oz. apple brandy**
**1½ oz. sweet vermouth**
**2 dashes orange bitters**

1. Fill mixing glass with ice
2. Add apple brandy, sweet vermouth and orange bitters
3. Shake
4. Strain into a chilled cocktail glass

## Stars and Stripes

**1 oz. grenadine**
**1 oz. heavy cream**
**1 oz. blue curaçao**

1. Pour grenadine into a pousse-café glass
2. Float cream on top
3. Float blue curaçao on top of that

## Stinger

**1½ oz. brandy**
**½ oz. white crème de menthe**

1. Fill mixing glass with ice
2. Add brandy and white crème de menthe
3. Stir
4. Strain into a chilled cocktail glass

## Stone Fence

3 oz. apple brandy
2 dashes Angostura bitters
sweet apple cider

1. Fill a rocks glass with ice
2. Pour in apple brandy and bitters
3. Fill glass with chilled cider

## Stone Sour

1½ oz. bourbon
½ oz. lemon juice
1 tsp. white crème de menthe
½ tsp. sugar (or to taste)
club soda

1. Fill a sour glass almost to the top with crushed ice
2. Pour in bourbon, lemon juice, white crème de menthe and sugar
3. Stir
4. Fill with club soda
5. Garnish with several sprigs of mint

## Stonewall

2 oz. apple cider
1 oz. Jamaican rum

1. Fill mixing glass with ice
2. Add apple cider and rum
3. Shake
4. Strain into a rocks glass filled with ice

# Stony Brook

**1½ oz. blended whiskey**
**½ oz. triple sec**
**½ egg white**
**2–3 drops almond extract**

1. Fill mixing glass with ice
2. Add blended whiskey, triple sec, egg white and almond extract
3. Shake
4. Strain into a rocks glass filled with ice
5. Garnish with a twist of lemon

# Stormin' Gorman

**1½ oz. vodka**
**juice of half a lemon**
**splash Cointreau**
**splash Mandarine Napoléon liqueur**

1. Fill mixing glass with ice
2. Add vodka, lemon juice, Cointreau and Mandarine Napoléon liqueur
3. Shake
4. Strain into a chilled martini glass

(Courtesy of Christine Gorman at Strings, Denver, Colorado)

# Straight Law

2½ oz. dry sherry
¼ oz. gin

1. Fill mixing glass with ice
2. Add dry sherry and gin
3. Shake
4. Strain into a chilled cocktail glass
5. Garnish with a twist of lemon

# Strawberry-Cranberry Frost

2 oz. vodka
4 oz. sliced frozen strawberries, in syrup, partially thawed
4 oz. cranberry juice cocktail

1. Fill blender with vodka, frozen strawberries, cranberry juice and 3 oz. crushed ice
2. Blend until smooth
3. Pour into a large goblet
4. Garnish with a whole strawberry and a sprig of mint

# Strawberry Shortcake

2 scoops vanilla ice cream
1 oz. crème de noyaux
½ oz. crème de cacao
6 whole strawberries, stems removed
whipped cream
1 tsp. strawberry liqueur

1. Combine vanilla ice cream, crème de noyaux, crème de cacao and 5 of the 6 strawberries in a blender
2. Blend until smooth
3. Pour into a large goblet
4. Top with whipped cream
5. Drizzle strawberry liqueur on top
6. Garnish with the 6th strawberry

# Strega Sour

1 oz. gin
½ oz. Strega
2 oz. sour mix

1. Fill mixing glass with ice
2. Add gin, Strega and sour mix
3. Shake
4. Strain into a chilled cocktail glass

# Suisesse

1 oz. Pernod
1 oz. lemon juice
1 egg white
club soda

1. Fill mixing glass with ice
2. Add Pernod, lemon juice and egg white
3. Shake
4. Strain into a rocks glass filled with ice
5. Top with club soda

# Summer Share

1 oz. vodka
1 oz. light rum
½ oz. tequila
1 oz. orange juice
1 oz. cranberry juice cocktail
1 dash apricot liqueur
7-Up

1. Fill mixing glass with ice
2. Add vodka, light rum, tequila, orange juice, cranberry juice and apricot liqueur

3. Shake
4. Strain into a chilled Collins glass
5. Add ice
6. Top with 7-Up
7. Garnish with a slice of orange

# Sunbeam

**1½ oz. Galliano**
**½ oz. sweet vermouth**

1. Fill rocks glass with ice
2. Add Galliano and sweet vermouth
3. Stir

# Sundowner

**2 oz. light rum**
**1 oz. lemon juice**
**3–4 dashes grenadine**
**tonic water**

1. Fill mixing glass with ice
2. Add light rum, lemon juice and grenadine
3. Shake
4. Strain into a highball glass filled with ice
5. Fill with tonic water

# Super Coffee

**¾ oz. brandy**
**¾ oz. Kahlúa**
**hot coffee**

1. Pour brandy and Kahlúa into a coffee mug or hot drink glass
2. Fill with hot coffee
3. Top with whipped cream

# Swamp Water

2 oz. rum
¼ oz. blue curaçao
1 oz. orange juice
½ oz. lemon juice

1. Fill mixing glass with ice
2. Add rum, blue curaçao, orange juice and lemon juice
3. Shake
4. Strain into a rocks glass filled with ice

# Swayze Swizzle

1½ oz. dark rum
passion fruit juice
orange juice
cranberry juice cocktail

1. Fill a highball glass with ice
2. Add dark rum
3. Fill glass with equal parts passion fruit juice, orange juice and cranberry juice
4. Stir

(Courtesy of Mulholland Drive Cafe, New York City, owned by Patrick Swayze)

# Swedish Lullaby

1½ oz. Swedish Punsch
1 oz. cherry liqueur
½ oz. lemon juice

1. Fill mixing glass with ice
2. Add Swedish Punsch, cherry liqueur and lemon juice
3. Shake
4. Strain into a chilled cocktail glass

# Sweet Cream

**1½ oz. Kahlúa**
**½ oz. Bailey's Irish Cream**

1. Pour Kahlúa into cordial glass or pousse-café
2. Float Bailey's on top

# Sweetie Baby

**2 oz. amaretto**
**5 oz. vanilla ice cream**
**½ oz. milk (optional)**

1. In a blender, combine amaretto, vanilla ice cream and milk
2. Blend at medium speed until smooth
3. Pour into a goblet or other large stemmed glass
4. Garnish with crushed almonds

# Sweet Patootie

**1 oz. gin**
**½ oz. triple sec**
**½ oz. orange juice**

1. Fill mixing glass with ice
2. Add gin, triple sec and orange juice
3. Shake
4. Strain into a chilled cocktail glass

# T

## Tahiti Club

2 oz. gold rum
½ oz. lime juice
½ oz. lemon juice
½ oz. pineapple juice
2–3 dashes maraschino liqueur

1. Fill mixing glass with cracked ice
2. Add gold rum, lime juice, lemon juice, pineapple juice and maraschino liqueur
3. Shake
4. Pour into a rocks glass
5. Garnish with a slice of orange

## Tango

1½ oz. gin
¼ oz. dry vermouth
¼ oz. sweet vermouth
¾ oz. orange juice
2–3 dashes curaçao

1. Fill mixing glass with cracked ice
2. Add gin, dry vermouth, sweet vermouth, orange juice and curaçao
3. Shake
4. Strain into a rocks glass filled with ice

# Tantalus

**1 oz. brandy**
**1 oz. lemon juice**
**¼ oz. Forbidden Fruit**

1. Fill mixing glass with ice
2. Add brandy, lemon juice and Forbidden Fruit
3. Shake
4. Strain into a rocks glass filled with ice

# Tawny Russian

**1 oz. amaretto**
**1 oz. vodka**

1. Fill a rocks glass with ice
2. Add amaretto and vodka
3. Stir

# Teddy Bear (shooter)

**½ oz. root-beer schnapps**
**½ oz. vodka**

Layer root-beer schnapps and vodka in a shot glass

# Temptation

**2 oz. blended whiskey**
**¼ oz. triple sec**
**¼ oz. Pernod**
**¼ oz. Dubonnet**

1. Fill mixing glass with ice
2. Add blended whiskey, triple sec, Pernod and Dubonnet

3. Shake
4. Strain into a chilled cocktail glass

## Tempter Cocktail

**1½ oz. port**
**1½ oz. apricot brandy**

1. Fill mixing glass with ice
2. Add port and apricot brandy
3. Shake
4. Strain into a rocks glass filled with ice

## Tennessee

**2½ oz. rye whiskey**
**½ oz. maraschino liqueur**
**½ oz. lemon juice**

1. Fill mixing glass with ice
2. Add rye, maraschino liqueur and lemon juice
3. Shake
4. Strain into a rocks glass filled with ice

## Tequila Collins

**1 oz. tequila**
**2 oz. sour mix**
**club soda**

1. Fill a Collins glass with ice
2. Add tequila and sour mix
3. Stir
4. Fill with club soda
5. Stir
6. Garnish with a cherry

# Tequila Daisy

1½ oz. tequila
2 tsp. lemon juice
¼ oz. raspberry syrup
club soda (optional)
dash Grand Marnier

1. Fill mixing glass with cracked ice
2. Add tequila, lemon juice and raspberry syrup
3. Shake
4. Pour into a highball glass
5. Fill with club soda (if desired)
6. Float Grand Marnier on top

# Tequila Ghost

2 oz. tequila
1 oz. Pernod
½ oz. lemon juice

1. Fill mixing glass with ice
2. Add tequila, Pernod and lemon juice
3. Shake
4. Strain into a rocks glass filled with ice

# Tequila Gimlet

1½ oz. tequila
1 oz. Rose's lime juice

1. Fill a rocks glass with ice
2. Add tequila and Rose's lime juice
3. Stir well
4. Garnish with a slice or wedge of lime

# Tequila Manhattan

2 oz. tequila
1½ oz. sweet vermouth

1. Fill mixing glass with ice
2. Add tequila and sweet vermouth
3. Stir
4. Strain into a chilled cocktail glass or a rocks glass filled with ice

# Tequila Martini

2 oz. tequila
½ oz. dry vermouth

1. Fill a rocks glass with ice
2. Add tequila and dry vermouth
3. Stir
4. Garnish with a twist of lemon or orange

# Tequila Old-Fashioned

1 sugar cube
3–4 dashes Angostura bitters
1½ oz. gold tequila
2–3 oz. water
2–3 drops lime juice (optional)

1. Place sugar cube in a rocks glass
2. Add bitters and muddle until sugar is dissolved
3. Fill the glass with ice
4. Pour in tequila
5. Add water
6. Add lime juice (if desired)
7. Stir
8. Garnish with a twist of lemon

# Tequila Popper (shooter)

**1 oz. tequila**
**½ oz. 7-Up**

1. Pour tequila into a shot glass
2. Fill with 7-Up
3. Place a napkin over the top of the glass and bang the glass down onto the table
4. Drink immediately


# Tequila Screwdriver

**1½ oz. tequila**
**5 oz. orange juice**

1. Fill a highball glass with ice
2. Add tequila
3. Fill with orange juice
4. Stir


# Tequila Shot (shooter)

**1½ oz. tequila (premium brand is recommended)**
**1 pinch salt**
**1 lemon or lime wedge**

1. Fill a shot glass with tequila (chilled, if desired)
2. Put salt between thumb and index finger of left hand
3. While holding shot glass in the same hand, and the lemon or lime wedge in the other hand, lick the salt and quickly drink the shot of tequila
4. Suck the lemon or lime juice immediately afterward

# Tequila Sour

**1½ oz. tequila**
**2–3 oz. sour mix**

1. Fill mixing glass with ice
2. Add tequila and sour mix
3. Shake
4. Strain into a sour glass
5. Add ice

# Tequila Stinger

**1½ oz. gold tequila**
**¾ oz. white crème de menthe**

1. Fill mixing glass with ice
2. Add gold tequila and white crème de menthe
3. Shake
4. Strain into a chilled cocktail glass

# Tequila Sunrise

**1½ oz. tequila**
**2–3 dashes lime juice (optional)**
**orange juice**
**½ oz. grenadine**

1. Fill a highball glass with ice
2. Add tequila (and lime juice, if desired)
3. Fill with orange juice
4. Stir
5. Pour grenadine down a spoon and let it rise from the bottom (do NOT stir)

# Tequila Sunset

1½ oz. tequila
2–3 dashes lime juice (optional)
orange juice
½ oz. blackberry brandy

1. Fill a highball glass with ice
2. Add tequila (and lime juice, if desired)
3. Fill with orange juice
4. Stir
5. Pour blackberry brandy down a spoon and let it rise from the bottom (do NOT stir)

# Tequini

1½ oz. tequila
½ oz. dry vermouth
dash Angostura bitters (optional)

1. Fill mixing glass with ice
2. Add tequila, dry vermouth and bitters
3. Stir
4. Strain into a chilled cocktail glass or a rocks glass filled with ice

# Texas Tea

1 oz. tequila
½ oz. vodka
½ oz. rum
½ oz. triple sec
1 oz. sour mix
cola

1. Fill mixing glass with ice
2. Add tequila, vodka, rum, triple sec and sour mix

3. Shake
4. Pour into a Collins glass
5. Add more ice, if necessary
6. Top with cola
7. Garnish with a lemon slice

# Thanksgiving Cocktail

**1 oz. gin**
**1 oz. dry vermouth**
**1 oz. apricot brandy**
**½ tsp. lemon juice**

1. Fill mixing glass with ice
2. Add gin, dry vermouth, apricot brandy and lemon juice
3. Shake
4. Strain into a rocks glass filled with ice
5. Garnish with a cherry

# Third Degree

**1½ oz. gin**
**½ oz. dry vermouth**
**½ tsp. Pernod**

1. Fill mixing glass with ice
2. Add gin, dry vermouth and Pernod
3. Stir
4. Strain into a chilled cocktail glass

# Third Rail

**1 oz. brandy**
**1 oz. apple brandy**
**1 oz. light rum**
**dash Pernod**

1. Fill mixing glass with ice
2. Add brandy, apple brandy, light rum and Pernod
3. Shake
4. Strain into a chilled cocktail glass

# Thistle

**1½ oz. scotch whiskey**
**¾ oz. sweet vermouth**
**3–4 dashes Angostura bitters**

1. Fill mixing glass with ice
2. Add scotch whiskey, sweet vermouth and bitters
3. Shake
4. Strain into a chilled cocktail glass

# Three Miles

**1 oz. brandy**
**½ oz. light rum**
**dash lemon juice**
**1 tsp. grenadine**

1. Fill mixing glass with ice
2. Add brandy, light rum, lemon juice and grenadine
3. Stir
4. Strain into a chilled cocktail glass

# Three Stripes

**1 oz. gin**
**½ oz. dry vermouth**
**½ oz. orange juice**

1. Fill mixing glass with ice
2. Add gin, dry vermouth and orange juice
3. Shake
4. Strain into a chilled cocktail glass

# Thunder

**2 oz. brandy**
**1 tsp. sugar syrup**
**1 egg yolk**
**pinch cayenne pepper**

1. Fill mixing glass with ice
2. Add brandy, sugar syrup, egg yolk and cayenne pepper
3. Shake
4. Strain into a rocks glass filled with ice

# Tidbit

**1 oz. gin**
**1 scoop vanilla ice cream**
**2–3 drops dry sherry**

1. In blender, combine gin, vanilla ice cream and dry sherry
2. Blend at low speed until smooth
3. Pour into a highball glass

# Tiger's Milk

**1 oz. Jamaican rum**
**1 oz. brandy**
**4 oz. heavy cream**
**¼ oz. sugar syrup**

1. Fill mixing glass with ice
2. Add Jamaican rum, brandy, heavy cream and sugar syrup
3. Shake
4. Strain into a rocks glass filled with ice

# Tiger Tail

**1½ oz. Pernod**
**dash curaçao**
**orange juice**

1. Fill a highball glass with ice
2. Add Pernod and curaçao
3. Fill with orange juice
4. Stir
5. Garnish with a slice of lime

# Tijuana Sunrise

**1½ oz. tequila**
**2–3 dashes lime juice (optional)**
**orange juice**
**½ oz. Angostura bitters**

1. Fill a highball glass with ice
2. Add tequila (and lime juice, if desired)
3. Fill with orange juice
4. Stir
5. Pour bitters down a spoon and let it rise from the bottom (do NOT stir)

# Tinton

**2 oz. port**
**2 oz. apple brandy**

1. Fill mixing glass with ice
2. Add port and apple brandy
3. Stir
4. Strain into a chilled cocktail glass

# Tintoretto

½ oz. pear puree
chilled champagne
dash pear brandy

1. Pour pear puree into a champagne glass
2. Fill with chilled champagne
3. Add dash of pear brandy

# Tiny Bowl (shooter)

1½ oz. vodka
1–2 drops blue curaçao
1 or 2 raisins

1. Combine vodka and blue curaçao with ice
2. Strain into a shot glass
3. Throw in 1 or 2 raisins

# Tipperary

1 oz. Irish whiskey
1 oz. green Chartreuse
1 oz. sweet vermouth

1. Fill mixing glass with ice
2. Add Irish whiskey, green Chartreuse and sweet vermouth
3. Shake
4. Strain into a chilled cocktail glass

# Tivoli

1½ oz. bourbon
½ oz. aquavit
½ oz. sweet vermouth
3–4 drops Campari

1. Fill mixing glass with ice
2. Add bourbon, aquavit, sweet vermouth and Campari
3. Shake
4. Strain into a chilled cocktail glass

# T.N.T.

1 oz. tequila
tonic water

1. Fill a highball glass with ice
2. Add tequila
3. Fill with tonic water
4. Stir
5. Garnish with a slice of lime

# Toasted Almond

½ oz. Kahlúa
½ oz. amaretto
2 oz. cream

1. Fill mixing glass with ice
2. Add Kahlúa, amaretto and cream
3. Shake
4. Strain into a highball glass
5. Add ice

# Tom and Jerry

1 oz. dark rum
1 oz. brandy
1 egg
½ oz. sugar syrup
hot milk or hot water

1. Separate the egg
2. Beat yolk and white separately
3. Fold together and combine with sugar syrup in a heat-proof mug
4. Slowly add dark rum and brandy
5. Beat mixture
6. Fill with hot milk or hot water
7. Garnish with ground nutmeg

# Tom Collins

1 oz. gin
2 oz. sour mix
club soda

1. Fill a Collins glass with ice
2. Add gin and sour mix
3. Stir
4. Fill with club soda
5. Stir
6. Garnish with a cherry

# Tootsie Roll

1 oz. Sabra
1 oz. orange juice

1. Fill a rocks glass with ice
2. Add Sabra and orange juice
3. Stir

(*Note:* 1½ oz. Kahlúa may be substituted for Sabra.)

# Top Shelf Margarita

**1½ oz. Cuervo gold tequila**
**½ oz. Grand Marnier**
**1 oz. sour mix**
**1 oz. lime juice**

1. Fill mixing glass with ice
2. Add Cuervo, Grand Marnier, sour mix and lime juice
3. Shake
4. Strain into a chilled cocktail glass or a rocks glass filled with ice

# Toreador

**1½ oz. tequila**
**½ oz. white crème de cacao**
**½ oz. cream**

1. Fill mixing glass with ice
2. Add tequila, white crème de cacao and cream
3. Shake
4. Strain into a chilled cocktail glass
5. Top with 1 tsp. whipped cream
6. Sprinkle with cocoa (if desired)

# Torpedo

**1½ oz. apple brandy**
**¾ oz. brandy**
**1–2 dashes gin**

1. Fill mixing glass with ice
2. Add apple brandy, brandy and gin
3. Shake
4. Strain into a chilled cocktail glass

# Tovarich

**1½ oz. vodka**
**¾ oz. kümmel**
**1 tbsp. lime juice**

1. Fill mixing glass with ice
2. Add vodka, kümmel and lime juice
3. Shake
4. Strain into a chilled cocktail glass

# Trade Winds

**2 oz. gold rum**
**½ oz. plum brandy**
**½ oz. lime juice**
**2 tsp. sugar syrup**

1. Fill blender with 3 oz. ice, gold rum, plum brandy, lime juice and sugar syrup
2. Blend until smooth
3. Pour into a large wineglass

# Traffic Light

**⅓ oz. green crème de menthe**
**⅓ oz. crème de banana**
**⅓ oz. sloe gin**

1. Pour green crème de menthe into a liqueur glass or a brandy snifter
2. Float crème de banana
3. Float sloe gin

# Trilby

1½ oz. bourbon
½ oz. sweet vermouth
2 dashes orange bitters

1. Fill mixing glass with ice
2. Add bourbon, sweet vermouth and orange bitters
3. Stir
4. Strain into a rocks glass filled with ice

# Trinidad Cocktail

1 oz. light rum
1 tbsp. lime juice
1 tsp. sugar
2–3 dashes Angostura bitters

1. Fill mixing glass with ice
2. Add light rum, lime juice, sugar and bitters
3. Shake
4. Strain into a chilled cocktail glass

# Trois Rivieres

1½ oz. Canadian whiskey
¾ oz. Dubonnet
½ oz. triple sec

1. Fill mixing glass with ice
2. Add Canadian whiskey, Dubonnet and triple sec
3. Shake
4. Strain into a rocks glass filled with ice

# Trolley

2 oz. bourbon
cranberry juice cocktail
pineapple juice

1. Fill a highball glass with ice
2. Add bourbon
3. Fill with equal parts cranberry juice and pineapple juice
4. Stir

# Trophy Room

½ oz. Amaretto de Saronno
½ oz. Vandermint
½ oz. Myers's dark Jamaican rum
hot coffee
½ oz. Tia Maria

1. Pour Amaretto, Vandermint and Myers's into a coffee mug
2. Fill with hot coffee
3. Top with whipped cream
4. Float Tia Maria on top

(Courtesy of Hotel Park, Tucson, Arizona)

# Tropical Cocktail

¾ oz. white crème de cacao
¾ oz. maraschino liqueur
¾ oz. dry vermouth
1 dash Angostura bitters

1. Fill mixing glass with ice
2. Add white crème de cacao, maraschino liqueur, dry vermouth and bitters
3. Stir
4. Strain into a chilled cocktail glass

# Tuaca Cocktail

**1 oz. vodka**
**1 oz. Tuaca**
**2 tbsp. lime juice**

1. Fill mixing glass with ice
2. Add vodka, Tuaca and lime juice
3. Shake
4. Strain into a chilled cocktail glass

# Tulip

**¾ oz. sweet vermouth**
**¾ oz. apple brandy**
**1½ tsp. apricot brandy**
**1½ tsp. lemon juice**

1. Fill mixing glass with ice
2. Add sweet vermouth, apple brandy, apricot brandy and lemon juice
3. Shake
4. Strain into a chilled cocktail glass

# Tumbleweed

**1 oz. white crème de cacao**
**1 oz. amaretto**
**2 oz. cream**

1. In blender, combine white crème de cacao, amaretto and cream with 3 oz. crushed ice
2. Blend until smooth
3. Pour into a goblet or large wineglass

# Turf

1 oz. gin
½ oz. dry vermouth
2 dashes anis
2 dashes maraschino liqueur
2 dashes Angostura bitters

1. Fill mixing glass with ice
2. Add gin, dry vermouth, anis, maraschino liqueur and bitters
3. Shake
4. Strain into a rocks glass filled with ice


# Turkey Shooter

¾ oz. 101-proof Wild Turkey Bourbon
¼ oz. white crème de menthe

1. Pour Wild Turkey into a liqueur glass or brandy snifter
2. Float white crème de menthe


# Tuxedo

2 oz. fino sherry
½ oz. anisette
3–4 dashes maraschino liqueur
3–4 dashes Angostura bitters

1. Fill mixing glass with ice
2. Add fino sherry, anisette, maraschino liqueur and bitters
3. Stir
4. Strain into a chilled cocktail glass

# Twin Hills

1½ oz. blended whiskey
2 tsp. Bénédictine
1½ tsp. lemon juice
1½ tsp. lime juice
1 tsp. sugar syrup

1. Fill mixing glass with ice
2. Add blended whiskey, Bénédictine, lemon juice, lime juice and sugar syrup
3. Shake
4. Strain into a chilled cocktail glass
5. Garnish with a slice of lemon and a slice of lime

# Twin Six

1 oz. gin
½ oz. sweet vermouth
2 tsp. grenadine
1 tbsp. orange juice
1 egg white

1. Fill mixing glass with ice
2. Add gin, sweet vermouth, grenadine, orange juice and egg white
3. Shake
4. Strain into a chilled cocktail glass

# Twister

2 oz. vodka
½ oz. lime juice, freshly squeezed
7-Up

1. Fill a highball glass with ice
2. Add vodka and lime juice
3. Top with 7-Up
4. Stir gently

# U

## Ulanda

1½ oz. gin
¾ oz. Cointreau
2–3 drops Pernod

1. Fill mixing glass with ice
2. Add gin, Cointreau and Pernod
3. Shake
4. Strain into a rocks glass filled with ice

## The Ultimate Margarita

1½ oz. Sauza Conmemorativo Tequila
¾ oz. Cointreau
1 oz. fresh lemon juice
½ oz. fresh lime juice
½ tsp. sugar

1. Fill mixing glass with ice
2. Add tequila, Cointreau, lemon juice, lime juice and sugar
3. Shake well
4. If desired, salt the rim of a large cocktail glass
5. Strain into glass
6. Garnish with a slice of lime

# Union Jack

1½ oz. gin
¼ oz. crème d'Yvette

1. Fill mixing glass with ice
2. Add gin and crème d'Yvette
3. Stir
4. Strain into a chilled cocktail glass

# Union League

2 oz. gin
1 oz. port
2 dashes orange bitters

1. Fill a rocks glass with ice
2. Add gin, port and orange bitters
3. Stir
4. Garnish with a twist of orange

# V

## Valencia

2 oz. apricot brandy
1 oz. orange juice
2–3 dashes orange bitters
chilled champagne

1. Fill mixing glass with ice
2. Add apricot brandy, orange juice and orange bitters
3. Shake
4. Strain into a chilled goblet or tulip glass
5. Fill with chilled champagne

## Vancouver Cocktail

2 oz. Canadian whiskey
1 oz. Dubonnet (rouge)
2 tbsp. lemon juice
½ egg white
½ tsp. maple syrup (sugar syrup may be substituted)
3–4 dashes Angostura bitters

1. Half-fill a mixing glass with cracked ice
2. Add Canadian whiskey, Dubonnet, lemon juice, egg white, maple syrup and bitters
3. Shake
4. Pour into a large wineglass or large cocktail glass

# Vanderbilt

**1½ oz. brandy**
**¾ oz. cherry brandy**
**1 tsp. sugar syrup**
**2 dashes Angostura bitters**

1. Fill mixing glass with ice
2. Add brandy, cherry brandy, sugar syrup and bitters
3. Stir
4. Strain into a chilled cocktail glass

# Vanity Fair Cocktail

**1½ oz. apple brandy**
**½ oz. cherry brandy**
**½ oz. cherry liqueur**
**1 tsp. crème de noyaux**

1. Fill mixing glass with 1–2 oz. cracked ice
2. Add apple brandy, cherry brandy and cherry liqueur
3. Shake
4. Pour into a cocktail glass
5. Float crème de noyaux on top

# Velvet Hammer

**½ oz. white crème de cacao**
**½ oz. triple sec**
**2 oz. cream**

1. Fill mixing glass with ice
2. Add white crème de cacao, triple sec and cream
3. Shake
4. Strain into a stemmed glass

# Velvet Kiss

1 oz. gin
½ oz. banana liqueur
½ oz. pineapple juice
1 oz. heavy cream

1. Fill mixing glass with ice
2. Add gin, banana liqueur, pineapple juice and heavy cream
3. Shake
4. Strain into a chilled cocktail glass

# Venetian Coffee

1 sugar cube
1 oz. brandy
hot coffee

1. Place sugar cube in a coffee mug
2. Pour in brandy
3. Fill with hot coffee
4. Top with whipped cream

# Vermouth Cassis

1 oz. sweet vermouth or dry vermouth (depending on taste)
1 oz. crème de cassis
club soda

1. Fill a highball glass with ice
2. Add vermouth and crème de cassis
3. Stir
4. Fill with club soda
5. Stir gently
6. Garnish with a twist of lemon

# Vermouth Frappe

1½ oz. sweet vermouth
dash Angostura bitters

1. Fill mixing glass with shaved ice
2. Add sweet vermouth and bitters
3. Stir
4. Strain into a chilled cocktail glass

# Verona

1 oz. gin
1 oz. amaretto
½ oz. sweet vermouth
1–2 dashes lemon juice

1. Half-fill mixing glass with cracked ice
2. Add gin, amaretto, sweet vermouth and lemon juice
3. Shake
4. Pour into a rocks glass
5. Garnish with a slice of orange

# Via Veneto

1½ oz. brandy
½ oz. sambuca
½ oz. lemon juice
1½ tsp. sugar syrup
½ egg white

1. Fill mixing glass with ice
2. Add brandy, sambuca, lemon juice, sugar syrup and egg white
3. Shake
4. Strain into a rocks glass filled with ice

# Victor

**1 oz. gin**
**1 oz. brandy**
**½ oz. sweet vermouth**

1. Fill mixing glass with ice
2. Add gin, brandy and sweet vermouth
3. Stir
4. Strain into a chilled cocktail glass

# Victory

**1½ oz. Pernod**
**¾ oz. grenadine**
**club soda**

1. Fill mixing glass with ice
2. Add Pernod and grenadine
3. Shake
4. Strain into a highball glass filled with ice
5. Fill with club soda

# Viking

**1½ oz. Swedish Punsch**
**1 oz. aquavit**
**1 oz. lime juice**

1. Fill mixing glass with ice
2. Add Swedish Punsch, aquavit and lime juice
3. Shake
4. Strain into a rocks glass filled with ice

# Virgin

1 oz. gin
½ oz. white crème de menthe
1 oz. Forbidden Fruit

1. Fill mixing glass with ice
2. Add gin, white crème de menthe and Forbidden Fruit
3. Shake
4. Strain into a rocks glass filled with ice

# Vodka and Tonic

1½ oz. vodka
5 oz. tonic water

1. Fill a highball glass with ice
2. Add vodka
3. Fill with tonic water
4. Stir
5. Garnish with a lime slice

# Vodka Collins

1 oz. vodka
2 oz. sour mix
club soda

1. Fill a Collins glass with ice
2. Add vodka and sour mix
3. Stir
4. Fill with club soda
5. Stir
6. Garnish with a cherry

# Vodka Cooler

1 oz. vodka
½ oz. sweet vermouth
7-Up

1. Fill mixing glass with ice
2. Add vodka and sweet vermouth
3. Shake
4. Strain into a Collins glass filled with ice
5. Fill with 7-Up

# Vodka Fizz

1 oz. vodka
2 oz. pineapple juice
1 tsp. lemon juice
1 tsp. powdered sugar
club soda

1. Fill mixing glass with ice
2. Add vodka, pineapple juice, lemon juice and sugar
3. Shake
4. Strain into a Collins glass
5. Add several ice cubes
6. Fill with club soda

# Vodka Gibson

2 oz. vodka
½ oz. dry vermouth

1. Fill mixing glass with ice
2. Add vodka and dry vermouth
3. Stir

4. Strain into a chilled martini glass or a rocks glass filled with ice
5. Garnish with a pearl onion

(*Note:* A Gibson is a martini with a pearl onion as garnish instead of an olive. As in a vodka martini, the drier the Gibson, the less vermouth is used in proportion to the vodka.)

## Vodka Gimlet

1½ oz. vodka
½ oz. Rose's lime juice

1. Fill rocks glass with ice
2. Add vodka and Rose's lime juice
3. Stir
4. Garnish with a lime slice

## Vodka Grand Marnier Cocktail

1½ oz. vodka
½ oz. Grand Marnier
2 tbsp. lime juice

1. Fill mixing glass with ice
2. Add vodka, Grand Marnier and lime juice
3. Shake
4. Strain into a chilled cocktail glass
5. Garnish with a slice of orange or a twist of orange

## Vodka Grasshopper

1 oz. white crème de cacao
1 oz. green crème de menthe
½ oz. vodka

1. Fill mixing glass with ice
2. Add white crème de cacao, green crème de menthe and vodka
3. Shake
4. Strain into a chilled cocktail glass

# Vodka Martini

**1½ oz. vodka**
**dash (approx. ⅛ oz.) dry vermouth**

1. Fill mixing glass with ice
2. Add vodka and dry vermouth
3. Stir
4. Strain into a chilled martini glass
5. Garnish with an olive

(*Note:* If serving "on the rocks," stir in a rocks glass filled with ice, garnish and serve.)

# Vodka Martini (dry)

**1½ oz. vodka**
**drop (approx. ⅒ oz.) dry vermouth**

1. Fill mixing glass with ice
2. Add vodka and dry vermouth
3. Stir
4. Strain into a chilled martini glass
5. Garnish with an olive

(*Note:* If serving "on the rocks," stir in a rocks glass filled with ice, garnish and serve.)

# Vodka Martini (very dry)

**1½ oz. vodka**
**approx. ¹⁄₁₂ oz. dry vermouth**

1. Fill mixing glass with ice
2. Add dry vermouth (In actuality, almost no dry vermouth is used. Let vermouth barely touch side of mixing glass.)
3. Add vodka
4. Stir
5. Strain into a chilled martini glass
6. Garnish with an olive

(*Note:* If serving "on the rocks," stir in a rocks glass filled with ice, garnish and serve.)

# Vodka Martini (extremely dry)

**2 oz. vodka**

Follow directions for other martini recipes. No vermouth is used. This translates to "vodka straight up" or "vodka on the rocks."

# Vodka on the Rocks

**2 oz. premium imported vodka**

1. Fill rocks glass with ice
2. Add vodka

(*Note:* Vodkas such as Absolut, Stolichnaya and Finlandia are extremely popular. To best enjoy the flavor, store the bottle of vodka in your freezer, allowing the alcohol to thicken. You may also serve it "straight up"—chilled, without ice.)

# Vodka Saketini

**2½ oz. vodka**
**½ oz. sake**

1. Fill mixing glass with ice
2. Add vodka and sake
3. Stir
4. Strain into a chilled cocktail glass or a rocks glass filled with ice
5. Garnish with a twist of lemon

# Vodka Stinger

**1½ oz. vodka**
**½ oz. white crème de menthe**

1. Fill mixing glass with ice
2. Add vodka and white crème de menthe
3. Stir
4. Strain into a chilled cocktail glass

# Volga Boatman

**1 oz. vodka**
**1 oz. cherry brandy**
**1 oz. orange juice**

1. Fill mixing glass with ice
2. Add vodka, cherry brandy and orange juice
3. Stir
4. Strain into a chilled cocktail glass

# W

## Wagon Wheel

1½ oz. cognac
2½ oz. Southern Comfort
1 oz. lemon juice
½ oz. grenadine

1. Fill mixing glass with ice
2. Add cognac, Southern Comfort, lemon juice and grenadine
3. Shake
4. Strain into a rocks glass filled with ice

## Waldorf

1½ oz. bourbon
¾ oz. Pernod
½ oz. sweet vermouth
dash Angostura bitters

1. Fill mixing glass with ice
2. Add bourbon, Pernod, sweet vermouth and bitters
3. Stir
4. Strain into a chilled cocktail glass

## Warday's Cocktail

1 oz. gin
1 oz. sweet vermouth
1 oz. apple brandy
1 tsp. yellow Chartreuse

1. Fill mixing glass with ice
2. Add gin, sweet vermouth, apple brandy and yellow Chartreuse
3. Shake
4. Strain into a chilled cocktail glass
5. Garnish with a cherry

# Ward 8

1 oz. whiskey
2 oz. sour mix
¼ oz. grenadine

1. Fill mixing glass with ice
2. Add whiskey, sour mix and grenadine
3. Shake
4. Strain into a sour glass
5. Add ice, if necessary
6. Garnish with a cherry

# Warsaw

1½ oz. vodka
½ oz. blackberry liqueur
½ oz. dry vermouth
¼ oz. lemon juice

1. Fill mixing glass with ice
2. Add vodka, blackberry liqueur, dry vermouth and lemon juice
3. Shake
4. Strain into a chilled cocktail glass

# Washington

1½ oz. dry vermouth
¾ oz. brandy
2 dashes sugar syrup
2 dashes Angostura bitters

1. Fill mixing glass with ice
2. Add dry vermouth, brandy, sugar syrup and bitters
3. Stir
4. Strain into a chilled cocktail glass

# Waterbury

**2 oz. cognac**
**½ oz. lemon juice**
**1 tsp. sugar syrup**
**½ egg white**
**2–3 dashes grenadine**

1. Fill mixing glass with ice
2. Add cognac, lemon juice, sugar syrup, egg white and grenadine
3. Shake
4. Strain into a chilled cocktail glass

# Watermelon

**¾ oz. vodka**
**¾ oz. Midori melon liqueur**
**3 oz. cranberry juice cocktail**

1. Fill a highball glass with ice
2. Add vodka, Midori and cranberry juice
3. Stir

# Wedding Belle

**½ oz. gin**
**½ oz. Dubonnet**
**¼ oz. cherry-flavored brandy**
**¼ oz. orange juice**

1. Fill mixing glass with ice
2. Add gin, Dubonnet, cherry-flavored brandy and orange juice

3. Shake
4. Strain into a rocks glass filled with ice

# Weekender

¾ oz. gin
¾ oz. dry vermouth
¾ oz. sweet vermouth
¾ oz. triple sec
3 dashes Pernod

1. Fill mixing glass with ice
2. Add gin, dry vermouth, sweet vermouth, triple sec and Pernod
3. Shake
4. Strain into a chilled cocktail glass

# Weep No More

1 oz. brandy
1 oz. Dubonnet
1 oz. lime juice

1. Fill mixing glass with ice
2. Add brandy, Dubonnet and lime juice
3. Shake
4. Strain into a chilled cocktail glass

# Wembley

1½ oz. gin
¾ oz. dry vermouth
3 dashes apple brandy

1. Fill mixing glass with ice
2. Add gin, dry vermouth and apple brandy
3. Stir
4. Strain into a chilled cocktail glass

# Which Way

**1 oz. brandy**
**1 oz. Pernod**
**1 oz. anisette**

1. Fill mixing glass with ice
2. Add brandy, Pernod and anisette
3. Shake
4. Strain into a chilled cocktail glass

# Whip

**1½ oz. dry vermouth**
**1 oz. brandy**
**1 dash curaçao**
**2 drops Pernod**

1. Fill mixing glass with ice
2. Add dry vermouth, brandy, curaçao and Pernod
3. Shake
4. Strain into a chilled cocktail glass

# Whippet

**2½ oz. blended whiskey**
**1 oz. peppermint schnapps**
**1 oz. white crème de cacao**

1. Fill mixing glass with ice
2. Add blended whiskey, peppermint schnapps and white crème de cacao
3. Shake
4. Strain into a rocks glass filled with ice

# Whirlaway

1½ oz. bourbon
¾ oz. curaçao
2–3 dashes Angostura bitters
club soda

1. Half-fill mixing glass with cracked ice
2. Add bourbon, curaçao and bitters
3. Shake
4. Pour into a rocks glass
5. Fill with club soda

# Whiskey and Water

1½ oz. whiskey
water

1. Fill a highball glass with ice
2. Add whiskey
3. Fill with water
4. Stir

# Whiskey Collins

1 oz. whiskey
2 oz. sour mix
club soda

1. Fill a Collins glass with ice
2. Add whiskey and sour mix
3. Stir
4. Fill with club soda
5. Garnish with a cherry and an orange slice

# Whiskey Daisy

1½ oz. blended whiskey
2 tsp. lemon juice
¼ oz. raspberry syrup
club soda (optional)
dash yellow Chartreuse (Grand Marnier or curaçao may be
    substituted)

1. Fill mixing glass with cracked ice
2. Add blended whiskey, lemon juice and raspberry syrup
3. Shake
4. Pour into a highball glass
5. Fill with club soda (if desired)
6. Float Chartreuse (or Grand Marnier or curaçao) on top

# Whiskey Fix

2 oz. scotch whiskey
1 oz. lemon juice
1 tsp. powdered sugar

1. Fill a Collins glass with crushed ice
2. Add scotch, lemon juice and powdered sugar
3. Stir
4. Garnish with fresh fruits in season

# Whiskey Highball

1 oz. whiskey
club soda or ginger ale

1. Fill a highball glass with ice
2. Add whiskey
3. Fill with club soda or ginger ale
4. Stir gently

# Whiskey Rickey

1½ oz. blended whiskey
½ oz. lime juice
1 tsp. sugar syrup
club soda

1. Fill a Collins glass with cracked ice
2. Add blended whiskey, lime juice and sugar syrup
3. Fill with club soda
4. Garnish with a slice of lime

# Whiskey Sour

1 oz. whiskey
2 oz. sour mix

1. Fill mixing glass with ice
2. Add whiskey and sour mix
3. Shake
4. Strain into a sour glass
5. Garnish with a cherry

# Whist

1 oz. apple brandy
½ oz. dark rum
½ oz. sweet vermouth

1. Fill mixing glass with ice
2. Add apple brandy, dark rum and sweet vermouth
3. Shake
4. Strain into a chilled cocktail glass

# White Baby

1 oz. gin
1 oz. triple sec
1 oz. heavy cream

1. Fill mixing glass with ice
2. Add gin, triple sec and heavy cream
3. Shake
4. Strain into a chilled cocktail glass

# White Bull

1 oz. tequila
¾ oz. Kahlúa
cream

1. Fill a rocks glass with ice
2. Add tequila and Kahlúa
3. Top with cream
4. Stir

# White Cargo

2½ oz. gin
½ oz. maraschino liqueur
2 dashes dry white wine
1 scoop vanilla ice cream

1. In a blender, combine gin, maraschino liqueur, wine and vanilla ice cream
2. Blend until smooth
3. Pour into a goblet

# White Elephant

½ oz. vodka
½ oz. white crème de cacao
2 oz. cream

1. Fill mixing glass with ice
2. Add vodka, white crème de cacao and cream
3. Shake
4. Strain into a chilled stemmed glass

# White Grape, Tangerine and Sparkling Wine Punch

48 oz. unsweetened white grape juice, chilled
6 oz. frozen tangerine juice concentrate, thawed
8 oz. club soda
3 oz. brandy
2 oz. lemon juice
1 bottle (25.4 oz.) sweet sparkling wine (e.g., asti spumante)
thin slices of tangerine

1. In a punch bowl, over a block of ice, combine white grape juice, tangerine concentrate, club soda, brandy and lemon juice
2. Mix
3. Cover punch bowl and refrigerate until cold
4. Just before serving, add the sparkling wine
5. Float thinly sliced tangerine on top

# White Heart

½ oz. sambuca
½ oz. white crème de cacao
2 oz. cream

1. Fill mixing glass with ice
2. Add sambuca, white crème de cacao and cream
3. Shake
4. Strain into a chilled stemmed glass

# White Heat

1 oz. gin
½ oz. triple sec
½ oz. dry vermouth
1 oz. pineapple juice

1. Fill mixing glass with ice
2. Add gin, triple sec, dry vermouth and pineapple juice
3. Shake
4. Strain into a rocks glass filled with ice

# White Lady (1)

1½ oz. gin
3 oz. sour mix
1 oz. cream

1. Fill mixing glass with ice
2. Add gin, sour mix and cream
3. Shake
4. Strain into a sour glass
5. Fill with ice
6. Garnish with a cherry and an orange slice

464

# White Lady (2)

½ oz. vodka
½ oz. crème de cacao
2 oz. cream

1. Fill mixing glass with ice
2. Add vodka, crème de cacao and cream
3. Shake
4. Strain into a chilled cocktail glass

# White Lily

1 oz. gin
1 oz. light rum
1 oz. triple sec
2–3 drops Pernod

1. Fill mixing glass with ice
2. Add gin, light rum, triple sec and Pernod
3. Shake
4. Strain into a rocks glass filled with ice

# White Lion

1½ oz. light rum
½ oz. lemon juice
1 tsp. sugar
½ tsp. grenadine
2 dashes Angostura bitters

1. Fill mixing glass with ice
2. Add light rum, lemon juice, sugar, grenadine and bitters
3. Shake
4. Strain into a chilled cocktail glass

# White Mint and Brandy Frappe

**2 oz. white crème de menthe**
**1 oz. brandy**

1. Fill a champagne glass with crushed ice
2. Pour in white crème de menthe and brandy

# White Rose

**1½ oz. gin**
**¾ oz. cherry liqueur**
**2 oz. orange juice**
**2 tbsp. lime juice**
**1 tsp. sugar**
**½ egg white**

1. Fill mixing glass with ice
2. Add gin, cherry liqueur, orange juice, lime juice, sugar and egg white
3. Shake
4. Strain into a rocks glass filled with ice

# White Russian

**1½ oz. vodka**
**1½ oz. Kahlúa**
**cream**

1. Fill a rocks glass with ice
2. Add vodka and Kahlúa
3. Float cream on top

# White Spider

**2 oz. vodka**
**1 oz. white crème de menthe**

1. Fill mixing glass with ice
2. Add vodka and white crème de menthe
3. Shake
4. Strain into a chilled cocktail glass

# White Wine Spritzer

**white wine**
**club soda**

1. Half-fill a tulip glass or a Collins glass with ice
2. Fill the glass halfway with chilled white wine
3. Fill with club soda
4. Stir gently
5. Garnish with a twist of lemon

# White Wine Super Sangria

**2 bottles dry white wine**
**½ cup Cointreau or triple sec**
**2 oz. brandy**
**1 cup orange juice**
**1 pint strawberries, hulled and quartered**
**1 lime, cut into thin slices**
**1 lemon, cut into thin slices**
**½ orange, cut into thin slices**
**1½ cups seedless green grapes**
**1½ cups seedless red grapes**
**1 oz. superfine granulated sugar**
**1½ cups club soda**

1. Combine all ingredients (except club soda) in a large bowl
2. Refrigerate for several hours
3. When ready to serve, add club soda
4. Stir
5. Serve in large wineglasses

# White Wing

**2 oz. gin**
**1 oz. white crème de menthe**

1. Fill mixing glass with ice
2. Add gin and white crème de menthe
3. Shake
4. Strain into a chilled cocktail glass

# Why Not

**1 oz. gin**
**1 oz. dry vermouth**
**½ oz. apricot brandy**
**dash lemon juice**

1. Fill mixing glass with ice
2. Add gin, dry vermouth, apricot brandy and lemon juice
3. Shake
4. Strain into a chilled cocktail glass

# Widow's Dream

**2 oz. Bénédictine**
**1 oz. heavy cream**
**1 egg**

1. Fill mixing glass with ice
2. Add Bénédictine, heavy cream and egg
3. Shake
4. Strain into a large chilled cocktail glass

# Widow's Kiss

1 oz. apple brandy
½ oz. Bénédictine
½ oz. yellow Chartreuse
dash Angostura bitters

1. Fill mixing glass with ice
2. Add apple brandy, Bénédictine, yellow Chartreuse and bitters
3. Shake
4. Strain into a chilled cocktail glass

# Wild Fling

1½ oz. DeKuyper WilderBerry schnapps
4 oz. pineapple juice
splash cranberry juice cocktail

1. Fill a highball glass with ice
2. Add WilderBerry schnapps
3. Fill with pineapple juice
4. Add a splash of cranberry juice
5. Stir

# Wild Irish Rose

1½ oz. Irish whiskey
1½ tsp. grenadine
½ oz. lime juice
club soda

1. Fill a highball glass with ice
2. Add Irish whiskey, grenadine and lime juice
3. Stir well
4. Fill with club soda

# Will Rogers

1½ oz. gin
½ oz. dry vermouth
dash triple sec
1 tbsp. orange juice

1. Fill mixing glass with ice
2. Add gin, dry vermouth, triple sec and orange juice
3. Shake
4. Strain into a chilled cocktail glass

# Wilson Cocktail

2 oz. gin
2 dashes dry vermouth
1 tbsp. orange juice

1. Fill mixing glass with ice
2. Add gin, dry vermouth and orange juice
3. Stir well
4. Strain into a chilled cocktail glass
5. Garnish with a twist of orange

# Wine Cooler

burgundy or rosé wine
7-Up

1. Half-fill a tulip glass or a Collins glass with ice
2. Fill the glass halfway with wine
3. Fill with 7-Up
4. Stir gently
5. Garnish with a cherry

# Wombat (shooter)

2 oz. dark rum
½ oz. strawberry liqueur
3 oz. orange juice
3 oz. pineapple juice
a mixing glass full of fresh watermelon, seeded
   (approximately 6 oz. fresh watermelon juice)

1. Pulverize fresh watermelon in a mixing glass and remove seeds
2. Combine with dark rum, strawberry liqueur, orange juice and pineapple juice
3. Shake well
4. Pour into shot glasses

(Yields approximately 4 shots)

(Courtesy of Bamboo Bernies, New York City)

# Woo Woo

¾ oz. vodka
¾ oz. peach schnapps
3 oz. cranberry juice cocktail

1. Fill a highball glass with ice
2. Add vodka, peach schnapps and cranberry juice
3. Stir

# Woo Woo (shooter)

½ oz. vodka
½ oz. peach schnapps
½ oz. cranberry juice cocktail

1. Fill mixing glass with ice
2. Add vodka, peach schnapps and cranberry juice
3. Stir
4. Strain into a shot glass

# Wyoming Swing Cocktail

1 oz. sweet vermouth
1 oz. dry vermouth
1 tsp. powdered sugar
2 oz. orange juice (preferably freshly squeezed)
½ tsp. sugar syrup, or to taste

1. Half-fill mixing glass with cracked ice
2. Add sweet vermouth, dry vermouth, powdered sugar, orange juice and sugar syrup
3. Shake
4. Pour into a highball glass
5. Add more ice, if necessary

# X

## Xango

**1½ oz. light rum**
**½ oz. triple sec**
**1 oz. grapefruit juice**

1. Fill mixing glass with ice
2. Add light rum, triple sec and grapefruit juice
3. Shake
4. Strain into a chilled cocktail glass

## Xanthia

**¾ oz. gin**
**¾ oz. yellow Chartreuse**
**¾ oz. cherry-flavored brandy**

1. Fill mixing glass with ice
2. Add gin, yellow Chartreuse and cherry-flavored brandy
3. Shake
4. Strain into a rocks glass filled with ice

## Xeres Cocktail

**2½ oz. dry sherry**
**1 dash orange bitters**

1. Fill mixing glass with ice
2. Add dry sherry and orange bitters
3. Stir
4. Strain into a chilled cocktail glass

# Xylophone

1 oz. tequila
½ oz. white crème de cacao
½ oz. sugar syrup
1 oz. cream

1. Fill blender with 3 oz. crushed ice, tequila, crème de cacao, sugar syrup and cream
2. Blend until smooth
3. Pour into a goblet or large wineglass
4. Garnish with a cherry

# XYZ

1½ oz. light rum
½ oz. triple sec
½ oz. lemon juice

1. Fill mixing glass with ice
2. Add light rum, triple sec and lemon juice
3. Shake
4. Strain into a chilled cocktail glass

# y

## Yale Cocktail

1½ oz. gin
½ oz. dry vermouth
3–4 dashes blue curaçao
dash Angostura bitters

1. Fill mixing glass with ice
2. Add gin, dry vermouth, blue curaçao and bitters
3. Stir
4. Strain into a chilled cocktail glass

## A Yard of Flannel

1 qt. ale
4 oz. gold rum
3 oz. superfine granulated sugar
4 eggs
½ tsp. grated nutmeg
½ tsp. ground cinnamon

1. Warm (don't boil) ale in a large saucepan over low heat
2. In a separate bowl, combine rum, sugar, eggs, nutmeg and cinnamon
3. Beat well
4. Pour mixture into a heat-resistant pitcher
5. Add ale slowly, stirring constantly
6. Stir until mixture is creamy
7. Pour into warmed mugs

# Yashmak

1½ oz. rye whiskey
¾ oz. dry vermouth
½ oz. Pernod
3–4 dashes Angostura bitters
½ tsp. sugar syrup, or to taste

1. Half-fill mixing glass with cracked ice
2. Add rye, dry vermouth, Pernod, bitters and sugar syrup
3. Shake
4. Pour into a highball glass

# Yellowbird

¾ oz. white crème de cacao
¾ oz. vodka
¾ oz. orange juice
¾ oz. cream
½ oz. Galliano

1. Fill mixing glass with ice
2. Add white crème de cacao, vodka, orange juice, cream and Galliano
3. Shake
4. Strain into a chilled champagne glass

# Yellow Fever

1½ oz. vodka
5–6 oz. lemonade

1. Fill a highball glass with ice
2. Add vodka
3. Fill with lemonade
4. Stir
5. Garnish with a slice of lemon

# Yellow Parrot

1 oz. apricot brandy
1 oz. Pernod
¾ oz. yellow Chartreuse

1. Fill mixing glass with ice
2. Add apricot brandy, Pernod and yellow Chartreuse
3. Shake
4. Strain into a rocks glass filled with ice

# Yellow Rattler

1 oz. dry vermouth
1 oz. sweet vermouth
1 oz. gin
3 oz. orange juice (preferably freshly squeezed)

1. Fill mixing glass with ice
2. Add dry vermouth, sweet vermouth, gin and orange juice
3. Shake
4. Strain into a chilled goblet

# Yellow Strawberry

1 oz. light rum
½ oz. banana liqueur
4 oz. frozen strawberries, thawed
1 oz. sour mix

1. Fill blender with 3 oz. ice, light rum, banana liqueur, frozen
   strawberries and sour mix
2. Blend
3. Pour into a goblet
4. Garnish with a banana slice

# Yodel

1½ oz. Fernet Branca
1½ oz. orange juice
club soda

1. Fill a rocks glass with ice
2. Add Fernet Branca and orange juice
3. Stir
4. Fill with club soda

# York Special

2½ oz. dry vermouth
½ oz. maraschino liqueur
3–4 dashes orange bitters

1. Fill mixing glass with ice
2. Add dry vermouth, maraschino liqueur and orange bitters
3. Stir
4. Strain into a chilled cocktail glass

# Z

## Zamboanga Hummer

½ oz. gold rum
½ oz. gin
½ oz. brandy
½ oz. curaçao or triple sec
2 oz. orange juice
2 oz. pineapple juice
½ oz. lemon juice
1 tsp. brown sugar

1. Fill mixing glass with 3 oz. ice
2. Add all ingredients
3. Shake well
4. Strain into a Collins glass filled with ice

## Zanzibar

2½ oz. dry vermouth
1 oz. gin
½ oz. lemon juice
1 tsp. sugar syrup
2–3 dashes orange bitters

1. Fill mixing glass with ice
2. Add dry vermouth, gin, lemon juice, sugar syrup and orange bitters
3. Shake
4. Strain into a chilled sour glass
5. Add ice, if desired
6. Garnish with a twist of lemon

# Zombie

1 oz. light rum
½ oz. crème de noyaux
½ oz. triple sec
1½ oz. sour mix
1½ oz. orange juice
½ oz. 151-proof rum

1. Fill mixing glass with ice
2. Add light rum, crème de noyaux, triple sec, sour mix and orange juice
3. Strain into a Collins glass filled with ice
4. Top with 151-proof rum
5. Garnish with a cherry

# Zoom

1½ oz. brandy
¼ oz. honey
½ oz. cream

1. Fill mixing glass with ice
2. Add brandy, honey and cream
3. Shake well
4. Strain into a chilled cocktail glass

# Nonalcoholic Drink Recipes

## Banana Milk Shake

**1 medium-sized ripe banana, peeled**
**½ pt. milk**
**1 tsp. honey**

1. Combine banana, milk and honey in a blender
2. Blend well
3. Pour into a rocks glass
4. Add ice

## Black Cow

**2 scoops vanilla ice cream**
**root beer**

1. Put ice cream into a Collins glass
2. Fill with cold root beer
3. Stir

## Café Mocha

**4 oz. strong hot black coffee**
**4 oz. hot chocolate**
**whipped cream**

1. Combine black coffee and hot chocolate in a large mug
2. Top with whipped cream
3. Sprinkle cinnamon and/or nutmeg on top

# Café Viennoise

**8 oz. strong cold black coffee**
**1 oz. heavy cream**
**1 tsp. chocolate syrup**
**several dashes cinnamon powder**

1. In blender, combine coffee, heavy cream, chocolate syrup and cinnamon
2. Blend until smooth
3. Pour into a goblet or large wineglass
4. Sprinkle nutmeg on top, if desired

# Center Court

**½ lb. strawberries, stems removed**
**½ pt. sweet cream**
**2 tsp. powdered sugar**
**½ tsp. powdered ginger**
**club soda**

1. Combine strawberries, sweet cream, sugar and ginger in a blender
2. Blend well
3. Pour into a pitcher
4. Add club soda and ice cubes
5. Stir

# Chocolate Almond Shake

**1 oz. chocolate syrup**
**1 oz. almond syrup**
**4 oz. cream**

1. In a blender, combine chocolate syrup, almond syrup, cream and 3 oz. crushed ice
2. Blend until smooth
3. Pour into a goblet or large wineglass

# Cola Float

**2 scoops vanilla ice cream**
**cola**

1. Put ice cream in a Collins glass
2. Fill with cola
3. Stir

# Cranberry Cooler

**2 oz. cranberry juice cocktail**
**½ oz. lime juice**
**club soda or ginger ale**

1. Fill mixing glass with ice
2. Add cranberry juice and lime juice
3. Shake
4. Strain into a rocks glass filled with ice
5. Fill with club soda or ginger ale

# Cranberry-Grape Drink

**3 oz. cranberry juice cocktail**
**3 oz. grape juice**

1. Fill a highball glass with ice
2. Add cranberry juice and grape juice
3. Stir

# Cranberry Sparkler

**3 oz. cranberry juice cocktail**
**3 oz. club soda**

1. Fill a highball glass with ice
2. Add cranberry juice and club soda
3. Stir gently

# Cranberry Splash

**5 oz. club soda**
**1 oz. cranberry juice cocktail**

1. Fill a highball glass with ice
2. Add club soda
3. Top with cranberry juice
4. Garnish with a slice of lemon and a slice of lime (optional)

# Dry Grape Vine

**2 oz. grape juice**
**1 oz. lemon juice**
**1 dash grenadine**

1. Fill mixing glass with ice
2. Add grape juice, lemon juice and grenadine
3. Shake
4. Strain into a chilled cocktail glass

# Easter Egg Hatch

**3½ oz. frozen vanilla yogurt**
**2 oz. orange juice**
**1 tbsp. sugar syrup**

1. In blender, combine frozen yogurt, orange juice, sugar syrup and 3½ oz. crushed ice
2. Blend
3. Pour into a goblet

(Courtesy of Beach Grill, Westminster, Colorado)

# Egg Cream

**1–1½ oz. chocolate syrup**
**cold milk**
**seltzer**

1. Pour chocolate syrup into a highball glass
2. Fill glass approximately ⅔ with milk
3. Top with seltzer
4. Stir

# Fruit Juice

**2 oz. pineapple juice**
**2 oz. orange juice**
**2 oz. grapefruit juice**
**2 oz. cranberry juice cocktail**

1. Combine all juices in a highball glass or Collins glass
2. Stir well

# Fruit Juice Cooler

**1½ oz. pineapple juice**
**1½ oz. orange juice**
**1½ oz. grapefruit juice**
**1½ oz. cranberry juice**
**2 oz. club soda or ginger ale**

1. Combine all juices in a highball glass or Collins glass
2. Stir well
3. Top with club soda or ginger ale

# Ginger Ale and Bitters

**6 oz. ginger ale**
**2–3 dashes Angostura bitters**

1. Fill highball glass with ice
2. Add ginger ale and bitters
3. Stir

# Grape Crush

**3 oz. grape juice**
**1 oz. cranberry juice cocktail**
**1 oz. sour mix**
**7-Up**

1. Fill a highball glass with crushed ice
2. Add grape juice, cranberry juice and sour mix
3. Stir well
4. Top with 7-Up

# Lemonade

**1½ oz. freshly squeezed lemon juice**
**2 tsp. superfine granulated sugar, or to taste**
**distilled or spring water**

1. Pour lemon juice into a Collins glass
2. Add sugar
3. Dissolve sugar
4. Fill with ice
5. Fill with water
6. Stir

# Lemonade Fizz

1 oz. lemon juice
2 tsp. powdered sugar
club soda

1. Combine lemon juice and sugar in a Collins glass
2. Stir until sugar is dissolved
3. Fill glass with ice cubes
4. Fill with club soda

# Limeade

1½ oz. freshly squeezed lime juice
3–4 tsp. sugar
distilled or spring water

1. Pour lime juice into a Collins glass
2. Add sugar
3. Dissolve sugar
4. Fill with ice
5. Fill with water
6. Stir

# Lime Cola

½ oz. freshly squeezed lime juice
cola

1. Fill a Collins glass with ice
2. Pour in lime juice
3. Fill with cola
4. Stir

# Lime Cooler

1 tbsp. lime juice
tonic water

1. Fill a Collins glass with ice
2. Add lime juice
3. Fill with tonic water
4. Garnish with a slice of lime

# Lime Rickey

1 oz. Rose's lime juice
club soda
dash of grenadine

1. Fill a highball glass with ice
2. Pour in lime juice
3. Fill with club soda
4. Stir
5. Add grenadine
6. Stir again

# Malted (chocolate)

2 scoops chocolate ice cream
1 cup milk
2 oz. chocolate syrup
2 tbsp. malt powder

1. Combine chocolate ice cream, milk, chocolate syrup and malt powder in a blender
2. Blend until smooth
3. Pour into a goblet or other large glass

# No-Gin Fizz

4 oz. lemon juice
1 oz. lime juice
1 tbsp. confectioners sugar
club soda

1. Fill a Collins glass with ice
2. Add lemon juice, lime juice and sugar
3. Stir until sugar is dissolved
4. Fill with club soda
5. Garnish with a lime wedge

# Old-Time Strawberry Milk Shake

4 oz. fresh strawberries, stems removed
8 oz. cold milk
1 tbsp. honey (sugar may be substituted)

1. Fill blender with several ice cubes, fresh strawberries, cold milk and honey or sugar
2. Blend until smooth
3. Pour into a goblet or large wineglass

# Orange Aid

6 oz. orange juice
1 tbsp. sugar syrup
club soda

1. Fill a Collins glass with ice
2. Add orange juice and sugar syrup
3. Stir well
4. Fill with club soda
5. Garnish with a slice of orange

# Orange and Tonic

**5 oz. orange juice**
**tonic water**

1. Fill a Collins glass with ice
2. Add orange juice
3. Fill with tonic water
4. Stir gently

# Orange Fizz

**5 oz. orange juice**
**1 oz. sour mix**
**club soda**

1. Fill a Collins glass with ice
2. Add orange juice and sour mix
3. Top with club soda

# Orange 'N' Bitters

**orange juice**
**2–3 dashes Angostura bitters**

1. Fill a highball glass with ice
2. Add orange juice and bitters
3. Stir

# Orange Sparkler

**3 oz. orange juice**
**3 oz. club soda**

1. Fill a highball glass with ice
2. Add orange juice and club soda
3. Stir gently

# Passion Fruit Spritzer

**4 oz. passion fruit juice**
**club soda**

1. Pour passion fruit juice over several ice cubes in a tulip glass
2. Fill with club soda
3. Garnish with a wedge of lime

# Pineapple-Cranberry Juice Punch

**2 qts. chilled unsweetened pineapple juice**
**2 qts. cranberry juice cocktail**
**16 oz. club soda**
**16 oz. ginger ale**

1. Combine all ingredients in a large punch bowl, over a block of ice
2. Stir
3. Garnish with pineapple slices

# Pineapple Milk Shake

**3 oz. pineapple juice**
**3 or 4 pineapple cubes**
**4 oz. cold milk**
**1 tbsp. honey (sugar may be substituted)**

1. Fill blender with several ice cubes, pineapple juice, pineapple, cold milk and honey or sugar
2. Blend until smooth
3. Pour into a goblet or large wineglass

# Prairie Oyster

1 egg
1 dash Tabasco
salt and pepper to taste

1. Combine all ingredients in a glass
2. Stir well
3. Drink down in one gulp

(*Note:* This drink is reputed to be a cure for hangovers.)

# Rainbow Sherbet Punch

8 oz. orange juice
8 oz. pineapple juice
8 oz. Hawaiian Punch
1 qt. rainbow sherbet
1 bottle club soda
1 bottle ginger ale

1. Combine juices in a punch bowl over ice
2. Before serving, add soda and scoops of rainbow sherbet

# Raspberry Cranberry Punch

12-oz. can frozen raspberry cranberry juice cocktail
   concentrate
36 oz. (3 cans) water
1 bottle (33.8 fluid oz.) 7-Up
raspberry sherbet

1. Combine all ingredients in a large punch bowl
2. Add ice
3. Serve in rocks glasses or punch glasses
4. Add a scoop of raspberry sherbet to each serving

# Raspberry Seltzer

**1 tsp. raspberry syrup**
**seltzer or club soda**

1. Pour raspberry syrup into a tall glass
2. Fill with cold seltzer
3. Add ice, if necessary


# Rose's Ruby Heart

**5 or 6 fresh strawberries**
**cream**
**1 oz. sour mix**

1. In blender, combine strawberries, cream and sour mix with 3 oz. crushed ice
2. Blend until smooth
3. Pour into a goblet


# Safe Sex on the Beach

**1 oz. peach nectar**
**3 oz. pineapple juice (or grapefruit juice)**
**3 oz. orange juice**

1. Pour peach nectar, pineapple juice (or grapefruit juice) and orange juice into a highball glass with several ice cubes
2. Stir


# Shirley Temple

**1 dash grenadine**
**ginger ale**

1. Fill a Collins glass with ice
2. Add grenadine
3. Fill with ginger ale
4. Decorate with a cherry and an orange slice

## Sober Spritzer

**3 oz. white grape juice**
**club soda**

1. Fill wineglass with several ice cubes
2. Add 3 oz. grape juice
3. Fill with club soda
4. Garnish with a twist of lemon

## Sober Thoughts

**3 oz. orange juice**
**3 oz. fresh lime juice**
**1 tbsp. grenadine**
**tonic water**

1. Fill a highball glass with ice
2. Add orange juice, lime juice and grenadine
3. Stir well
4. Fill with tonic water

## Soda and Bitters

**5 oz. club soda**
**2–3 dashes Angostura bitters**

1. Fill a highball glass with ice
2. Fill with club soda
3. Add bitters
4. Stir

# Summer Cooler

¼ lb. strawberries, stems removed
¼ pt. plain yogurt
½ pt. milk
sugar or honey, to taste

1. Combine strawberries, yogurt, milk and sugar or honey in a blender
2. Blend well
3. Fill rocks glasses with ice cubes and pour in mixture
4. Garnish with strawberry slices

# Swamp Water

3 oz. root beer
3 oz. orange soda

1. Fill a highball glass with ice
2. Add equal amounts of root beer and orange soda
3. Stir

# Tequila Sunset

2 oz. orange juice
1 tbsp. grenadine

1. Fill a rocks glass with ice
2. Pour in orange juice
3. Slowly add grenadine, by pouring over the back of a spoon. Let it rise from bottom of the glass.

# Tropical Fruit Punch

four 46-oz. cans pineapple juice
two 6-oz. cans orange juice concentrate
two 6-oz. cans lemonade concentrate
8 oz. fresh lime juice
8 oz. grenadine

1. Pour all ingredients over a block of ice in a punch bowl
2. Stir
3. Garnish with lime slices and fresh sprigs of mint

# Very Lemon Lemonade

2 oz. sour mix
club soda
7-Up

1. Fill a Collins glass with ice
2. Add sour mix
3. Fill with equal parts club soda and 7-Up
4. Stir gently

# Virgin Madras

3 oz. cranberry juice cocktail
3 oz. orange juice

1. Fill a highball glass with ice
2. Add cranberry juice and orange juice
3. Stir

# Virgin Margarita

1½ oz. sour mix
½ oz. Rose's lime juice
½ oz. orange juice

1. Fill mixing glass with ice
2. Add sour mix, lime juice and orange juice
3. Shake
4. Strain into a chilled cocktail glass or a rocks glass filled with ice

# Virgin Mary

**4 oz. tomato juice**
**½ oz. lemon juice**
**3 drops Tabasco sauce**
**3 drops Worcestershire sauce**
**pinch celery salt**
**pinch pepper**
**dab horseradish (squeeze out liquid)**

1. Combine tomato juice, lemon juice and seasonings (to taste) in a well-chilled shaker
2. Shake
3. Pour into an oversized wineglass or a chilled Collins glass
4. Garnish with a lime slice or a celery stalk

# Virgin Piña Colada

**1 oz. pineapple juice**
**3 or 4 pineapple chunks (optional)**
**1 oz. cream of coconut**
**1 tsp. orange juice**
**1 tbsp. cream**

1. Combine pineapple juice, pineapple chunks, cream of coconut, orange juice and cream with 3 oz. ice in a blender
2. Blend until smooth
3. Pour into a goblet or large wineglass
4. Garnish with a cherry and an orange slice

# Virgin Sea Breeze

3 oz. grapefruit juice
3 oz. cranberry juice cocktail

1. Pour grapefruit juice and cranberry juice into a highball glass filled with ice
2. Stir

# Yogurt Supreme

1 oz. lemon juice
1 oz. orange juice
1½ oz. milk
1½ oz. plain yogurt
½ tsp. honey

1. Combine lemon juice, orange juice, milk, yogurt and honey in a blender
2. Blend well
3. Pour into a goblet and add ice

# Index by Ingredients

*(NA = NONALCOHOLIC)*

## Amaretto Drinks

## Amer Picon

## Anise and Anisette Drinks

## Apple Brandy/Apple Liqueur

## Apricot Brandy/ Apricot Liqueur Drinks

## Aquavit Drinks

## Bailey's Original Irish Cream Drinks

## Banana Liqueur/ Creme de Banana Drinks

## Beer and Ale Drinks

## Bénédictine Drinks

## Blackberry Brandy/Liqueur Drinks

## Blueberry Schnapps

# Bourbon Drinks

# Brandy Drinks

## Campari Drinks

## Canadian Whiskey

## Caramel Liqueur Drinks

## Chambord Drinks

## Chambraise

## Champagne and Sparkling Wine Drinks

## Chartreuse Drinks

## Cherry Brandy

## Cherry/Maraschino Liqueur Drinks

## Chocolate Liqueur

## Chocolate Mint Liqueur

## Coffee Drinks

# Coffee Liqueur

# Cognac Drinks

# Cointreau Drinks

# Cranberry Liqueur Drinks

# Cream and Milk Drinks

## ■ Crème de Almond ■

## ■ Crème de Cacao Drinks ■

## Crème de Cassis

## Crème de Menthe Drinks

Roman Stinger, 375
Snowball, 405
Spanish Moss, 409
Stinger, 411
Stone Sour, 412
Tequila Stinger, 425
Traffic Light, 435

Turkey Shooter, 439
Virgin, 448
Vodka Grasshopper, 450
Vodka Stinger, 453
White Spider, 466
White Wing, 468

## Crème de Noyaux Drinks

Banana Split, 99
Cupid's Kiss, 158
Fern Gully, 184
Lillet Noyaux, 276
Old Etonian, 322
Pink Almond, 346

Rockaway Beach, 374
Ruptured Duck, 380
Scorpion, 390
Strawberry Shortcake, 414
Vanity Fair Cocktail, 444
Zombie, 480

## Crème de Violette Drinks
## (Crème d'Yvette)

Jupiter Cocktail, 258
Rainbow Pousse-Café, 366

Snowball, 405
Union Jack, 442

## Curaçao Drinks

After Dinner, 76
Alabama, 77
Alabazam, 78
Azteca, 95
Betsy Ross, 101
Big Blue Sky, 107
Blue Carnation, 114
Blue Denim, 114
Blue Hawaiian, 115
Blue Margarita, 115
Blue Moon, 116
Blue Shark, 116
Bombay, 118
Booster, 118
Breakfast Eggnog, 125
Chicago, 142
City Slicker, 145
Coronado, 154
Diamond Head, 165
Drawbridge, 169
Dream, 170

El Presidente Edwardo, 177
Eve, 178
Fair and Warmer, 181
Fare-Thee-Well, 183
Frostbite, 196
Gloom Chaser, 209
Go-Go Juice, 211
Golden Margarita, 214
Gorilla Punch, 216
Grapeshot, 219
Green Eye-Opener, 221
Green Room, 222
Hammerhead, 225
Harper's Ferry, 227
Hawaiian Orange Blossom, 229
Hula-Hula, 238
Ichbien, 241
Il Magnifico, 242
Irish, 245
Jade, 251
Jamaica Ginger, 252

# Drambuie Drinks

# Dubonnet Drinks

# Dry Vermouth Drinks

514

## Dubonnet Drinks

## Fernet Branca

## Forbidden Fruit

## Framboise

## Frangelico Drinks

## Galliano Drinks

# Gin Drinks

# Grand Marnier Drinks

# Ice Cream Drinks

# Irish Mist

# Irish Whiskey

# Kahlúa Drinks

## Kirsch

## Kummel Drinks

## Lillet Drinks

# Madeira

# Malibu

# Mandarine Napoléon Liqueur

# Metaxa

# Midori Drinks

# Ouzo

# Peach Brandy/ Peach Liqueur Drinks

# Peach Schnapps

Brain, 120
Cerebral Hemorrhage, 137
Frozen Bikini, 197
Hairy Navel, 225
Halley's Comfort, 225

Killer Kool-Aid, 263
Royal Peach Freeze, 377
Sex on the Beach, 395
Sex on the Beach in Winter, 395

# Peanut Liqueur

Brown Bomber, 120

# Pear Brandy

Tintoretto, 431

# Peppermint Schnapps

Adrienne's Dream, 74
Adult Hot Chocolate, 75
After Five, 76
Apres Ski, 89
Cold Deck, 151
Girl Scout Cookie, 208
Ground Zero, 223
Hot Pants, 235
Hot Peppermint Patty, 235

Hot Shots (shooter), 236
Interplanetary Punch, 244
Old Pale, 323
Peppermint Patty, 339
Polynesian Punch, 354
Snow Shoe, 406
Snuggler, 406
Whippet, 458

# Pernod Drinks

Bombay, 118
City Slicker, 145
Death in the Afternoon, 163
Depth Charge, 164
Duchess, 172
Earthquake, 174
Eve, 128
Foggy Day, 190
Hawaiian Eye, 228
Henry Morgan's Grog, 230
Iceberg, 240
Irish, 245
Kiss Me Quick, 267
Ladies, 270
Last Round, 272
Lawhill, 273

Linstead, 277
London, 280
Millionaire, 302
Modern (1), 306
Modern (2), 306
Montreal Club Bouncer, 308
Moonshine Cocktail, 308
Morning, 309
Morning Glory, 309
New Orleans, 316
Nineteen, 318
Nineteen Pick-Me-Up, 318
Pernod Cocktail, 340
Pernod Flip, 340
Pernod Frappe, 340
Phoebe Snow, 341

# Peter Heering

# Pimms

# Plum Brandy

# Port Wine Drinks

# Punt e Mes

# Raspberry Liqueur

Teddy Bear (shooter), 420

# Rum Drinks

## Sabra Drinks

## Sake

## Sambuca Drinks

## Scotch Drinks

## Sherry Drinks

## Sloe Gin Drinks

## Southern Comfort Drinks

## Strawberry Liqueur Drinks

## Strega Drinks

## Swedish Punsch Drinks

## Sweet Vermouth Drinks

## Tequila Drinks

## Tia Maria Drinks

## Triple Sec Drinks

## Tuaca Drinks

## Vandermint Drinks

## Vodka Drinks

## Whiskey Drinks

# WilderBerry Schnapps

# Wine Drinks

# Index by Type

*(NA = NONALCOHOLIC)*

## Blender Drinks

# Cobblers

Brandy Cobbler, 121

# Collins

Butterscotch Collins, 128
Joe Collins, 256
John Collins, 256
Rum Collins, 379

Tequila Collins, 421
Tom Collins, 433
Vodka Collins, 448

# Coolers

Chablis Cooler, 138
Coffee Cooler, 150
Cooler by the Lake, 153
Country Club Cooler, 154
Cranberry Cooler (NA), 483
Cuban Cooler, 158
Emerald Isle Cooler, 177
Fruit Juice Cooler (NA), 485
Jamaica Cooler, 251
Java Cooler, 254
Kerry Cooler, 263

Klondike Cooler, 267
Lime Cooler (NA), 488
Mint Cooler, 304
Negroni Cooler, 314
Rouffy Party Punch Cooler, 375
Rum Curaçao Cooler, 379
Summer Cooler (NA), 495
Vodka Cooler, 449
Whiskey Collins, 459
Wine Cooler, 470

# Daiquiris

Apple Daiquiri, 87
Banana Daiquiri (frozen), 98
Chambord Daiquiri (frozen), 138
Cherry Daiquiri (frozen), 142

Frozen Daiquiri, 198
Frozen Fruit Daiquiri, 198
Frozen Mint Daiquiri, 200
Gin Daiquiri, 206

# Exotic Drinks

Atlantic Breeze, 93
Bahama Mama, 97
Banana Mama, 99
Big Blue Sky, 107
Blue Hawaiian, 115
Blue Margarita, 115
Boardwalk Breezer, 116
Cherry Bomb, 141
Club Med, 148
Coco-Loco, 148
Diamond Head, 165
Dominican Coco Loco, 168
Fogcutter, 190

Frozen Daiquiri, 200
Gorilla Punch, 216
Hawaiian Eye, 228
Ice Palace, 240
Kappa Colada, 260
Mai Tai, 288
Malibu Monsoon, 288
Mandarine Colada, 289
Melon Colada, 299
Peach Treat, 336
Piña Colada, 344
Planter's Punch, 352
Scorpion, 390

## Fizzes

## Flip

## Frappes

## Frozen Drinks

# Hot Drinks

# Margaritas

# Pousse-Cafés

# Punches

# Rickey

# Shooters

After Eight, 76
After Five, 76
Alabama Slammer, 78
Anti-Freeze, 86
Baby Ruth, 96
Bubble Gum, 126
Buffalo Sweat, 127
Chocolate-Covered Cherry, 144
Deep Throat, 163
Green Lizard, 222
Hawaiian Punch, 229
Hot Shots, 236
Indian Summer, 243
Jell-O Shots, 254
Kamikaze, 260
Lemon Drop, 275
Lion Tamer, 278
Meltdown, 299
Mexican Flag, 300
Mexican Missile, 301
Mission Accomplished, 304

Nutty Irishman, 320
Out of the Blue, 328
Pancho Villa, 331
Pineapple Bomber, 345
Pink Lemonade, 347
Prairie Fire, 358
The Purple Hooter Shooter, 362
Russian Quaalude, 382
Silk Panties, 399
Slimeball, 402
Snow Cap, 405
Snow Shoe, 406
S.O.B. Shooter, 406
Sour Grapes, 407
Teddy Bear, 420
Tequila Popper, 424
Tequila Shot, 424
Tiny Bowl, 431
Wombat, 471
Woo Woo, 471

# Sours

Aalborg Sour, 71
Apricot Sour, 90
Bourbon Sour, 120
Frisco Sour, 196
Midori Sour, 302
Picon Sour, 342
Pisco Sour, 351

Rum Sour, 380
Scotch Stone Sour, 391
Stinger Sour, 412
Stone Sour, 412
Strega Sour, 415
Tequila Sour, 425
Whiskey Sour, 461

# Index of New Drinks
# for the Nineties

*(NA = NONALCOHOLIC)*

# Index of
# Low-calorie Drinks

# Rockaway Beach

1½ oz. light rum
½ oz. dark rum
½ oz. tequila
1 oz. orange juice
½ oz. pineapple juice
½ oz. cranberry juice cocktail
1 tsp. crème de noyaux

1. Fill mixing glass with 4 oz. cracked ice
2. Add light rum, dark rum, tequila, orange juice, pineapple juice, cranberry juice and crème de noyaux
3. Shake
4. Strain into a chilled Collins glass
5. Add ice
6. Garnish with a cherry

# Rocky Green Dragon

1½ oz. gin
½ oz. green Chartreuse
½ oz. cognac

1. Fill mixing glass with ice
2. Add gin, green Chartreuse and cognac
3. Shake
4. Strain into a rocks glass filled with ice

# Rolls Royce

1½ oz. gin
½ oz. dry vermouth
½ oz. sweet vermouth
3–4 dashes Bénédictine

374

# Glossary

**Abisante** a pale green, anise-flavored liqueur

**Absinthe** a redistilled alcohol containing wormwood; it is illegal in the United States

**Advokaat** an eggnog liqueur originally from Holland

**Akvavit** (aquavit) Scandinavian; made from rye with an infusion of caraway

**Aperitif** an alcoholic drink taken before a meal, or any of several wines and bitters, such as vermouth

**Ale** a beer similar to lager but with a more bitter taste

**Amaretto** an almond-flavored liqueur made from apricot pits; the original amaretto is Amaretto di Saronno, from Italy

**Amer Picon** a French aperitif, made from quininc, oranges and gentian

**Anise; anisette** licorice-flavored liqueur made from anise seeds

**Apple brandy** an apple liqueur, such as Calvados or applejack

**Apricot liqueur** a cordial made from apricot pits

**Armagnac** a high-quality brandy like cognac, but distilled only once and available in vintages

**Banana liqueur** (crème de banana) a sweet liqueur made from bananas

**Beer** an alcoholic beverage brewed from malted barley; flavored with hops after fermentation

**Bénédictine** an herb liqueur made from a secret formula by the Benedictine monks in France

**Bitters** a sweet to dry flavored drink made from aromatic plants, usually spirit-based; considered an aperitif

**Blackberry liqueur** a cordial made from blackberries

**Blended whiskey** a combination of different whiskeys that have been "married" in casks; more common than straight whiskey

**Bourbon whiskey** a brown liquor made from at least 51 percent corn and aged for at least two years in white oak casks

**Brandy** a single distillate or

mixture of distillates obtained from wine or the fermented juice of fruit; some brandies have caramel added for color

**Canadian whiskey** a liquor made from corn, rye and barley; always blended and usually aged for six or more years in charred oak casks

**Chambord** a French liqueur made from small black raspberries

**Chambraise** a French liqueur made from wild strawberries

**Chartreuse** an herb-based cordial that comes in either yellow or green varieties; created by Carthusian monks in France in the early seventeenth century and made from a secret recipe

**Chaser** a mild drink, such as beer, taken after a hard liquor

**Cherry Heering** a Danish liqueur made from cherries

**Cherry Marnier** a French cherry liqueur with a hint of almond

**Cocktail** a chilled alcoholic drink made from a combination of liquors and flavoring ingredients; the term is used fairly broadly these days to describe most mixed drinks

**Coffee liqueur** a coffee-flavored drink

**Cognac** a fine brandy from the Cognac region of France

**Cointreau** a high-quality orange-flavored liqueur, made from the skins of curaçao oranges; the generic term is curaçao, which if redistilled clear is called triple sec

**Collins** a tall drink made with liquor (usually gin or vodka), sour mix and club soda; the Tom Collins, made with gin, is the most famous variety

**Cooler** a drink made with wine or another spirit and a carbonated mixer

**Cordials** sweetened spirits distilled from fruits, seeds, herbs and peels; the same as liqueurs

**Cranberry liqueur** a cranberry-flavored cordial

**Cream of coconut** a coconut syrup used in many exotic drinks, especially Piña Coladas

**Crème liqueurs** a group of liqueurs (cordials) with a high sugar content, resulting in a consistency similar to that of cream, e.g. crème de ananas (from pineapples), crème de cacao (dark or white—from cacao), crème de cassis (from black currants), crème de menthe (green or white—from mint) or crème de vanille (from vanilla beans)

**Curaçao** a delicate orange-flavored liqueur; comes in orange and blue

**Drambuie** a sweet liqueur with a Scotch malt whiskey base

**Dubonnet** a light, zesty aperitif from France

**Falernum** a fruity sweetener with a spicy, limey taste; available in liquor stores and specialty stores

**Fix** a sour drink, usually made with pineapple syrup and crushed ice

**Fizz** similar to a Collins, made with sour mix, sugar and club soda; sometimes an egg is used, as in the Ramos Fizz

**Forbidden Fruit** a drink of shaddock-infused brandy

**Fortified wine** a wine, such as port or sherry, with extra alcohol added to it

**Fraises** a strawberry liqueur with a high sugar content

**Framboise** a raspberry liqueur with a high alcohol content

**Frangelico** a hazelnut-flavored liqueur from Italy

**Frappe** a drink made by packing a glass with crushed ice and pouring the liqueur or liquor of your choice over it

**Galliano** (Liquore Galliano) a piquant golden Italian liqueur made from herbs and spices; most familiar as an ingredient of the Harvey Wallbanger

**Garnish** an ingredient used to decorate or top off a drink, such as fruit, olives or nutmeg

**Gin** a liquor distilled from juniper berries and other botanicals, such as herbs, seeds, berries and roots; English gin (the most common variety) is made from a base spirit of 75 percent corn, 15 percent barley malt and 10 percent other grains

**Grand Marnier** an orange-flavored, cognac-based liqueur from France

**Grenadine** a sweet red flavoring made from pomegranates

**Highball** a basic drink containing ice, 1½ to 2 ounces of liquor and 6 to 10 ounces of a mixer such as soda or juice

**Irish cream liqueur** a sweet, rich liqueur made from cream, Irish whiskey and sweetener; the original is Bailey's Original Irish Cream

**Irish Mist** an Irish whiskey-based liqueur flavored with honey and orange

**Irish whiskey** a light-colored liquor made from malted and unmalted barley and heated in a kiln; the only whiskey that is distilled three times

**Kahlúa** a premium coffee-

flavored liqueur from
Mexico

**Kirsch** (kirschwasser) a
liqueur distilled from black
cherries

**Kümmel** a caraway-flavored
brandy

**Liqueur** see Cordial

**Liquor** an alcoholic
beverage most often
distilled, rather than
fermented

**Lillet** an aperitif wine from
France; comes in red or
white

**Lowball** (also called an old-
fashioned) a type of drink
served "on the rocks" in a
rocks glass (also called an
old-fashioned glass)

**Malibu** a coconut rum
liqueur

**Mandarine** a tangerine-
flavored, cognac-based
liqueur

**Maraschino** technically a
brandy, but usually
considered a liqueur;
cherry-and-almond flavored

**Metaxa** a sweetened Greek
brandy

**Midori** a honeydew-flavored
liqueur produced in Japan

**Mixing glass** part of the
cocktail shaker set, used to
mix drinks

**Neat** refers to any liquor
(usually whiskey) served
straight in a shot glass; can
be taken with a chaser

**"On the rocks"** a term
used to describe wine or

spirits served over ice,
usually in a rocks glass

**Orgeat** almond syrup

**Ouzo** an anise-flavored Greek
aperitif

**Parfait Amour** a purple
cordial made from citron

**Passion fruit liqueur** a
liqueur from Hawaii,
flavored with either peach
or mango

**Peach liqueur** a brandy- or
neutral spirit-based liqueur
flavored with fresh and/or
dried peaches

**Pear liqueur** a liqueur from
pears, made in Hungary;
one brand, Williams Pear
Liqueur, has a whole pear
in the bottle

**Penaut Lolita** a liqueur
made from peanuts

**Peppermint schnapps** a
light, minty liqueur

**Pernod** a licorice-flavored
liqueur

**Peter Heering** a brand-name
cherry liqueur from
Denmark

**Pineapple liqueur** a liqueur
made from pineapples,
usually from Hawaii or the
Caribbean

**Pousse-Café** a drink made
by floating one ingredient
on top of another in layers

**Proof** the alcoholic content
of a spirit; determined in
the United States by
doubling the percentage of
alcohol (an 80-proof liquor,
for example, has a 40

percent alcohol content)

**Prunelle** a liqueur made from meat, plum pits, figs and vanilla beans

**Punch** a mixture of spirits, wines, flavorings, sweeteners and fruit, sometimes combined with carbonated beverages or other ingredients, usually made in a large bowl, but also in single-serving portions

**Rickey** a drink made with a spirit such as gin and lime juice, club soda and ice

**Rock and Rye** a liqueur made from rye whiskey and rock candy

**Rum** a liquor distilled from fermented sugar cane or molasses; lighter rums are distilled at a higher proof than darker rums; certain rums, especially Puerto Rican rums, are aged

**Rye or American whiskey** liquor made from at least 51 percent rye; aged in oak casks

**Sabra** an orange liqueur with a hint of chocolate; from Israel

**Sambuca** a well-known Italian licorice-flavored liqueur; often served with 3 coffee beans floating on top

**Sangaree** a chilled tall drink made using liquor, wine or beer; it is sweet and topped with nutmeg

**Scotch whiskey** a liquor made from grain and malt, distilled in copper coil stills and heated over peat; most scotch is blended, but many single-malt varieties are available; scotch sold in the United States must be aged for at least four years

**Shooter** whiskey or other spirit poured directly into the glass from the bottle; the term can also be used to describe a mixed drink that has been strained into a shot glass and is taken in one gulp.

**Slivovitz** a brandy distilled from plums

**Sloe gin** a fruity liqueur made from sloe berries steeped in gin

**Sour** a tart drink served in a sour glass; made from a liquor or liqueur and sour mix (lemon, lime and sugar); whiskey sours are the best known

**Sour mix** (also called sweet and sour mix) a combination of lemon and lime juice and sugar; used in many mixed drinks, including sours, Collinses and fizzes; fresh juices can be used instead, or there are several commercial pre-mixes on the market (see recipe for sour mix on p. 20)

**Southern Comfort** a high-proof liqueur made from

bourbon, peach liqueur and fresh peaches

**"Straight up"** any spirit served chilled and without ice

**Straight whiskey** a whiskey made from one strain of barley malt

**Strawberry liqueur** a liqueur made from strawberries; imported versions are called Fraises or Fraise de Bois, which translates "wild strawberries"

**Strega** a sweet Italian liqueur made from a variety of herbs and spices

**Swedish Punsch** a citrus-flavored liqueur with a rum base

**Tequila** a liquor distilled from the fermented sap of the mezcal plant; produced near the city of Tequila in Mexico; gold tequila is aged in oak casks for two to four years

**Tia Maria** a coffee-flavored liqueur from Jamaica

**Toddy** a mixture of sweetened spirits and hot water, usually with a lemon slice or peel and one or more spices; traditionally a hot drink, but there are also cold versions

**Tonic** a tall drink made with ice, spirits and tonic water

**Tonic water** a carbonated beverage flavored with quinine, lemon and lime

**Triple sec** an orange-flavored liqueur

**Tuaca** an Italian brandy-based liqueur with citrus flavors; sometimes called "milk brandy" since there is milk in it

**Vandermint** a Dutch chocolate-mint liqueur

**Vermouth** a dry or sweet aperitif wine, flavored with aromatic herbs

**"Virgin"** used to indicate mixed drinks made without alcohol (e.g., Virgin Piña Colada is made without rum)

**Vodka** a liquor distilled from a fermented mash of grain and distilled at high proof so it has little taste; it is not aged

**Wild Turkey Liqueur** a bourbon-based liqueur that is lightly flavored with spices

**Wine** a beverage made from the fermented juice of grapes

**Yukon Jack** a Canadian-whiskey based liqueur, with citrus and herb flavors